TRANSFORMING TALK

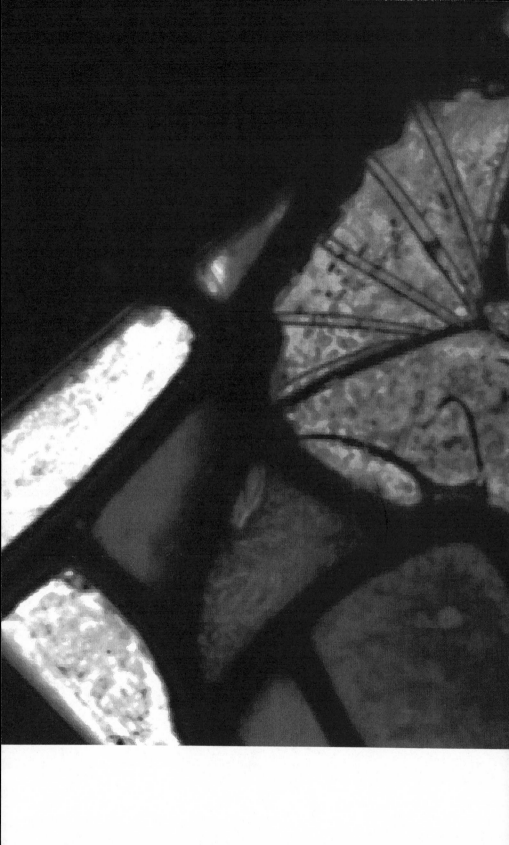

TRANSFORMING TALK

The Problem with **Gossip in Late Medieval England**

SUSAN E. PHILLIPS

THE PENNSYLVANIA STATE UNIVERSITY PRESS
University Park, Pennsylvania

Library of Congress Cataloging-in-Publication Data

Phillips, Susan E., 1970–
Transforming talk : the problem with gossip in late
medieval England / Susan E. Phillips.
p. cm.
Includes bibliographical references and index.
ISBN-13: 978-0-271-02995-5 (pbk: alk. paper)
ISBN-10: 0-271-02995-1 (pbk: alk. paper)
1. English literature—Middle English, 1100–1500—History and criticism.
2. Gossip in literature.
3. Social interaction in literature.
4. Chaucer, Geoffrey, d. 1400—Criticism and interpretation.
I. Title.

PR275.G67P55   2007
820.9'353—dc22
2006036757

The Pennsylvania State University Press
is a member of the Association of
American University Presses.

It is the policy of
The Pennsylvania State University Press to
use acid-free paper. This book is printed on stock that meets
the minimum requirements of American National
Standard for Information Sciences—
Permanence of Paper for Printed Library Material,
ANSI Z39.48–1992.

Frontispiece: "The Gossips," stained-glass window from the church
of St. Nicholas, Stanford-upon-Avon. Reproduced by kind
permission of the Parish of Stanford-upon-Avon,
Northamptonshire. (Photo by Keith Barley)

For BECKY *and* BOATS

CONTENTS

ACKNOWLEDGMENTS

It is a great pleasure to be able to thank publicly the many people whose time, energy, and encouragement helped to bring this project to fruition. I am especially grateful to my former colleagues at the University of Iowa, Matt Brown, Huston Diehl, Kevin Kopelson, Rob Latham, Kathy Lavezzo, Phillip Round, Claire Sponsler, Doug Trevor, Jon Wilcox, and David Wittenberg, and to my colleagues at Northwestern University, Katherine Breen, Nick Davis, Kasey Evans, Richard Kieckhefer, Robert Lerner, Jeffrey Masten, Barbara Newman, Bill Paden, Marco Ruffini, Helen Thompson, Wendy Wall, and Will West. Students at Iowa and Northwestern have also contributed a great deal to this project; I am particularly grateful to Vickie Larsen for her intellectual curiosity and enthusiasm and to Joanne Diaz and Josh Smith for their incisive questions and for their invaluable assistance in fact-checking, proofreading, and indexing the manuscript. Participants in the Harvard Medieval Doctoral Conference offered useful suggestions on some of this material at various stages of the project's development, and I would like to thank, in particular, Mary Jo Arn, Charles Blythe, Bob Epstein, Lianna Farber, Katharine Horsley, Carla Mazzio, and Jane Tolmie, for their insights. At the book's earliest stages, I had the good fortune of working at Harvard University with incredibly generous teachers, and I am deeply indebted to Larry Benson, Dan Donohue, Marjorie Garber, Rebecca Krug, Barbara Lewalski, and to Derek Pearsall, who first introduced me to Chaucer, shepherded me through my doctoral work, and continues to be a wonderful mentor.

Many scholars have read and commented on parts of this project. I would like to thank David Benson and Susanna Fein for reading the entire manuscript with great care and understanding. I am also grateful to Susan Lohafer and Jon Wilcox for their helpful comments on an early version of the manuscript, to Ed Craun for his invaluable insights into Chapter 1, to Paul Strohm for his timely suggestions on material in Chapters 1 and 2, and to Kathy Lavezzo, Claire Sponsler, and Nicholas Watson for their thoughtful responses to an early version of Chapter 4. Conversations with Elizabeth Allen, Seeta Chaganti, Kathy Sanok, Claire Waters, and other participants in the

Medieval Writing Workshops, as well as members of Metalürgy, enabled me to reformulate key points of my argument, and I am deeply grateful for their warmth, intelligence, and friendship. As I wrote this book, colleagues and friends provided me with invaluable advice, not only about the book but also about academic and professional life more generally. I thank David Benson, Melissa Deem, Chris Gaggero, Brian Goldberg, Sara Levine, and Lara Trubowitz for their kindness and encouragement.

I am grateful to Peter Potter for his immediate support of this project, and to everyone at Penn State Press for their help in guiding the manuscript through the publication process. I thank the staff at the British Library, the Cambridge University Library, the Pierpont Morgan Library, the Newberry Library, and the Houghton Library for their aid in using their collections. I would also like to thank the Masters and Fellows of Corpus Christi College, Cambridge, for allowing me to reproduce the *Troilus* frontispiece, the Huntington Library for allowing me to reproduce woodcuts from the *Gospelles of Dystaues*, and Judith Wiggins, the Parish of Stanford on Avon, Northamptonshire, and Keith Barley of Barley Studios for allowing me to reproduce "the Gossips." An early version of material from Chapter 1 appeared in *Hands of the Tongue: Essays on Deviant Speech*, ed. Edwin D. Craun (Kalamazoo: Medieval Institute Publications, 2007). Material from Chapters 1 and 2 appeared in *Twenty-first Century Approaches to Literature: The Middle Ages*, ed. Paul Strohm (Oxford: Oxford University Press, 2007). Revised versions appear here by kind permission of the Medieval Institute Publications and the Oxford University Press. This book was written with the help of a University of Iowa Old Gold Research Fellowship, as well as travel and research funding from Northwestern University, the University of Iowa, and the Woodrow Wilson Foundation.

Finally, I am profoundly grateful to my mother, Susan Abdel Aziz, whose love and encouragement made this book possible. My grandmother, Nancy Phillips, my father, Mohamed Abdel Aziz, my sister, Hebah, my brothers, Hani, Mohamed, and Omar, and my oldest friends, Elizabeth Elsas, Rachael Burger, Tara Altebrando, Susan Livingston, Michele Jaffe, and Hilary Bart-Smith have contributed to this book in numerous ways and I appreciate their love and support. I owe a great debt to Susan Lazorchick for her unwavering encouragement and friendship and to Phil Round for being a wonderful coach as well as a dear friend. Finally, I would like to express my deepest gratitude to Becky Krug—the best advisor, reader, and friend I could ever have hoped for. Her generosity, insight, and patience know no bounds. I could not have finished this book without her.

INTRODUCTION

My sone, be war, and be noon auctour newe
Of tidynges, wheither they been false or trewe.
Whereso thou come, amonges hye or lowe,
Kepe wel thy tonge and thenk upon the crowe.
—Geoffrey Chaucer, *The Manciple's Tale*, lines 359–62

Gossips beware. The literature of late medieval England abounds with cautionary tales concerning the dangers of idle talk. Whether in penitential manuals, courtesy books, or literary compilations, English writers repeatedly tell the story of gossip's "euele werke," revealing the dire consequences facing anyone who engages in unproductive speech. On the pages of moralizing texts, industrious devils record idle words in their account books, while uncompromising authorities sever wagging tongues and place gossiping bodies on ignominious public display. But perhaps nowhere are the repercussions of this speech more vividly depicted than in Manciple's tale of the chattering crow. Here the effects of idle talk are nothing short of physical transformation: because he cannot hold his tongue about the adultery of his master's wife, the pure white crow becomes pitch black and his mellifluous speech is reduced to a discordant cry. The Manciple renders into fable pastoral commonplaces about idle talk as a morally corrosive force, declaring that gossip's idle words turn a trusted servant into a traitor and a miraculous voice into harsh noise. Yet for the Manciple, as for late medieval English culture more generally, idle talk accomplishes far more than the transformation of virtue into vice.

Prompted by a fear of small talk and closing with a fifty-line *moralitas* that cannot hold its tongue about "janglyng" (idle talk) (IX. 350), the *Manciple's Tale* does not simply recount the exemplum of the crow; it tells the story of idle talk—its uses as well as its consequences.¹ On one level, his story is familiar, the received wisdom of medieval and modern authorities alike. The Manciple engages in a deeply self-interested exemplarity; he uses his cautionary tale to contain the animus he incited when he ridiculed the inebriated Cook in the tale's prologue. Concerned that the Cook might later revenge himself by speaking "smale thynges" (IX. 73) about his shady business dealings, the Manciple tries to preempt this retaliatory gossip by recounting an exemplum that not only illustrates the dangers of such speech but also reveals its problematic associations. Here, the crow appears not as corrupted virtue, but as the social subordinate whose idle talk has the power to undo his superiors. Attached to this story of the upstart underling, the exemplum's moral, with its proliferating commonplaces about idle talk, serves less as an occasion for moral instruction than as the opportunity to affirm the connection between "janglyng" and social inferiors. For the duration of the seemingly endless barrage of proverbs, the Manciple ventriloquizes his mother's voice, attributing the loquacity of the *moralitas* to her. The Manciple thus introduces his "dame" not as an "auctoritee" on idle talk but as an emblem of it—a comic reminder of gossip's traditional associations.

The narrative about insubordinate speech, however, is merely a cover story. What it occludes is a much more interesting tale—a story in which gossip is not a vice but a narrative and pastoral strategy, not a tool of the underling but a tactic deployed by authority. Although the Manciple attempts to tell the tale of other people's gossip, he loses control of this narrative, revealing instead his own dependence on idle talk. Not only does he chatter on about the Cook's drunkenness in order to insinuate his exemplum into the tale-telling rotation, he also uses idle talk to breathe new life into his fable from "olde bookes" (IX. 106). Pretending to let his fellow pilgrims in on the privy details of his characters' lives, he recounts the overly familiar details of classical narrative and antifeminist commonplace as if they were the latest news: "if the sothe that I shal sayn, / Jalous he was" (IX. 143–44). More strikingly, he makes his philological speculations appear as inside jokes. Discussing whether the term "lemman" (lover) is more appropriate for a poor wench than a noble wife, he elbows his audience knowingly: "God it woot, myne owene deere brother, / Men leyn that oon as lowe

---

1. Unless otherwise noted, all Chaucer quotations come from the *Riverside Chaucer*, ed. Larry D. Benson (Boston: Houghton Mifflin, 1987).

as lith that oother" (IX. 221–22). In addition to making the "textueel" appear colloquial, the Manciple uses idle talk here to make his audience into his conversational kin, closing the gap between himself and the "lordynges" (IX. 309) he addresses. That is, gossip is a device through which the Manciple both reinvents his narrative and renegotiates his relationship with his audience. In this context, his mother's *moralitas,* rather than merely suggesting that idle talk is women's work, transforms a compendium of learned *auctoritates*—the wisdom of Solomon, Cato's *Distichs,* Seneca's *De Ira,* Biblical proverb and Flemish saying—into gossip. Both the narrative and its moral participate in the "janglyng" they condemn, as the Manciple's exemplum functions less as a cautionary tale than as an illustration of idle talk's talent for discursive appropriation. Despite his claims to the contrary, for the Manciple, gossip's idle words are productive; they have the ability to blur boundaries not simply between vice and virtue, but between acquaintances and kin, narrative and news, idle talk and pastoral practice.

The story of gossip in late medieval England is the story of this transforming talk. As I argue throughout this book, idle talk performs a wide range of social, pastoral, and literary functions. Gossip appropriates pastoral practice, turning idle talk into confession and confession into idle talk. It performs generic alchemy—making fabliaux read like exempla and changing sermon exempla into the latest news. And it restructures social relationships, converting neighbors into sisters, confessors into lovers, and idle women into trusted advisors. I begin my discussion with the Manciple's failed exemplum because it illustrates gossip's ability to subvert pastoral practice and remake conventional narrative, and to disempower literary authority and forge social bonds. But the *Manciple's Tale* does more than suggest the complicated ways in which gossip functioned in late medieval England; it reveals the inadequacy of contemporary gossip theory to account for these functions, for this cautionary tale about insubordinate speech with all its occlusions is one that critics continue to tell.

In recent decades, scholars have endeavored to explicate gossip's work. While early theorists focused on the destructive qualities of idle talk, providing epidemiological models for this discursive "virus," more recently the discussion has turned to the vital social role that gossip plays.[2] Two compet-

2. Gordon W. Allport and Leo Joseph Postman, *The Psychology of Rumor* (New York: H. Holt, 1947). This viral model has had a lasting effect on gossip theory. See, for example, Gary Alan Fine, *Manufacturing Tales: Sex and Money in Contemporary Legends* (Knoxville: University of Tennessee Press, 1992); and Karen C. Adkins, "Poison Pens: Gossip's Viral Knowledge," paper

ing models have predominated in gossip theory. The first, largely espoused by anthropologists, identifies gossip as an instrument of social control. Idle talk, the theory argues, both establishes membership in a community and polices that community's morals.[3] In certain groups, gossip acts as a feared social regulator, enforcing standards of behavior and promoting competition through its approval and disapproval.[4] Critiquing this model of social control, sociologists and social psychologists have focused on the ways in which gossip serves the individuals engaged in it.[5] This second model defines idle talk as a "social exchange," in which information is traded for status, money, and services.[6] The last decade has seen a reformulation of these two methodological extremes, as gossip theorists across several disciplines have sought models that combine social and individual perspectives.[7] Robin Dunbar's recent intervention into the debate reveals the possibilities of this combined approach; he argues that gossip is the evolution of primate grooming, a mechanism through which humans establish and maintain social bonds. As social networks expanded, humans needed a more practicable method of maintaining social connections than physical grooming. According to Dunbar, human language developed in order to fill that role. In short, humans learned to talk so that they could gossip with one another.[8]

Literary critics have imported these sociological models in order both to investigate and to account for gossip's all-pervasive presence in Western literature; in the process they have shifted the terms of the debate. Building

---

presented at Dirt: An Interdisciplinary Conference, Center for Literary and Cultural Study, Harvard University (March 1996).

3. Max Gluckman, "Gossip and Scandal," *Current Anthropology* 4, no. 3 (1963): 307–16. Sally Engle Merry has recently questioned the applicability of this model to all communities, suggesting that in an urban environment, gossip's effect is diffused. "Rethinking Gossip and Scandal," in *Toward a General Theory of Social Control*, vol. 1, *The Fundamentals*, ed. Donald Black (New York: Academic Press, 1984), 271–302.

4. John Beard Haviland, *Gossip, Reputation, and Knowledge in Zinacantan* (Chicago: University of Chicago Press, 1977).

5. Robert Paine was the first to suggest that gossip's primary function was individual advancement. "What Is Gossip About? An Alternative Hypothesis," *Man: The Journal of the Royal Anthropological Institute* 2, no. 2 (1967): 278–85.

6. Ralph L. Rosnow and Gary Alan Fine, *Rumor and Gossip: the Social Psychology of Hearsay* (New York: Elsevier, 1976).

7. Luise White, "Between Gluckman and Foucault: Historicizing Rumor and Gossip," *Social Dynamics* 20, no. 1 (1994): 75–92; and Jörg R. Bergmann, *Discreet Indiscretions: The Social Organization of Gossip*, trans. John Bednarz, Jr. (New York: Aldine de Gruyter, 1993). White provides a helpful survey of contemporary gossip theory.

8. Robin Dunbar, *Grooming, Gossip, and the Evolution of Language* (Cambridge: Harvard University Press, 1996).

on the pioneering work of Patricia Spacks, scholars have interpreted gossip as a mode of resistance, a subversive speech that *"will not be suppressed."*[9] Feminists, queer theorists, and scholars of minority discourses have suggested the larger social and literary stakes of this subversive speech, arguing that gossip is the "resistant oral discourse of marginalized groups," a means of critiquing majority culture and protecting community interests.[10] While critics have explored gossip across the range of historical periods, discussion has focused primarily on nineteenth- and twentieth-century fiction, as scholars have pursued Spacks's claim that gossip is integral to novelistic narration.[11] Those few scholars, such as Karma Lochrie, who address medieval gossip, have embraced the current trend in gossip theory, interpreting idle talk as a transgressive social phenomenon—the resistant speech of that most marginalized of social groups, medieval women.[12] Such an assumption, however, obscures as much as it reveals.

As I argue in this book, transformation rather than transgression is the principle underlying this discursive phenomenon. Although the models provided by contemporary gossip theorists provide insight into individual aspects of gossip's multifaceted work, none of them adequately accounts for the role of idle talk in late medieval England and the concern it produced in civil and ecclesiastical authorities alike. While medieval English writers do exploit gossip's capacity for social transgression, depicting women whose idle talk threatens to subvert official discourse, to reduce gossip to the status of marginalized speech is to overlook the ways in which it influences and

9. Patricia Meyer Spacks, *Gossip* (New York: Knopf, 1985), 263. I am indebted to Spacks's richly suggestive study, particularly her first two chapters on gossip's reputation and its "problematics."

10. Karma Lochrie, *Covert Operations: The Medieval Uses of Secrecy* (Philadelphia: University of Pennsylvania Press, 1999), 57. See also Karen C. Adkins, "The Real Dirt: Gossip and Feminist Epistemology," *Social Epistemology* 16, no. 3 (2002): 215–32; Patricia A. Turner, *I Heard It Through the Grapevine: Rumor in African-American Culture* (Berkeley and Los Angeles: University of California Press, 1993); Deborah Jones, "Gossip: Notes on Women's Oral Culture." *Women's Studies International Quarterly* 3, nos. 2–3 (1980): 193–98; and Jennifer Coates, "Gossip Revisited: Language in All-Female Groups," in *Women in Their Speech Communities: New Perspectives on Language and Sex,* ed. Jennifer Coates and Deborah Cameron (London: Longman, 1988), 94–122.

11. "Novelistic narrators often arouse in readers the kind of intense interest in personal detail that gossip generates, and they may attempt to establish with their readers a kind of relationship approximating that of gossip." Spacks, *Gossip,* 10. See also Jan B. Gordon, *Gossip and Subversion in Nineteenth-Century British Fiction: Echo's Economies* (Basingstoke, Eng.: Macmillan, 1996).

12. Lochrie, *Covert Operations,* 56–92. See also Sylvia Schein, "Used and Abused: Gossip in Medieval Society," in *Good Gossip,* ed. Robert F. Goodman and Aaron Ben-Ze'ev (Lawrence: University Press of Kansas, 1994), 139–53.

structures orthodox literary and religious practices. Idle talk is not simply women's speech in late medieval England; it is both the obstacle and the tool of priests and pastoral writers. And it is a device that enables vernacular poets to reinterpret Latin textual culture.[13] Moreover, to reduce all idle talk to women's work is both to miss the complicated ways in which Middle English writers represented women's gossip and to underestimate its power. Gossip was certainly as transgressive in the Middle Ages as it is in contemporary culture, but to focus exclusively on the idea of transgression ignores the discursive appropriations that make idle talk both so problematic and so productive in late medieval England.

My focus on gossip's idleness has both a practical and methodological dimension. In Middle English, "gossip" refers not to speech but to a pastoral office, connoting not triviality but spiritual responsibility. A gossip was a godparent, a baptismal sponsor bound in spiritual kinship to both the godchild and its parents.[14] The talk we now recognize as "gossip" was known as "jangling" or "ydel talke," a Sin of the Tongue that encompassed a range of verbal transgressions: excessive chatter, impudent and unproductive speech, tale-telling, news, disturbing reports, bawdy jokes, lies, and scorning one's neighbor.[15] To claim that idleness was the defining feature of medieval gos-

---

13. Nicholas Watson's work on vernacularity has forced scholars to reconsider the status and influence of vernacular writing in fourteenth- and fifteenth-century England. The texts I discuss in this book both attest to Watson's claims about the complicated negotiations between Latin and vernacular cultural production and reveal the influential role that idle talk played in those negotiations. Nicholas Watson, "Censorship and Cultural Change in Late-Medieval England: Vernacular Theology, the Oxford Translation Debate, and Arundel's Constitutions of 1409," *Speculum* 70, no. 4 (1995): 822–64; and Jocelyn Wogan-Browne, Nicholas Watson, Andrew Taylor, and Ruth Evans, eds., *The Idea of the Vernacular: An Anthology of Middle English Literary Theory, 1280–1520* (University Park: The Pennsylvania State University Press, 1999).

14. *Oxford English Dictionary*, s.v. "gossip"; and the *Middle English Dictionary*, s.v. "god-sib(be."

15. First catalogued by Guillaume Peyraut in his *Summa de vitiis*, the Sins of the Tongue became a standard tool for pastoral writers treating verbal transgression. Most Middle English manuals reduce Peyraut's list of twenty-four sins to ten (the branches of the tree of wicked tongue), conflating several categories. As a result, idle talk—*ociosa verba*—comes to include *multiloquium, rumor, scurrilitas, turpiloquium*, and *bonorum derisio*. On the discourse of the Sins of the Tongue, see Edwin D. Craun's thorough and insightful study, *Lies, Slander, and Obscenity in Medieval English Literature: Pastoral Rhetoric and the Deviant Speaker* (Cambridge: Cambridge University Press, 1997), 10–24. I explore in detail the placement and explication of idle talk within this larger context in "'Janglynge in cherche': Gossip and the Exemplum," in *The Hands of the Tongue: Essays on Deviant Speech*, ed. Edwin D. Craun (Kalamazoo: Medieval Institute Publications, 2007), 61–94, esp. 63–69.

sip does not distinguish it from this speech in contemporary culture. As Spacks has argued, "Gossip insists on its own frivolity. Even the most destructive gossip does not announce its destructive intent; the talk's alleged 'idleness' protects its participants."[16] But while frivolity might protect modern speakers from recrimination, in late medieval England, idleness was what made jangling so deeply problematic, so detrimental to participants, implicating them in all manner of venial and deadly sin. As penitential manuals were fond of warning, on Judgment Day, gossiping parishioners would be required to render accounts for every idle word they spoke.[17] In medieval England, it was gossip's triviality that made it so consequential.

Ecclesiastical and civil authorities denounced jangling as a dangerously paradoxical discourse: unproductive speech with an unlimited capacity for sin. As one fourteenth-century penitential manual warns parishioners, "Men clepen [call] hem idele wordes, but þei beþ not ydel, for þei beþ wel dere and ful of harm and wel perilous."[18] At once idle and prolific, jangling was identified as the cause of a range of spiritual ills. Priests and penitential writers complain bitterly that gossip's idle tales corrupted parishioners and interfered with pastoral instruction, distracting attention from devotion and stripping the heart of all virtue to fill it with vanities. Preachers railed against the frivolous chatter that disrupted their sermons, deploying all the tools in their pastoral arsenal to silence it. What is more, idle talk was as much a social menace as a spiritual one. Jangling not only maligned good men; it disturbed the peace, causing civil and spiritual unrest with its unsettling tales.

Implicated in countless sins, yet never reducible to any of them, gossip was problematic for medieval authorities not simply because it was an ever-present interruption but also because it proved an elusive foe, contaminating the pastoral discourse levied against it. In the precise and ordered rhetoric of penitential manuals, which carefully enumerated the divisions and subdivisions of sin, jangling was a disruptive force, blurring categories and crossing boundaries. Attempts to define and describe it produced confusion

16. Spacks, *Gossip*, 6.

17. A commonplace in pastoral discussion of idle talk, the passage originates in Matthew 12:36: "Dico autem vobis quoniam omne verbum otiosum quod locuti fuerint homines reddent rationem de eo in die iudicii." *Biblia sacra iuxta Vulgatam versionem*, ed. Robert Weber, 3rd ed. (Stuttgart: Deutsche Bibelgesellschaft, 1983).

18. *The Book of Vices and Virtues*, ed. W. Nelson Francis, EETS, o.s. 217 (London: EETS, 1942), 55/20–22.

and contradiction. Where other vices are described in concrete terms as the leaves, branches, or parts of sin, idle talk has "maners," a word referring as much to form as content, suggesting that how one engages in idle talk is just as consequential as what one says. Moreover, while most manuals catalogue the same five manners of idle speech, readers seem to have had great difficulty drawing the appropriate distinctions between them; medieval scribes and printers, as well as modern editors, both exaggerate and underestimate the number of sins gossip entails.[19] Explication proves even more difficult than enumeration. In their attempts to warn parishioners of the dangers posed by this supposedly frivolous speech, pastoral writers define idle talk through competing terms that make this unprofitable speech seem profitable. Jangling, penitential manuals declare, is at once light and heavy, trifling and consequential, worthless and costly. These paradoxical binaries are doctrinally consistent; however, because idle talk exists solely in these oppositions, it becomes speech with the ability to move between opposites, changing one into the other. Gossip's capacity for transformation thus becomes apparent even at the level of pastoral explication.

Pastoral practice provides the backdrop for my discussion of medieval gossip because—whether on the pages of penitential manuals or in the stanzas of narrative poems—for vernacular writers, idle talk and pastoral rhetoric are deeply intertwined.[20] For ecclesiastical authorities, idle talk poses both a practical problem and an institutional threat; two of the Church's most important tools of instruction and social control—confession and sermon—are both contaminated by and implicated in idle talk. Preachers do not simply rail against gossip; they traffic in it, enticing parishioners with detailed stories that come dangerously close to the congregation's unlicensed taletelling: exemplarity emulates jangling. Similarly, although authorities express anxiety about gossip's propensity to breach confessional secrecy, they

19. In his *Ryal Book*, William Caxton declares that there are "vi maners," while listing the same five as appear elsewhere (fol. F3v). The scribe of British Library, MS Additional 17103, who denotes all other subspecies of deviant speech with individual capitulum marks, identifies only three manners though his text lists all five (fols. 17v–18r). And Richard Morris, the first modern editor of the *Ayenbite of Inwyt* notes only four manners in his marginal comments, even though his text explicitly states that there are five. *Ayenbite of Inwyt; or, Remorse of Conscience*, ed. Richard Morris, EETS, o.s. 23 (London: Trübner, 1866), 58.

20. Given scholarly interest in court intrigue, it might seem that a social rather than pastoral setting would provide a more obvious framework for a discussion of medieval gossip. English writers, however, appear to have been less interested in gossip's courtly machinations than in its pastoral indiscretions and appropriations. That is, the Church rather than the court informs late medieval literary representations of idle talk.

demand that parishioners deliver complete and detailed penitential narratives that share much with idle talk.

What is more, poets exploit the slippage between these ecclesiastical tools and the gossip they are designed to contain. English authors represent jangling as the sinful, unproductive, distorting, and proliferating speech condemned by their clerical contemporaries. Yet even as they appear to confirm this rhetoric, writers reveal the literary and social transformations gossip enables. Indeed, Chaucer recuperates those aspects of jangling deemed so problematic by ecclesiastical authorities. Idle talk in all its pastoral infamy enables the narrative experimentation so fundamental to Chaucerian poetics. Few Middle English authors treat gossip as sympathetically as Chaucer, but many share his interest in the intersections between pastoral practice and the idle talk it condemns. When late medieval literary characters gossip, they do not merely converse, they recount unorthodox exempla, deliver co-opted saints' lives, and participate in an alternative form of confession—a mutual exchange of secrets that is both more compelling and more effective than its orthodox rival. Gossip's ability to appropriate pastoral discourse is acknowledged even by those writers who attempt to neutralize jangling by dismissing it as the pastime of idle women. The Gossips who appear in late medieval literature are not just wives who chatter idly about their husbands' "wares," but women whose conversation remakes orthodox textual and pastoral practice.

By exploring the ways in which pastoral practice is informed by idle talk for preachers as well as poets, this book does not simply illustrate gossip's powers of transformation; it shifts the focus of current critical paradigms for late medieval confession and exemplarity. The advent of New Historicism in Medieval Studies has produced much-needed revisions to existing models of late medieval pastoral practice, taking into account the social and political dimensions of these ecclesiastical tools. Whereas earlier scholarly models of the exemplum represented this narrative form as a passive instrument of Church doctrine, recent scholarship has demonstrated that these sermon stories have an ideological power all their own.[21] Although this rich work

---

21. The first and most wide-ranging of these studies is Larry Scanlon's *Narrative, Authority, and Power: The Medieval Exemplum and the Chaucerian Tradition* (Cambridge: Cambridge University Press, 1994). For more recent interventions into this debate, see Mark Miller, "Displaced Souls, Idle Talk, Spectacular Scenes: *Handlyng Synne* and the Perspective of Agency," *Speculum* 71, no. 3 (1996): 606–32; Judith Ferster, *Fictions of Advice: The Literature and Politics of Counsel in Late Medieval England* (Philadelphia: University of Pennsylvania Press, 1996); and Elizabeth

has recuperated the often-overlooked complexities of medieval exemplarity, scholars have been primarily concerned with the intentions of the religious and political authorities who deploy these narratives, rather than the audiences who experience, and indeed resist, them.[22] As a result, this scholarship has failed to account for the ways in which late medieval exemplary practice caters to the tastes of unruly parishioners, competing with and adopting the tactics of the congregation's idle talk. Confession, too, has been both illuminated and obscured by the scholarly focus on "authority." Heavily influenced by Foucault, historicists have interpreted confession as a tool of surveillance—a technology of truth-production that requires self-revelation.[23] But gossip's penitential disruptions—the stories it tells both during and about confession—generate a strikingly different paradigm. As I demonstrate in the pages that follow, confessional practice consisted of taletelling as much as surveillance, and confessional theory was as concerned with narrative as with truth-production.

This book investigates the intersection between unofficial speech, pastoral practice, and literary production in late medieval England. Beginning with preachers who employ jangling as a device for reframing their authorized tales and concluding with the Gossips who use idle talk to restructure their social world, its chapters move from an exploration of gossip's role in narrative practice toward an examination of the social ramifications of this narrative strategy. Accompanying this progression is an increasing concern with the gendering of idle talk, as the chapters turn from gossip as the tool of male priests and narrators to gossip as women's work. Yet as each of the book's chapters attests, whether on the tongues of clerics, poets, or female characters, idle talk's discursive appropriations inspire both unofficial narratives and unorthodox pastoral care.

Chapters 1 and 2 explore gossip's role in pastoral and poetic practice. " 'Janglynge in cherche': Pastoral Practice and Idle Talk," analyzes the methods late medieval preachers and moralizing poets used to both depict and diffuse the threat of idle talk. More than an incidental problem for ecclesiastical authority, gossip poses a fundamental challenge to pastoral practice.

Allen, *False Fables and Exemplary Truth in Later Middle English Literature* (New York: Palgrave Macmillan, 2005).

22. Allen's insightful exploration of the reading practices necessitated by late medieval exemplarity is a notable exception to this trend.

23. For a recent formulation of this argument, see Lochrie, *Covert Operations*, 12–55.

Jangling in church, the chapter argues, is institutionally embedded, integral to both theory and the practice of pastoral instruction; it not only contaminates but also provides the model for the very pastoral tools designed to silence it. "Chaucerian Small Talk" investigates the ways in which Chaucer incorporates gossip into his poetry, both as a means to explore a discourse condemned by ecclesiastical authority and as a way to experiment with narrative itself. This second chapter discusses Chaucer's theory of gossip as it is sketched in the *House of Fame* and his practice of it in the *Canterbury Tales*. Idle talk catalyzes not only narrative exchanges that seem to reproduce actual gossip but also the generic alchemy so central to the *Canterbury Tales*, as fabliaux become exempla and exempla become idle tales. Turning literary "auctoritee" into "small talk," Chaucer, I argue, uses gossip as means to transform his old sources into new tales.

Taking the Wife of Bath's secret-sharing as a template, the book's final two chapters raise the question of how gossip becomes women's work. "'Sisteris in schrift': Gossip's Confessional Kinship," investigates the conversational communities of the wives and widows depicted in Chaucer's *Shipman's Tale* and Dunbar's *Tretis of Twa Mariit Wemen and the Wedo*. Represented as establishing kinship through their adaptation of confession, the women in these texts supplant relationships based on consanguinity and marriage with alliances forged through idle talk to become "sisteris in schrift." As the chapter demonstrates, these conversational siblings do not limit their co-optation of pastoral practice to confession alone, but rather are depicted as translating into a kind of wifely vernacular the products and practices of Latin textual and pastoral culture. "The Gospel According to Gossips, or How Gossip Got Its Name" takes as its subject the medieval Gossips—those suspect women who proliferate in late medieval carols, ballads, and narrative poems—focusing in particular on the communities of women depicted in the *Gospelles of Dystaues* and the *Fyftene Joyes of Maryage*. The women discussed in this final chapter are gossips in the original sense of the word, baptismal sponsors who reinvent their pastoral offices. Rather than inducting a newborn into the community of the faithful, these sponsors initiate young women into the community of Gossips, instructing them in female textual and cultural practice. That the label "gossip" becomes a particularly English way of diffusing this problematic female erudition is the chapter's ultimate claim as it explores how baptismal sponsors become the idle talk in which they engage.

This book is not just about frivolous talk. It explores a discursive phenomenon that fundamentally shaped the culture of late medieval England. If we as scholars want to understand medieval pastoral theory and practice, we have to consider not only the ecclesiastical authorities who regulated it, but also the wayward parishioners and less than perfect priests who "jangle" in church. More often than not, sermons were delivered before chattering congregations to whose tastes preachers' "authorized" narratives were obliged to cater. And while confession certainly enabled priests to probe the souls of their flock, it also licensed narratives, penitential and otherwise, which both participate in and circulate as idle talk. Similarly, if we want to account fully for the status of the vernacular in medieval England, we need to consider not simply the justifications offered by erudite theological and literary theoretical texts, but the surprising strategies through which popular vernacular poetry staged its contest with Latin textual culture—strategies that are indebted to idle talk.

"JANGLYNGE IN CHERCHE":
PASTORAL PRACTICE AND IDLE TALK

Among the more surprising aspects of late medieval ecclesiastical authority is the fact that its most serious challenge comes not from heretical uprisings but from the seemingly frivolous discourse of idle talk. Although heresy certainly poses an undeniable threat to the Church in late medieval England, the intense scholarly focus on heresy in recent decades has obscured our view of the less obvious, though no less serious, problems with which authorities grappled. Gossip is the most glaring of these omissions, for concern over it is almost universal. Indeed, complaint about gossip is the most consistent feature of Middle English pastoral literature.[1] On the pages of penitential manuals, sermon collections, and religious treatises, writers denounce the evils of "jangling in church," condemning the idle talk that disrupts pastoral instruction.[2] Jangling transcends ideological boundaries,

---

1. According to G. R. Owst, idle talk during the divine service was so common that "hardly an English sermon collection fails to deal with it" (173–74). *Preaching in Medieval England: An Introduction to Sermon Manuscripts of the Period c. 1350–1450* (New York: Russell and Russell, 1965). While a complete list of all Middle English pastoral literature addressing the problem of "jangling in church" would be too cumbersome, the following is a representative sample: the *Book of Penance* (c. 1300), *Handlyng Synne* (c. 1303), *Ayenbite of Inwit* (c. 1340), the *Book of Vices and Virtues* (c. 1375), *Speculum Vitae* (c. 1375), *A Myrour to Lewede Men and Wymmen* (c. 1400), *Jacob's Well* (c. 1425), and both Mirk's *Festial* (c. 1425) and his *Instructions for Parish Priests* (c. 1425).

2. While "gossip" itself does not acquire the signification of idle and trifling talk until the nineteenth century (*Oxford English Dictionary*, s.v. "gossip"), its medieval godparent is "jan-

disturbing the attempts of both orthodox and heterodox preachers to gain verbal control over their audiences.[3] Whether secular or monastic, male or female, urban or rural, learned or "lewed," all congregations gossip in church.[4] So pervasive is the problem that it merits its own devil, Tutivillus, the recording demon who is invoked by clerics with such frequency that he becomes part of the cultural imagination.[5] Despite the ubiquity of clerical condemnation of idle talk, gossip's institutional challenge has been largely ignored as a subject of inquiry, not only because scholars have been preoccupied with heresy, but also because gossip's deceptive frivolity would seem to argue against its being taken seriously. Yet it is precisely gossip's triviality, its status as idle amusement, that renders it so institutionally problematic.

Even as medievalists have emphasized the significance of the social structures underlying institutional threats to the Church, they have dismissed gossip as a straightforwardly social problem. Overlooking gossip's institutional implications, critics, when they discuss the topic at all, have interpreted jangling in church as the practical problem of individual preachers trying to control their chattering congregations, a social interaction that frustrates particular individuals but does not threaten pastoral practice in any significant way.[6] Those scholars who have explored the pastoral implica-

gling," the idle speech that scorns neighbors, tells new and distressing tales, and never ceases (*Oxford English Dictionary*, s.v. "jangling"; *Middle English Dictionary*, s.v. "jangling").

3. Texts as ideologically divergent as the *Lanterne of Liȝt*, the *Pricke of Conscience*, and the *Lay Folks Mass Book* clamor in unison about gossip's evil work. *The Lanterne of Liȝt*, ed. Lilian M. Swinburn, EETS, o.s. 151 (London: Kegan Paul, Trench, Trübner, 1917), 50–57; the *Pricke of Conscience*, ed. Richard Morris (London: Philological Society, 1863), lines 3478–81; and the *Lay Folks Mass Book*, ed. Thomas Frederick Simmons, EETS, o.s. 71 (London: Kegan Paul, Trench, Trübner, 1879), 4–5.

4. Even the sisters of Sion Abbey are not above jangling during the divine service, as the *Myroure of Our Ladye* reveals. *The Myroure of Oure Ladye*, ed. John Henry Blunt, EETS, o.s. 19 (London: Trübner, 1873), 46–47.

5. In addition to being invoked in countless Middle English penitential manuals and sermon collections, Tutivillus appears on manuscript flyleaves and stars in morality plays. For a complete account of the demon's popularity as well as an extensive catalogue of his literary and pastoral appearances, see Margaret Jennings's exhaustive study, "Tutivillus: The Literary Career of the Recording Demon," *Studies in Philology* 74, no. 5 (1977): 1–95. Kathy Cawsey's recent provocative essay extends Jennings's study, exploring the ways in which the Tutivillus figure serves as a nexus for a range of issues threatening late medieval English social and religious authorities. "Tutivillus and the 'Kyrkchaterars': Strategies of Control in the Middle Ages," *Studies in Philology* 102, no. 4 (2005): 434–51. See also Susanna Greer Fein's discovery of Tutivillus' appearance in the Audelay MS. "A Thirteen-Line Alliterative Stanza on the Abuse of Prayer from the Audelay MS," *Medium Ævum* 63, no. 1 (1994): 61–74.

6. Most studies of late medieval preaching practice gloss over jangling in church as an amusing and inevitable obstacle. See, for example, Owst, *Preaching in Medieval England*, 173–80; Siegfried Wenzel, *The Sin of Sloth: Acedia in Medieval Thought and Literature* (Chapel Hill: Uni-

tions of verbal transgression have treated gossip incidentally, as the trivial and self-evident cousin of more dangerous types of speech, such as lying and blasphemy.[7] Yet gossip's idle words are no trivial matter for ecclesiastical authorities. Idle talk is far more than an incidental problem—more than simply an unavoidable professional hazard for the late medieval preacher. Gossip poses a fundamental challenge to ecclesiastical authority, for jangling in church is not merely the pastime of unruly congregations, it is the strategy of the clerics who instruct them and the ever-present obstacle with which late medieval pastoral practice must contend.

Gossip's institutional challenge inheres in its contamination, as well as its disruption, of pastoral practice. Two of the Church's most important tools of instruction and social control, confession and the exemplum, are continually vulnerable to gossip's idle tales. On the tongues of priests and parishioners alike, idle talk turns confession into a forum for the latest news and transforms authorized exempla into idle tales. We might be inclined to dismiss these transgressions as the consequence of wayward parishioners and less than perfect priests, the fault, that is, of flawed individuals. Jangling in church, however, is institutionally embedded, integral to both theory and the practice of pastoral instruction. Both confession and the exemplum are structured by their recounting of narrative detail. Just as exempla instruct through detailed stories, so confession's penitential narratives are defined by their diligent recitation of specific details. While specificity is what makes these practices effective as pastoral tools, it is also what renders them susceptible to idle talk. As I will argue in this chapter, gossip, through its trafficking in specific details, does not simply contaminate pastoral practice; it provides the model for the very pastoral tools designed to silence it.

---

versity of North Carolina Press, 1960), 113 and 150–54; and H. Leith Spencer, *English Preaching in the Late Middle Ages* (Oxford: Clarendon Press, 1993), esp. 1–3 and 64–76. A notable exception is Mark Miller, who explores Robert Mannyng's concern about the relationship between idle talk and his pastoral project. For Miller, however, idle talk is not gossip but ineffective pastoral speech. Miller, "Displaced Souls," 606–32.

7. The most thorough account of pastoral writing on verbal transgression is Edwin Craun's insightful exploration of the Sins of the Tongue. Because Craun's study covers such a broad range of Latin and vernacular treatises, tracing their influence on late medieval English literature, he is unable to address all types of sinful speech, relegating idle talk to the margins of his discussion. Craun, *Lies, Slander, and Obscenity*. See also, Carla Casagrande and Silvana Vecchio, *Les Péchés de la langue*, trans. Philippe Baillet (Paris: Les Éditions du Cerf, 1991) and Joan Heiges Blythe, "Sins of the Tongue and Rhetorical Prudence in 'Piers Plowman,'" in *Literature and Religion in the Later Middle Ages*, ed. Richard G. Newhauser and John A. Alford (Binghamton, N.Y.: Medieval and Renaissance Texts and Studies, 1995), 119–42.

Tracing the institutional consequences of idle talk does more than recuperate gossip from its trivial reputation, more, that is, than expose an overlooked challenge facing ecclesiastical authority; it requires us to reassess our understanding of late medieval pastoral practice. More specifically, examining pastoral practice through the lens of idle talk reveals the limitations of current critical paradigms for both confession and exemplarity. In recent years, Larry Scanlon's study, *Narrative, Authority, and Power,* has stood as the definitive text on medieval exemplarity. Rejecting earlier scholarship that reduced these narratives to passive vehicles of Church doctrine, Scanlon argues that the exemplum wields a persuasive power dependent on and, indeed, "constituted by its rhetorical specificity as narrative."[8] Concerned with the ways in which authoritative political and religious structures deploy exempla in order to shore up their own, often unstable, moral authority, he reads exemplary practice as a mechanism for perpetuating forms of social power. Extending Scanlon's discussion, scholars have recuperated the exemplum as political, pastoral, and literary tool.[9] While bringing to light both the richness of individual narratives and the complex exemplary strategies practiced by late medieval clerics, this body of scholarship, because it is concerned with the authorities who use exempla rather than the congregations who hear them, has overlooked the limitations and problematic appropriations that are endemic to late medieval exemplarity. Elizabeth Allen has quite rightly called into question the stability of exemplary narratives and thus their efficacy as instruments of cultural power. For Allen, exempla are inherently unstable; they "continually exceed or call into question the univocal doctrine they are designed to convey."[10] As such, medieval exemplary practice requires discerning readers who are actively engaged in negotiating between moral generalities and narrative specificity—an audience who recognizes that "reading constitutes moral activity."[11] In attending to the audience of the exempla, Allen makes a much-needed intervention. Her rich and suggestive study uncovers a great deal about the complex negotiations inherent in late medieval exemplary practice; however, her focus on reading as a "moral activity" nonetheless assumes an audience sympathetic to the intentions of the priest or moralizing poet. Consequently, she, like Scanlon

---

8. Scanlon, *Narrative, Authority, and Power,* 31.
9. See, for example, Mark Miller's investigation of how Robert Mannyng uses the exemplum to explore and establish his own unstable moral authority. Miller, "Displaced Souls."
10. Allen, *False Fables,* 11.
11. Ibid., 16.

and others, have ignored those resistant and recalcitrant parishioners who tell idle tales, reinterpret official narratives, and jangle in church. Yet late medieval exemplarity was practiced in relation to precisely these parishioners. Preachers and penitential writers used exempla to substitute authorized narratives for the idle tales of their audiences, simultaneously railing against and catering to their sinful tastes.

Recent discussions of confession have similarly focused on the institutional efficacy of pastoral practice, exploring confession's role as a tool of surveillance and interrogation. In her work on medieval secrecy, Karma Lochrie has argued that confession was a technology for producing both the truth and the self through its negotiation of secrets.[12] Although Lochrie does investigate the means through which individual sinners might resist confessional practice, interpreting confession as a "complicated mesh of seductions and manipulations," she nonetheless assumes that a consistent and untroubled logic of truth-production underlies confessional theory.[13] Like Lochrie, Dyan Elliott is interested in the ways that ecclesiastical authorities deployed confession as a mechanism for producing truth.[14] Her comprehensive study of female spirituality and inquisitional culture demonstrates the slippage between ecclesiastical and juridical confession, as authorities increasingly used confessional practice both to prove orthodoxy and to supply information about heresy. For Elliott, this slippage is most obvious in, and indeed draws its authorization from, the canons of the Fourth Lateran Council, which privileged juridical as well as sacramental confession; thus, the document mandating private auricular confession both assumed and exploited confession's capacity for truth-production. Idle talk's confessional ruptures, however, reveal a practice motivated by the art of tale-telling, not one based solely on interrogation and surveillance. Rather than constituting a breach of confessional decorum, this tale-telling arises from the adherence to penitential rules. That is, confessional theory is based in narrative exchange.

My discussion of jangling in church begins with the preacher of *Jacob's Well*, an early fifteenth-century cleric whose sermon cycle explicitly stages the battle between pastoral instruction and idle talk. His understudied text reveals just how central a problem jangling in church might have been.

12. Lochrie, *Covert Operations*, 12–55.
13. Ibid., 37.
14. Dyan Elliott, *Proving Woman: Female Spirituality and Inquisitional Culture in the Later Middle Ages* (Princeton: Princeton University Press, 2004), 9–43.

More than a practical problem to be solved, jangling fundamentally shapes his preaching practice. Relentlessly browbeating his audience with exempla about the dangers of idle talk, this preacher reveals both the limitations and the pitfalls of late medieval exemplary practice. From the battle for verbal control waged in *Jacob's Well,* I turn to the narrative substitution practiced by Robert Mannyng. Representing his text *Handlyng Synne* as a replacement for his congregation's idle tales rather than a condemnation of them, Mannyng appropriates idle talk as a narrative mode. He trades on the illicit specificity of his narratives, catering to the tastes of his audience by transforming his exempla into a kind of officially sanctioned gossip. In the second half of this chapter, I move from priests' stories to sinners' tales, examining confession, the pastoral practice in which idle talk is most deeply embedded. Not simply a matter of how confession is enacted by individuals, gossip's tale-telling, I argue, structures confessional exchange.

The Battle for Verbal Control

In late medieval England, no priest or penitential writer was more preoccupied with idle talk than the preacher of *Jacob's Well*.[15] Although little is known with any certainty about the professional life of this cleric, scholars have concluded that he ministered to a rural congregation located near Suffolk.[16] Drawing on two major sources—the *Speculum Vitae*, a Middle English verse edition of Lorens d'Orléans's *Somme le Roi,* and the *Alphabetum*

15. I follow Leo Carruthers and Clinton Atchley in taking the author at his word that these sermons were in fact delivered. Leo Carruthers, "The Liturgical Setting of *Jacob's Well*," *English Language Notes* 24, no. 4 (1987): 11–23 and "Allegory and Bible Interpretation: The Narrative Structure of a Middle English Sermon Cycle," *Literature and Theology* 4, no. 1 (1990): 1–14; and Clinton Parham Edwin Atchley, "The 'Wose' of *Jacob's Well*: Text and Context" (Ph.D. diss., University of Washington, 1998), 40–66. For a more cautious account, see Spencer, *English Preaching*, 214–15. The first fifty sermons of *Jacob's Well* were edited by Arthur Brandeis, *Jacob's Well*, part I, EETS, o.s. 115 (London: Kegan Paul, Trench, Trübner, 1900); the remaining forty-five have recently been edited in Atchley's *Wose*.

16. On the basis of dialectal evidence, Carruthers has argued convincingly that the extant copy of *Jacob's Well* was produced in the center or north of Suffolk, "in the region between Bury St. Edmunds and Ipswich, although excluding both towns." Carruthers, "Where Did *Jacob's Well* Come From? The Provenance and Dialect of MS Salisbury Cathedral 103," *English Studies* 4 (1990): 335–40, 339. Carruthers goes on to suggest that this dialect and locale were also shared by the original author, especially given that he has borrowed material from another Suffolk writer, Richard of Lavynham. On the basis of internal evidence, Atchley argues that the preacher's congregation may have consisted of clergymen as well as lay men and women. Atchley, *Wose*, 28–32.

Narrationum[17]—the preacher composed his sermon cycle during the first quarter of the fifteenth century and may have performed it annually during the liturgical period between Ash Wednesday and Pentecost.[18] His ambitious project, a ninety-five-day sermon cycle that covers all aspects of the pre-scribed pastoral syllabus, resounds with complaints about the idle chatter that disrupts his service.[19] He organizes his lessons by means of an extended metaphor, teaching his congregation how to transform the shallow pit of the body into a pure well of virtue by purging the ooze of sin. While he initially refers to the members of that congregation as his "frendys" (4/31), as early as day two, he acknowledges the adversarial nature of his relation-ship with his flock, admonishing parishioners for their lack of attention. Such condemnation quickly becomes almost as consistent a feature of the three-and-a-half-month cycle as the details that sustain its structuring meta-phor. Attempting to maintain the attention of his audience, this preacher delivers weekly diatribes against his congregation's idle talk, which he incor-porates into the fabric of his lessons.[20] Condemnation is so frequent that

17. Carruthers suggests that the *Speculum Vitae* is "the principal text lying behind *Jacob's Well*." Carruthers, "Where Did *Jacob's Well* Come From?" 339. While the preacher borrows much of his pastoral material from the *Speculum Vitae*, as Joan Gregg has argued, he draws the vast majority of his numerous exempla from the *Alphabetum Narrationum*. Joan Young Gregg, "The Narrative Exempla of *Jacob's Well*: A Source Study with an Index for *Jacob's Well* to *Index Exemplorum*" (Ph.D. diss., New York University, 1973), and "The Exempla of 'Jacob's Well': A Study in the Transmission of Medieval Sermon Stories," *Traditio* 33 (1977): 359–80.

18. There is evidence to suggest that other preachers followed in his footsteps; the single surviving manuscript of *Jacob's Well* is not the author's monograph but a copy that the scribe has corrected according to a now lost exemplar. Moreover, two late fifteenth-century readers composed a subject index for the collection; each entry summarizes the content of the sermons, thus serving as a quick-reference guide for locating particular topics. Atchley, *Wose*, 7. Although they disagree on which sermon would have been performed on Easter Sunday, both Carruthers and Atchley contend that these daily sermons were delivered during the period from Ash Wednesday to Pentecost. Though the precise date of the sermon cycle remains uncertain, most scholars place its composition during the first quarter of the fifteenth century. Carruthers, "Litur-gical Setting"; Atchley, *Wose*, 1–3; Brandeis, *Jacob's Well*, x–xii; and Robert R. Raymo, "Jacob's Well," in *A Manual of the Writings in Middle English, 1050–1500*, ed. Albert E. Hartung (New Haven: Connecticut Academy of Arts and Sciences, 1967), 7:2262.

19. During the course of the sermon cycle, the preacher not only addresses all the topics on Archbishop John Pecham's syllabus, *Ignorantia sacerdotum* (1281), but expands the list, treating excommunication, tithe payment, the prohibited degrees of kindred and affinity, confession, the seven deadly sins, the bodily and spiritual senses, the virtues and vices, good works, the creed, the sacraments, the commandments, the precepts, the works of mercy, the Ave, and the Lord's Prayer. For a discussion of Pecham's syllabus and its influence on English preaching practice, see, Spencer, *English Preaching*, 201–27. The text of *Ignorantia sacerdotum* is provided in F. M. Pow-icke and C. R. Cheney, eds., *Councils and Synods with Other Documents Relating to the English Church, II: 1205–1313*, 2 vols. (Oxford: Clarendon, 1964), 2:900–905.

20. Discussions of jangling in church occur in chapters 2 (excommunication), 16 (sloth), 17

parishioners must have wondered whether there was any topic that did not have a connection to this transgressive speech. The preacher does not simply discuss idle talk in the context of its traditional associations—as a species of gluttony and the sins of the mouth or as the kind of speech endemic to sloth's idleness—rather, he insists on the connection between idle talk and most aspects of the pastoral syllabus.[21] Whether he is discussing pride or humility, prayer or confession, temperance or chastity, restitution or righteousness, he finds a way to insinuate his congregation's chatter into the lesson, even going so far as to interpret jangling in church as a violation of the Fourth Commandment, in which parishioners dishonor their "gostly fadyr" with their idle talk.[22] Given both the frequency and the increasing virulence of his condemnation, jangling in church was not simply an occasional professional hazard for the preacher of *Jacob's Well*. It was *the* problem of his pastoral endeavor.

Although the preacher avails himself of every pastoral tool designed to control idle talk, he relies most often on the exemplum, deploying an astonishing number of stories in his struggle for verbal control.[23] Emphasizing the

---

(sloth), 24 (lechery), 27 (confession), 28 (confession), 29 (satisfaction), 36 (idleness), 37 (humility), 42 (the "grauel of mysgouernaunce"), 46 (righteousness and steadfastness), 59 (chastity), 61 (temperance), 82 (the third commandment), and 83 (the fourth commandment). By week three, the author has more than compensated for the early hiatus. After Easter—chapter 45, if we accept Atchley's argument about liturgical setting—condemnation for jangling occurs less frequently, though with no less vehemence. For a discussion of liturgical setting, see Atchley, *Wose*, 49–58.

21. Although many late medieval penitential manuals discuss idle talk in the context of sloth, the vast majority attach the Sins of the Tongue to gluttony and the sins of the mouth. A notable exception to this tradition is the *Parson's Tale*, which connects verbal transgression to wrath. Craun discusses in detail the origins, placement, and development of treatises on the Sins of the Tongue. Craun, *Lies, Slander, and Obscenity*, 10–24. For a re-evaluation of the relation between the *Parson's Tale* and other penitential manuals, see the essays in David Raybin and Linda Tarte Holley, eds., *Closure in* The Canterbury Tales: The Role of The Parson's Tale (Kalamazoo: Medieval Institute Publications, 2000).

22. Atchley, *Wose*, 440–41.

23. The preacher of *Jacob's Well* relies on conventional pastoral condemnations of idle talk—those *sententiae*, definitions, biblical passages, and lists of verbal transgressions that originate with Peyraut's *Summa de vittis et virtutibus* and are found throughout the penitential literature of the later Middle Ages. This preacher, however, greatly amplifies those standard practices. For example, where other pastoral texts contain one or possibly two lists of verbal transgressions, *Jacob's Well* has three: the ten branches of the tree of "wicked tongue" (148–56)—a popular device in Middle English penitential manuals, especially those stemming from the *Somme le Roi*; the twenty-two misconducts of the tongue, a list quite close to Peyraut's twenty-four (260–63); and finally, the "sins of the mouth," a seemingly endless list containing everything from bearing false witness to foolish laughter and including nearly sixty verbal transgressions (294–95). This compulsive thoroughness is not a characteristic of the volume more generally; rather the preacher reserves it exclusively for verbal transgression. His bias is particularly clear when he discusses the

significance of idle talk's supposedly trivial words, the preacher relentlessly browbeats his congregation with the moral that talking in church leads to damnation. So many narratives are employed to exemplify this moral that it functions as the sermon cycle's refrain. In fact, he devotes more than 10 percent of his narratives, either entirely or in part, to the condemnation of idle talk—a remarkable statistic considering the comprehensive scope of his pastoral project. Like the majority of his clerical contemporaries, the preacher of *Jacob's Well* attempts to draw on the persuasive power of the exemplum, using narrative to focus his audience's attention on his particular lesson. His fixation on idle talk, however, compromises the effectiveness of his narratives. Rather than demonstrating the ideological power of the exemplum, his sermons expose the pitfalls and limitations of late medieval exemplary practice.

Perhaps the most popular exemplum for the vilification of idle speech is the story of Tutivillus, that famous recording demon who takes written account of jangling in church. The narrative first appears in Jacques de Vitry's *Sermones Vulgares,* but by the late fourteenth century, Tutivillus had become a commonplace, appearing on church walls and misericords as well as in a vast number of penitential, sermonizing, and literary texts.[24] Given this preacher's preoccupation with idle talk, it is hardly surprising that he privileges this narrative above all others, delivering the tale not once but three times.[25] Ordinarily, the Tutivillus story consists of two distinct strains, en-

---

various types of "mysgouernaunce" attributed to one's heart, one's tongue, and one's deeds: he devotes six lines to the misconduct of the heart, nine to deeds, and more than a hundred to the tongue's transgressions (260–64). Other English texts that include this tripartite listing of sins provide roughly the same number of transgressions for heart, mouth, and deed. See Richard Rolle's *Form of Living. Richard Rolle: Prose and Verse, Edited from MS Longleat 29 and Related Manuscripts,* ed. S. J. Ogilvie-Thomson, EETS, o.s. 293 (Oxford: Oxford University Press, 1988), 11–12.

24. Thomas Frederick Crane, ed., *The Exempla or Illustrative Stories from the Sermones Vulgares of Jacques de Vitry* (London, 1890), #239 and #19. In the appendices to her study, Jennings catalogues the demon's textual appearances. Jennings, "Tutivillus," 85–91. The misericord in Ely Cathedral is particularly vivid in its detailed representation of the Tutivillus exemplum: in the center, the demon sits on two jangers' shoulders; on the right-hand side, he is depicted tugging at the scroll with his teeth. In addition to the Ely misericord, Tutiviullus appears in wall paintings at Peakirk, Seething and Little Melton, Melbourne, and Colton, in a stained window at St. Nicholas, Stanford on Avon, and in misericords at Gayton and Enville. M. D. Anderson, *Drama and Imagery in English Medieval Churches* (Cambridge: Cambridge University Press, 1963), 173–77. See also Jonathan Alexander and Paul Binski, *Age of Chivalry: Art in Plantagenet England, 1200–1400* (London: Royal Academy of Arts, 1987), esp. 444–46, and Edward Clive Rouse, *Medieval Wall Paintings* (Princes Risborough, Eng.: Shire Publications, 1991), esp. 68–69.

25. The repetition of exempla in this sermon collection is rare. In all other instances, the repeated exemplum is used for two different purposes, as in the narrative of the half-burned

abling preachers to select the version most appropriate for their audience: one features the sack carrier who collects words skipped by clerics in the performance of their offices; the second depicts a writing demon who records lay verbal transgression.[26] But while most preachers and penitential writers either recount one version exclusively or treat the two versions on separate occasions, the preacher of *Jacob's Well* delivers both at the same time, using one as the prologue for the other.

His compulsion to repeat the Tutivillus exemplum throughout his sermon cycle structures his narration of the tale itself. When he first introduces his congregation to the recording demon, he begins with a short narrative about a "feend" who bears a heavy sack filled with the "stolyn" verses of negligent clerics (115/1–5). Quickly invoking the vice of his congregation, he explicates this first exemplum with a moral not about priestly sloth but about his parishioners' idle chatter: "fforsothe, þanne I trow [believe] þe feend hath a gret sacche full of ȝoure ydell woordys, that ȝe iangelyn in cherche in slowthe" (115/6–7). Rather than attempting to make sense of his moral by drawing an analogy between the cleric's dereliction and his congregation's slothful recitation of their prayers, the preacher announces that the story is really about idle talk, offering a second exemplum as proof.[27] He has already warned his audience that the devil keeps track of their words, yet he repeats this lesson several more times before his concluding moral. Tutivillus, he explains, sat in church one morning recording the idle chatter and persistent whispering of a particularly garrulous congregation. Running out of room on his scroll, he attempted to stretch it out with his teeth, but as he did so, the parchment broke and he banged his head on the church wall. A holy man, witnessing this spectacle, asked the demon to explain himself, and

woman, who first appears as a quarrelsome noblewoman (95) and later as a talkative nun (231). In *Jacob's Well*, as in many other texts that Jennings cites, the recording demon is not named.

26. Jennings, "Tutivillus," 8. Tubach catalogues the two strains as #1630a and b. Frederic C. Tubach, *Index Exemplorum; a Handbook of Medieval Religious Tales* (Helsinki: Suomalainen Tiedeakatemia, 1969).

27. In light of Atchley's claim that the *Jacob's Well* was directed at a hybrid lay-clerical audience, we might be tempted to interpret the preacher's recounting of both strains as an attempt to address separately the transgressions of both halves of his audience. Atchley, *Wose*, 28–31. Yet the preacher uses both versions of the story to illustrate the same moral, a moral directed at his congregation's idle chatter. Although some penitential writers do adapt the sack-carrier narrative for lay audiences, suggesting that the devils collects the words that lay folk mumble or skip in prayer, the idea that the devil collects the syllables of idle talk is unconventional. See Jennings, "Tutivillus," 10–34.

Tutivillus responded as follows: "I wryte þise talys of þe peple in þis cherche, to recordyn hem a-fore god at þe doom for here dampnacyoun, and my book is to narwe to wryten on alle here talys; þei say so manye. þerfore I drawe it out braddere, þat none of here talys schulde be vnwretyn" (115/ 13–17). By explaining his task in such detail, Tutivillus in effect repeats the exemplum, just in case the congregation missed it the first (or indeed second) time. Other versions of the narrative avoid this repetition by omitting either the demon's response or the opening explanation—the subject of the devil's writing is not revealed until he speaks. But for the preacher of *Jacob's Well*, repetition is fundamental to his strategy for gaining verbal control. The demon does not simply repeat the exemplum; he reinforces the preacher's stern warning about the consequences of idle talk, explaining that he records jangling to secure the congregation's damnation. At the same time, the demon echoes the beleaguered preacher's frustration, complaining about the burdensome nature of his task in "þis cherche," where "þei say so manye"—a telling narrative embellishment that is unique to *Jacob's Well*.[28]

As the preacher highlights and repeats those aspects of the exemplum designed to dissuade against idle talk, he omits those details that might soften the impact of this lesson. The majority of late medieval pastoral writers draw explicit attention to the narrative's humor. In some versions of the tale, the thud of the demon's head against the wall is so loud that it startles the whole congregation; in others, the holy man who sees the devil hit his head laughs out loud, disrupting the service and earning a reprimand from his superior.[29] But for the preacher of *Jacob's Well*, jangling in church is no laughing matter. Neither the holy man nor our preacher cracks a smile; even the demon is deadly serious about his task. Just as this preacher's lack of

---

28. In no other version of the story does Tutivillus complain about the garrulity of the congregation. In fact, the demon's voice is rarely heard in Middle English versions of the narrative. While the *Myroure of Our Ladye* recounts the devil's complaints, there the sack carrier laments not the burdens of a garrulous congregation but the beatings he will receive if he does not meet his quota of sacks "full of faylynges, & of neglygences in syllables and wordes" (54). Moreover, *An Alphabet of Tales*, a text that according to Joan Gregg shares a common source text, the *Alphabetum Narrationum*, with *Jacob's Well*, remains silent on the subject, stating only that "he tolde hym all þat is befor said." *An Alphabet of Tales*, ed. Mary Macleod Banks, EETS, o.s. 126, 127 (London: Kegan Paul, Trench, Trübner,1904), 581/20. Gregg, *Narrative Exempla*.

29. "How to hear mass," *The Minor Poems of the Vernon Manuscript*, ed. Carl Horstmann. EETS, o.s. 98, 117 (London: Kegan Paul, Trench, Trübner, 1892), 501/313–18; Jennings, "Tutivillus," 26–27. In some versions, Mary intervenes on the holy man's behalf, and the exemplum becomes an illustration of power of Mary's intercession rather than a lesson about gossip.

humor sets him apart from his fellow penitential writers, so does his pessi-mism.[30] Most other versions of the narrative conclude with the fictional congregation's penitence and the erasure of the scroll.[31] John Mirk, for ex-ample, suggests that janglers can be rehabilitated. In his version of the story, the priest confronts two gossiping women with their idle talk, reading to them from the devil's scroll and shaming them into repentance.[32] The preacher of *Jacob's Well*, however, offers no such possibility. The devil's scrolls will be read against his parishioners on Judgment Day.[33] Indeed, this preacher's attitude toward gossip is so uncompromising that he does not grant the men in his audience their usual exemption when it comes to idle talk. Resisting the cultural wisdom of the later Middle Ages, this preacher does not identify the "janglers" in his narrative as women.[34] Where wall paintings and stained glass windows, most medieval poets, and many mod-ern dictionaries all gender gossip as women's work, the author of *Jacob's Well* recognizes it as an all-too-universal occupation.[35]

Despite the preacher's relentless insistence that the devil's accounting will indict every chattering parishioner, the moral he delivers suggests that his

30. Gregg takes note of the preacher's austere tendencies more generally: "By rigidly exclud-ing any tale which could even remotely be suspected of levity, the English sermon composer evinces an unwillingness to compromise his homiletic material which was not wholly typical of his age." Gregg, "Exempla of 'Jacob's Well,'" 374.

31. This pattern originates in the first version of the exemplum found in Jacques de Vitry's *Sermones Vulgares*, Thomas F. Crane, ed., *The Exempla or Illustrative Stories from the Sermones Vulgares of Jacques de Vitry* (London, 1890), #239. See also Jennings, "Tutivillus," 41.

32. John Mirk, *Festial*, part I, ed. Theodor Erbe, EETS, e.s. 96 (London: Kegan Paul, Trench, Trübner, 1905), 279–80.

33. While the narrative, in its many versions, stages a competition between the oral and the written, between the words of parishioners and a scribal culture that can record and condemn it, the contest emphasized by the author of *Jacob's Well* is not primarily that of an oral culture vs. a scribal one, but rather that of two competing kinds of speech. For a discussion of the larger cultural implication of Tutivillus's scroll, see Cawsey, "Tutivillus and the 'Kyrkchaterars.'"

34. Jennings argues that identification of the "female presence" in the narrative comes to be one of its most consistent characteristics. Jennings, "Tutivillus," 27. Among the Middle English versions of the narrative, Mirk's *Festial*, the *Book of the Knight of the Tower*, the *Lay Folks Mass Book*, and *Handlyng Synne* all explicitly identify the janglers as women.

35. Mirk, for example, in addition to having Tutivillus sit on women's shoulders, offers an extended discussion of women's loquacity in his sermon on the Visitation, observing that since Mary spoke only four times in the Gospels, contemporary women should curtail their speech. *Festial* (London, 1491), fols. R₁r–R₃v. The translation of Peyraut's *Summa* contained in BL MS Harley 6571 departs from its source to offer a similar argument in a discussion of loquacity (fols. 67r–v). This text has been edited by F. N. M. Diekstra, *Book for a Simple and Devout Woman: A Late Middle English Adaptation of Peraldus's Summa de Vitiis et Virtutibus and Friar Laurent's Somme le Roi, edited from British Library Mss Harley 6571 and Additional 30944*, Mediaevalia Groningana, 24. (Groningen: Egbert Forsten, 1998), 296.

audience is unaffected by his pastoral strategies. Instead of concluding with a generic statement of moral instruction, such as the Vernon manuscript's exhortation to think on God's wrath or Robert Mannyng's advice to janglers to hold their tongues,[36] the preacher of *Jacob's Well* speaks with all-too-vivid specificity about the relevance of this tale to his wayward congregation: "I drede me þanne, þe feend hath a gret book aȝens [against] ȝou, wretyn of ȝoure ianglynges in cherch, & ȝit ȝe excusyn ȝow þere-in and seyn: 'me must | speke to hym þat spekyth to me'" (115/18–20). Even as he warns his parishioners that the devil has enough evidence against them to fill "a gret book," let alone a single piece of parchment, he demonstrates their immunity to such condemnation, voicing their nonchalant dismissal of his stern remarks. By staging this contentious dialogue with his audience, the preacher of *Jacob's Well* does more than demonstrate the difficulty a habitual sinner has in recognizing and renouncing his sin. He reveals the explicit defiance of an audience that considers idle talk an unavoidable social obligation.

While we might interpret the preacher's ventriloquizing as an attempt to circumvent his audience's rationalization, the moral he adds to a subsequent rendition of this exemplum suggests that the congregation's resistance is far from hypothetical. After a brief but characteristically repetitive recounting of the Tutivillus story, he concludes with a warning that details the egregiousness of his congregation's chatter: "I trowe þe feend hath nede to drawe lengere & braddere his rolle here; for it is ellys to lytel to wryten on alle þe talys tolde in þis cherch, for it is neuere lefte, but it be at sacre [communion], for prechyng, ne schryfte, ne schame, ne dreed of god ne of þe world" (232/15–19). Using the moral to repeat the narrative yet again, he is able to depict the demon's recording practices three times in the space of ten lines. As he does so, however, he makes explicit the parallel between the demon's exasperation and his own, demonstrating the inefficacy of his exemplary practice. Unless the tongues of his parishioners are weighed down by the Eucharist, he complains, they are forever occupied with idle talk. Nothing, it seems, will stop the jangling in "þis cherche": not prayer, not confession, not the fear of God, not his litany of exempla. The depiction of jangling, here, is far more immediate, more persistent, and more threatening than could be accounted for through the conventional pastoral depiction of sin

---

36. "How to Hear Mass," *Vernon Manuscript*, 503/395–400; and *Handlyng Synne*, ed. Idelle Sullens (Binghamton, N.Y.: Medieval and Renaissance Texts and Studies, 1983), lines 9312–13.

as ever-present and all-pervasive. A far cry from Scanlon's description of the penitential manual as a "closed, stable text" whose authority is "total and unassailable," these sermons from *Jacob's Well* suggest that even that space in which the preacher's authority should be unimpeachable—the moment of pastoral explication—is compromised by jangling in church.[37]

That the preacher's moralizing commentary manifests not his pastoral authority or polemical skill but his inability to silence his audience is evident in all those narratives which traffic in idle talk. Although he typically concludes his exempla with sweeping, unspecific statements of pastoral advice, such as "cast out þis wose [ooze] of enuye" (88/12) and "beeth ware of þis wose of glotonye," he becomes threatening and personal when it comes to jangling. Frustration turns to aggression when he delivers a gruesome exemplum about a chaste nun who delighted in gossip. When this talkative nun died, the preacher explains, she was buried in the churchyard, but the following evening, the church caretaker saw her being dragged by devils to an infernal altar. After cutting the nun in half with their burning saws, these devils set the top half of her body ablaze, burning her "for her ydell woordys" (232/27) while leaving intact the lower, chaste part of her body.[38] The story, described by a late-fifteenth-century reader of *Jacob's Well* as a particularly good narrative about idle talk, would seem sufficiently arresting to silence the congregation.[39] But when our preacher arrives at his moral, his virulence is at its height and composed advice gives way to taunting threats: 'I drede me, þanne, ȝe that arn ydell in woord, thouȝt, & dede, schal be

37. Scanlon, *Narrative, Authority, and Power*, 13.

38. This popular exemplum (Tubach #723) has a number of variants, none of which is so relentlessly focused on idle talk. Although Gregory discusses the nun's foolish words, he uses the narrative to illustrate not the consequences of idle talk but the fact that church burial does not guarantee one's bodily safety. Gregory I, *Saint Gregory the Great, Dialogues*, trans. Odo John Zimmerman (Washington: Catholic University Press, 1959), IV. 53. In Caesarius of Heisterbach, though prompted by women's chattering in church, the tale is told about a shrewish and quarrelsome noblewoman whose wrathful tongue leads her to eternal flames. Caesarius, *Dialogue on Miracles*, trans. H. von E. Scott and C. C. Swinton Bland (London: Routledge, 1929), IV. 22. Robert Mannyng, by contrast, intimates that the nun's speech was less than chaste, thereby explaining the chaste-unchaste binary of the nun's two halves (lines 1547–1600 and again briefly at lines 8297–300). Far more concerned with jangling rather than with lechery, the preacher of *Jacob's Well* has removed the foulness from the nun's "foly speech."

39. In one of the rare instances in which the marginal glosses to the manuscript offer evaluative commentary, the reader identifies this story as a "narracio bona contra verba ociosa." Both Brandeis and Atchley argue that the hands that provide the subject-index to the manuscript and the side notes are from the second half of the fifteenth century. Brandeis, *Jacob's Well*, xiii; Atchley, "Wose," 4–8.

brent & sawyd wel werse þan sche was but ȝe leuyn it" (233/1–2). No other priest or penitential writer delivers such a venomous moral.[40] Indeed, when the preacher of *Jacob's Well* himself delivered this narrative earlier in a sermon on wrath, his tone was altogether different: rather than launching into a hostile second-person attack, he delivers a detached third-person address, warning the wrathful that they will "in soule be brent" if they do not seek equity (95/19). When the transgression is idle talk, however, our preacher replaces this concerned warning with an exasperated rant. Petty and aggressive in its tone—what, for example, would it mean to be burnt and sawed worse than this half-charred nun?—his moral compromises his pastoral efficacy. In the struggle for verbal control, the preacher loses control of his exemplum as well as his congregation.

The preacher's relentless campaign against idle talk reveals more about limitations of late medieval exemplary practice than simply his congregation's immunity to particular narratives. That his pastoral advice devolves into petty threats is just one way in which his moralizing strategies undermine his exemplary practice. Although the late medieval exemplary archive contains a few popular narratives about the dangers of idle speech, given the preacher of *Jacob's Well*'s preoccupation with jangling, this limited repertoire proves insufficient to meet his needs. Consequently, the preacher must modify numerous exempla in order to address the garrulity of his audience. Many of these narratives are not conventionally used to condemn idle talk. Indeed, the majority of them when told elsewhere make absolutely no mention of jangling. The preacher employs an ingenious variety of interpolative strategies to adapt his archive, demonstrating the versatility of the exemplum as a pastoral tool. Yet as he does so, he exposes to his congregation the manipulative strategies inherent in exemplary practice.

At his least invasive, the preacher inserts idle talk into his narratives as additional detail, which particularizes but does not dramatically transform the conventional version of these exempla. A devil, who elsewhere tempts monks from the Divine Office by means of a generic assortment of potions, here has a draft concocted specifically to promote idle chatter.[41] Similarly, those familiar demons who run through congregations wreaking havoc by

---

40. Cf. Mannyng's advice that we rid ourselves of "foule" speech so that "we be nat wiþ here brent / Yn helle fere" (lines 1597–98); and Mirk's explanation that "By þys ensampull ȝe may know, how gret synne hyt ys to speke of rybawdy" (Mirk, *Festial*, 97).

41. *Jacob's Well*, 115–16. Tubach #210.

poking parishioners in the eyes to induce sleep and appearing in the likeness of women to inspire lust are accompanied in *Jacob's Well* by demons, "blewe as men of Inde," (237/17) who rub a devilish ointment onto parishioners' lips in order to incite jangling.[42] Just as devils become explicitly concerned with idle talk, so characters who are not known elsewhere for their tendency to gossip here become janglers in addition to their other transgressions. During a sermon on excommunication, the preacher recounts the tale of Odo of Magdeburg, a wealthy priest who defied the Church's authority, died while still under the "gret curse," and suffered numerous infernal punishments as a result. Attempting to implicate idle talk in this most serious of transgressions, the preacher both augments Odo's gruesome punishments and has the devil explain their relevance. In addition to being forced to drink molten metal because he was gluttonous and being made to bathe in boiling pitch because he pampered himself with soft sheets and "swete bathys" (9/26), Odo must spend eternity roasting on an infernal griddle for his "iangelyng in cherche" (10/4).[43] While the preacher's interpolations do not disrupt these narratives, they are far from subtle, making obvious his tactic of inserting jangling into every available narrative.

The preacher's manipulative exemplarity becomes both more palpable and more problematic in those narratives whose conventional use he radically alters. Although he transforms a number of exempla throughout his sermon cycle,[44] perhaps nowhere are the limitations of his exemplary practice more evident than in during a sermon he delivers on sloth barely two weeks into his project.[45] Infuriated by the incessant chattering of his parishioners, the preacher uses the moral of his exemplum to give them an ultimatum: they must listen in silence or gossip and be damned, for a devil records

42. Tubach #1165. No other version of the narrative, which originates in the *Verba Seniorum*, mentions the lip balm that causes jangling. *Verba Seniorum, Patrologia Latina*, ed. J. P. Migne (Paris, 1849), vol. 73, col. 765, #43.

43. This third punishment is not found in any other version of the narrative. For a discussion of exemplum's extant variants, see Gregg, *Narrative Exempla*, 244–52.

44. In the preacher's revision of many popular exempla, he does not simply add idle talk to the narrative; he uses it to replace other sins. For example, when the crucifix stops its ears in other pastoral writings, it does so against usurers, those who could not bear to hear God mentioned, and those who would not listen to any sermon, rather than against mere janglers. Tubach #1844; *Jacob's Well*, 110. Similarly, the young man who is told that penitential medicine cannot work while he continues to consume unwholesome food is given to lechery, not idle words, in all the pastoral texts in which he appears. Tubach #3253; *Jacob's Well*, 230–32.

45. During his two-day sermon on sloth, the preacher singles out idle talk as this sin's most ubiquitous and problematic species, devoting all four exempla to its condemnation.

every syllable of their "idell woordys, ianglyng, & [their] rownyng in cherche" (111/21). While his moral is by now all too familiar, the exemplum he
uses as a vehicle for it is not. Rather than recounting the story of Tutivillus,
the preacher delivers a narrative conventionally used to illustrate labor's
hidden virtues.[46] In his version of the story, a hermit, weary from the daily
task of drawing water at a distant well, succumbs to sloth and resolves to
move his dwelling closer to the water supply. The moment he makes this
decision, he realizes not only that is he being followed by an angel, but that
the angel is counting his footsteps as he walks back from the well. Puzzled
by this development, the curious hermit stops to ask for an explanation and
discovers that the angel records each step of his labor as a good deed, in
order to render a full account of them before God "aȝens þe feend" (111/13).
Such vigilant accounting is necessary, the angel cautions, because angels are
in direct competition with devils, who "noumbre þe steppys of man & wom-
man to synne warde," including "alle rownynges & ianglynges in dyvyn seru-
yse, for to schewe þe noumbre of hem a-for god to mannys dampnacyoun"
(111/14–17). Hearing the angel's account and desiring earnestly to increase
his virtuous steps, the hermit quickly moves his cell five miles farther away.

The preacher's moral about idle talk is not so much prompted by the
exemplum as forced into it. Presenting his lesson as an objective truth articulated within the story rather than as explication of the tale, the preacher
attempts to camouflage his moral as narrative detail. The moral he interpolates, however, is peculiarly reductive. Instead of making a general claim
about sloth, he condemns idle talk in particular, a subject not mentioned in
any other version of the narrative and one that seems out of place even
here.[47] At the same time, the preacher omits from the story any details that
might distract attention from this very particular lesson. Rather than depicting the hermit as a sympathetic character who comically voices frustration
with his daily chores, as is the case in other versions of the narrative, the
preacher reduces him to a caricature of sloth who, like his congregation, is
badly in need of reform. Just as he flattens out the complexities in the hermit's character, so he strips the plot of its dramatic tension. In other versions

---

46. Tubach #2143. Originating in the *Verba Seniorum* (*P.L.* 73, col. 900, #31), the tale appears in Jacques de Vitry, Odo de Cheriton, the *Speculum Laicorum*, and the *Alphabet of Tales*, to
name a few.

47. Of all the slothful acts the hermit might commit, jangling in church is unlikely to be one
of them. On the originality of this didactic interpolation, see Gregg, *Narrative Exempla*, 179–80
and 267–68.

of the narrative, the angel is not immediately recognizable as an angel. Instead both the hermit and the audience encounter an unidentified man tallying footsteps. This uncertainty prompts the question, "Who are you?" and enables a dramatic revelation: "I am þe aungell off God."[48] The unveiling of the angel's identity is as central to the plot of these other versions as his occupation because the dramatic articulation of both precipitates the narrative's resolution. In contrast, for the preacher of *Jacob's Well*, the goal of the plot is the specific identification of sinward steps with jangling in church, a revelation that all but supplants the exemplum's narrative resolution. The hermit's decision to move his cell is rendered superfluous, and the angel becomes little more than a mouthpiece for this overly reductive lesson, as he scolds the wayward congregation. Idle talk, for this preacher, is a problem with which even angels are preoccupied.

What the preacher of *Jacob's Well* demonstrates in his revision of this exemplum is more than simply his fixation with idle talk. By embedding his moral within the story, he reveals an awareness of narrative's capacity for distraction—an awareness, that is, of the pitfalls inherent in the tools of his trade. While he certainly attempts to draw on the persuasive power of exemplary narrative, he also recognizes that the details of that narrative can undermine its pastoral function. His solution is to cut off all potential for distraction, first by removing the opportunity for parishioners to be waylaid by a compelling character or a miraculous development, and then by relentlessly directing their attention toward a single idea. The image he attempts to leave in the minds of his congregation is not of a reformed monk and his angel tutor, but of a devil who records their every word. Yet in reducing his exemplum to its moral, the preacher renders it unpersuasive as a narrative. The details he inserts disrupt the story because they act outside its narrative logic: the idle talk of lay men and women has no connection to a reclusive hermit, however slothful he might be. As a result, the exemplum becomes legible as a transparent and therefore ineffective attempt to silence the congregation. By forcing the exemplum to submit to, rather than illustrate, his lesson—that is, by compromising its "rhetorical specificity as narrative"—the preacher strips his pastoral tool of its ideological power.[49] However, in

48. *Alphabet*, no. 426, 293/5. Cf. the *Verba Seniorum*, "Angelus Domini sum." *P.L.* 73, col. 900, #31. Jacques de Vitry is a notable exception. But while his exemplum contains no dramatic identification, he uses the narrative to exemplify the rewards of virtue rather than the wages of sin, making no mention of idle talk. Crane, *Exempla*, #128.

49. Scanlon, *Narrative, Authority, and Power*, 31. For Scanlon, the exemplum's powers of

his attempt to separate the exemplum's capacity for distraction from its powers of persuasion, the preacher exposes both the limitations of his own rigid exemplarity and, more important, the vulnerability inherent in late medieval exemplary practice.

Exemplary Jangling

Idle talk poses a problem for the exemplum, not merely by resisting the particular stories levied against it, but by undermining the ideological power of a tool that had become indispensable to late medieval preaching practice.[50] Idle talk's influence on exemplary practice extends far beyond the failed efforts of an individual priest whose preoccupation with jangling undermines his pastoral authority. Moreover, concern about the potential for distraction intrinsic to exemplary narrative is not unique to the preacher of *Jacob's Well.* Even as clerics championed the exemplum's persuasive powers, anxiety over the questionable use of these stories was widespread as authorities attempted to prescribe acceptable sources for pastoral narratives.[51] Chaucer's Parson articulates the orthodox critique of exemplary practice, proclaiming his complete distrust of these unruly stories:

> Thou getest fable noon ytoold for me,
> For Paul, that writeth unto Thymothee,
> Repreveth hem that weyven [turn aside from] soothfastnesse
> And tellen fables and swich wrecchednesse.
> (X. 31–34)

The words of the gospel and not gossipy tales—those "ineptas autem aniles fabulas" (foolish old wives' tales) prohibited by St. Paul and peddled by

---

persuasion inhere in its status as narrative: "The Church valued the exemplum not because it passively submitted to Christian doctrine, but, on the contrary, because the exemplum's status as narrative gave it an ideological power doctrine often lacked. That ideological power is constituted by its rhetorical specificity as narrative."

50. As Thomas Heffernan has argued, "the use of the exemplum was the single most important development in the success of the *ad populum* sermon of late medieval England." "Sermon Literature," in *Middle English Prose: A Critical Guide to Major Authors and Genres,* ed. A. S. G. Edwards (New Brunswick, N.J.: Rutgers University Press, 1984), 177–207, 183.

51. While most orthodox commentators accept patristic writers as exemplary sources, they cast suspicion on chronicles, romances, and classical texts. See Spencer, *English Preaching,* 78–91.

Chaucer's Pardoner—are the proper vehicles for pastoral instruction.[52] As Edwin Craun has argued, the Parson uses Paul's words to establish the "binary opposition of salvific teaching and loquacity" conventionally articulated by ecclesiastical authorities.[53] In his invocation of this pastoral binary, the Parson does more than condemn those stories that distract from the truth; he equates exemplary practice with idle talk.[54] Practicing what he preaches, he excludes all exempla from his "myrie tale" (X. 46).[55]

The Parson's condemnation of exemplarity is precisely the accusation heterodox writers levy against orthodox preaching practice. Wyclif fiercely condemns those "nouelries," "fablis & newe soteltes," which become incontrovertible evidence of the orthodoxy's failed preaching: "þei techen opynly fablys, cronyklis and lesyngis [lies] and leuen cristis gospel and þe maundementis of god."[56] Such condemnation occurs with great frequency in late medieval heterodox polemic. According to De Officio Pastorali, priests under the pope's authority are far more likely to sin in their sermons than to teach their congregations about sin; instead of preaching from Scripture, these deliquent clerics tell "iapis & gabbingis or oþere tryuolis" (jokes, idle tales, or other trifles).[57] Similarly, the Lanterne of Liȝt complains that clerics who

52. 1 Tim. 4:7. Just as Chaucer surveys the clerical ranks and the spectrum of abuses associated with them, so he covers the range of clerical opinion on exemplarity.

53. The binary, Craun explains, was constructed by Alain of Lille, in his Summa de arte praedicatoria, and popularized by Peyraut. Craun, Lies, Slander, and Obscenity, 216.

54. Chaucerians have long debated the intent behind the Parson's rejection of "fables," interpreting it variously as a condemnation of the Host's less than virtuous tastes and as a rejection of all narrative including those that comprise the Canterbury Tales. For Paul Strohm, the Parson rejects "fabulation itself," radically altering the conditions of the tale-telling competition and leading pilgrims away from the "rampant narrativity" that has characterized their collective endeavor. Paul Strohm, Social Chaucer (Cambridge: Harvard University Press, 1989), 176. For Craun, the Parson's injunction against tales is not absolute but rather speaks only of those tales that are morally unproductive. Craun, Lies, Slander, and Obscenity, 217–21.

55. The Parson's ban on exempla has one curious exception. He includes a single exemplum about an angry schoolmaster who is taught a lesson in patience by the words of his wayward student (X. 670–73). It is perhaps not coincidental that this single "tale" follows quickly on the heels of his catalogue of the Sins of the Tongue, which concludes with idle talk, jangling, and japes. It is as if the Parson, having completed his critique of idle and deviant speech, is compelled to offer a tale that illustrates the tongue's proper use—a tale about speaking "sothe" and counseling virtue. While this exemplum would seem to be a long way from the "wrecchednesse" he denounces in others' fables, the source of the narrative is unknown. Thus, without scriptural foundation—or indeed, authority of any kind—it is a tale that, for all its preoccupation with the idea of speaking "sooth," might in itself be one of the those false "fables" the Parson so abhors.

56. John Wyclif, Comment on the Testament of St. Francis, The English Works of Wyclif, ed. F. D. Matthew, EETS, o.s. 74 (London: Kegan Paul, Trench, Trübner, 1902), 50; The Order of Priesthood, English Works, 175; Of the Leaven of Pharisees, English Works, 16.

57. English Works, 442.

deploy exempla are preachers in the devil's church, for they "prechen crony-
clis; wiþ poyses & dremyngis / & manye oþir helples talis; þat riȝt nouȝt
availen."⁵⁸ With their emphasis on the novel, the trifling, and the subtle, the
exemplary narratives of orthodox clerics more closely resemble news than
pastoral instruction. By relying on exempla, orthodox preachers and penitential writers run the risk of engaging in the idle chatter that they have been
trying to suppress.

This thin line between idle tales and orthodox exemplary practice is nowhere more blurred than in Robert Mannyng's *Handlyng Synne,* a popular
Middle English penitential manual composed in Lincolnshire in the first
decade of the fourteenth century.⁵⁹ Rather than camouflaging morals as narrative detail, Mannyng's exemplary practice celebrates narrative specificity,
emphasizing the kind of details so often omitted by the preacher of *Jacob's
Well.* His method trades on the entertainment value of the exemplum, a
practice he makes explicit in the introduction to his text. He has undertaken
the task of translating this work into English, he declares, because so many
parishioners love "to lestene trotouale" (48)—that is, they delight in listening to idle tales and foolish talk.⁶⁰ Taking advantage of the fact that so many
men "wyl bleþly [happily] here" tales in any venue—"Yn gamys, yn festys, &
at þe ale" (47)—Mannyng entices his audience into pastoral instruction
through the promise of compelling stories of his own. By substituting his
authorized narratives for his congregation's idle tales, Mannyng attempts to
replace sinful recreation with the more spiritually productive work of religious devotion, recognizing all the while, however, that he can achieve this
substitution only by catering to the sinful tastes of his audience.

While this practice does not distinguish Mannyng from numerous other
priests and pastoral writers, his explicit admission of his tactic places him in
questionable company. Announcing his strategy of narrative substitution,

58. *Lanterne of Liȝt,* 55/26–28.
59. In the prologue to his poem, Mannyng explains that he is a native of Bourne in Lincolnshire, that he lived in the Gilbertine priory of Sempringham, and that he began writing his text
in 1303 (61–75). Heavily anthologized in recent decades, *Handlyng Synne* survives in three complete copies: Bodleian Library MS Bodley 415, Folger Library MS V.b.236, and British Library MS
Harley 1701. Parts of the text have been preserved in at least six other manuscripts. For a complete
account of the manuscript tradition, see Sullens, *Handlynge Synne,* xviii–xxxiii.
60. As Miller observes, "trotouale" appears to be a "favorite term" of Mannyng's. Miller,
"Displaced Souls," 619 n. 14. In fact, Mannyng is one of the few English writers to use the word
at all; and whereas the other texts in which the word appears offer only a unique instance,
Mannyng uses "trotouale" four times in *Handlyng Synne. Oxford English Dictionary* and *Middle
English Dictionary,* s.v. "trotevale."

Mannyng acknowledges and asserts not the persuasive power of the exemplum but its ability to entertain, a principle that Chaucer's Pardoner, that
master storyteller and moneymaker, understands well:

> Thanne telle I hem ensamples many oon
> Of olde stories longe tyme agoon.
> For lewed peple loven tales olde;
> Swiche thynges kan they wel reporte and holde.
>
> (VI. 435–38)

The Pardoner ensures his audience, and by extension, his profit, by recounting numerous exempla—these ever-popular, old stories. His motive in employing this practice, however, is far from simple. He tells tales not merely
because his audience delights in them and therefore will pay him, nor purely
because his audience can "holde" them, learning and continuing to gain
spiritual benefit from them after the sermon is over—the exempla continuing to act on the conduct through memory—but because his audience can
"wel reporte" them. Either the Pardoner wants his audience to report the
tales they hear to their neighbors, encouraging them to gossip about his
exempla as a means of ensuring and enlarging his next audience; or, he is
encouraging his audience to repeat the exempla in order to educate those
neighbors. Both readings suggest that the practice of authorized tale-telling
might have dangerous side effects. What the Pardoner imagines here is a
kind of alternative religious/moral community telling its own exempla, with
their own morals—morals that may or may not be those of the Church. In
either interpretation, this alternative community is problematic, taking away
the authority of priests, providing a space for heresy, or making the Church
complicit in its idle talk. The Pardoner's appraisal of his exemplary practice
complicates the warnings of anti-exemplum polemic, for the problem he
reveals here is not the source of exemplary narratives but the ways in which
they circulate. That is, exempla are equivalent to idle tales not simply because they are narratives that have the potential to distract from and usurp
scripture, but because they can so easily devolve into the congregation's
jangling.

   Although Mannyng embraces the exemplum's ability to entertain, he recognizes that his narratives have this dangerous affinity with idle talk. The
concern he reveals and repeats, however, is not of providing his congregation with more material about which to chatter, nor of supplanting the Gos-

pels with classical fables and new verse chronicles. Instead, he acknowledges that pastoral storytelling, even when performed by an authorized preacher and derived from an authoritative source, might still constitute a species of idle talk. When he describes the contents of his text, Mannyng asserts that his exemplary practice is above reproach, offering the following protective disclaimer:

> Talys shalt þou fynde þer ynne,
> And chauncys þat haue happyd for synne;
> Merueylys, some as y fond wretyn,
> And ouþyr þat haue be seye & wetyn;
> None be þer ynne more ne lesse
> But þat y fond wrete or hadde wytnesse.
> Þarfore may hyt & gode skyle why,
> Handlyng synne be clepyd oponly.
> For hyt touchyþ no pryuyte,
> But opon synne þat callyd may be.
>   (131–40)

[You shall find tales therein and adventures that have happened because of sin; marvels, some as I found them written and others that have been witnessed or known. There are no stories, more or less, contained therein unless I found them written or had testimony to them. Therefore it (this book) may for good reason be openly called "Handlyng Synne," for it touches no private matters except that which may be called open/public sin.][61]

He will tell many marvelous stories but will reveal "no pryuyte." Unlike the transgressive details of other people's private and backbiting gossip, his stories are in the realm of the public—tales that are already well known or that at least speak of sins already revealed.[62] Yet even as Mannyng establishes the legitimacy of his narratives, he advertises them as compelling. More prominent in this disclaimer than the fact that his text abjures private matters is

---

61. Unless otherwise noted, all translations are my own.

62. Mannyng's preoccupation with committing this verbal sin is evidenced by the fact that he makes a similar disclaimer even earlier in the text, as he outlines his project: "Of pryuytees speke y nouȝt; / Þe pryuytees wyle y nouȝt name / For noun þarfore shuld me blame" (30–32). It is almost as if the very premise of Handlyng Synne requires such a disavowal.

the fact that it contains no more or less than all the tales, adventures, and marvels that have ever been recorded. While Mannyng insists that his exempla have proper authority, the nature of that authority is suspect, for he claims to rely not only on traditional *auctoritas*, what has already been written, but also on his own experience and on the experience of his acquaintances. Moreover, Mannyng's assertion of authority through stories that have "be seye & wetyn" or that he "hadde wytnesse" is dangerously close to gossip's own verifying rhetoric.[63]

Throughout his text, Mannyng acknowledges the potential slippage between exemplarity and gossip, as he reminds both himself and his congregation that his tale-telling sermons are always in danger of spilling over into the realm of idle talk's "ydel tales." At the conclusion to one exemplum, appropriately about a backbiting monk, Mannyng quickly catches himself before committing the sin that he expounds:[64]

> Þys tale y wote and vndyrstande
> Where hyt fyl yn ynglande,
> At a ful namecouth abbeye
> Þat y ne wyle telle ne bewreye.
> Swych peyne ys for hem dyght
> Þat kun nat kepe here tung ryght.
> (3617–22)

[I know and understand where this tale took place—in England at a very famous abbey that I will not tell nor betray/reveal. Such pain is prepared for those who cannot rightly hold their tongues.]

Mannyng's concluding warning, here, is a provocative variation on Scanlon's argument about the relationship between the exemplum and its moral. Here, not only is the moral "apprehended narratively," growing organically out of, and confirming, the narrative, but also it runs the risk of being too successful a confirmation, coming dangerously close to being another instance of that narrative.[65] Whereas the preacher of *Jacob's Well* uses the

---

63. "I heard it from so-and-so who was there," "I saw it with my own eyes," etc. Cf. the speech tags that accompany tidings in Chaucer's *House of Fame*, lines 2051–54.

64. Tubach #4907.

65. Scanlon, *Narrative, Authority, and Power*, 30: "the moral can only be apprehended narratively. Indeed, it can only be apprehended narratively because it is produced narratively." The

moral to bridle the narrative, Mannyng runs the risk of letting the narrative contaminate his moral. Proclaiming that he is withholding information in order to protect both himself and his audience from sin, he first assures them that he knows the identity of the abbey and then refuses to reveal its name. By claiming that his tale took place in a famous abbey in England that shall remain nameless, Mannyng renders his exemplum more immediate, more transgressive, more like the tales of his chattering congregation. These moments on the verge of transgression and the tenuous disclaimers that accompany them are precisely what make Mannyng's exempla so engaging and persuasive. The problem with his sensationalizing rhetoric, however, is that it renders the exemplum an instance of that which it seeks to control. Even while this posturing gives the exemplum its power to bridle the congregation's chatter, it makes the exemplum complicit in that taletelling.

Mannyng's identification of backbiting as the sin to which his exemplary practice is susceptible is a complicated mixture of advertising, confession, and diversion, for the sin he commits here is not backbiting. He nonetheless insists on his need to be vigilant about that particular sin. In fact, this is one of the few instances in which Mannyng calls for a general, communal shriving: "Of þys synne y rede [advise] we vs shryue / And take oure penaunce by oure lyue" (3631–32). Whereas his moralizations usually address the congregation in the second-person plural, here he includes himself in the company that needs to atone for this specific transgression.[66] Yet Mannyng clearly stays within the letter of the law on backbiting. Not only have the monk's transgressions have been recounted in numerous exempla, but also Mannyng does not traffic in the monk's "privitee": he does not disclose either the abbey's identity or the monk's name. Although the monk reveals his identity to his former colleague within the narrative—"and tolde hys name" (3604)—Mannyng does not convey this private information to his audience. Nor does he attempt to slander surreptitiously this anonymous English monk. This is not, for example, the Pardoner's barely concealed

Manciple's Tale provides a humorous echo of Mannyng's concern. To his exemplum about the dangers of not holding one's tongue, the Manciple adds a fifty-line _moralitas_, in which he ventriloquizes his mother's voice. What she provides in the form of advice from parent to child is a monotonous list of proverbs and parables about idle speech. In its seemingly endless repetition of injunctions against too much speaking, however, the Manciple's _moralitas_ (or at least his mother's) commits the sin against which it speaks, with jangling triumphing over its condemnation.

66. This communal shriving is not found in Mannyng's source, the _Manuel de pechiez_.

slander, through which the audience knows the subject of his story despite the Pardoner's omission of proper names: "For though I telle noght his propre name, / Men shal wel knowe that it is the same, / By signes, and by othere circumstances" (VI. 417–19). Mannyng's exemplum is not malicious nor is it unprofitable, for its content is morally useful to its audience, or at least has the intent of being so. Yet, with its emphasis on the "curiouse" and the sensational, Mannyng's storytelling is a manner of deviant speech; rather than backbiting, however, it is the jangling of idle talk. By claiming that Mannyng jangles, I am not attributing to him the ineffectual and unproductive speech that Mark Miller suggests haunts Mannyng throughout his text: the fear that his well-intentioned words might fail to be profitable despite his best efforts.[67] Nor do I mean to charge him with the jangling that preoccupies Langland—the idle speech that inappropriately debates matters of religion.[68] Mannyng's transgression is both more problematic and more unconventional than these two clerical pitfalls, for he traffics in the curious details and sensational rhetoric of idle talk. By foregrounding his precarious avoidance of backbiting, Mannyng camouflages his gossip.

For all his disclaimers to the contrary, throughout this text, Mannyng plays blatantly and deliberately with the line between idle talk and productive salvific speech, repeatedly reminding his readers that his tales are no "tryfyls" even as he draws on the attention-grabbing power of the "trotouale." More than a favorite term or even a constant preoccupation, "trotouale" is his narrative mode. It is the mechanism through which he transforms narratives derived from exemplary authorities into the new and exciting tales in which his audience so delights. While he begins his text with "a tale of autoryte" (168) "wretyn al and sum / Yn a boke of vitas patrum" (169–70), his citation of patristic authority quickly gives way to the advertising rhetoric of the "trotouale": "Y shal ʒow telle what me was told / Of a prest þat sagh and fond / Þys chaunce yn þe holy lond" (1252–54). Despite this titillating introduction, the narrative preceded by this claim does not come from the firsthand account of a priest who traveled to the Holy Land, but directly from Mannyng's source, the *Manuel de pechiez*.[69] That is, Mannyng

67. Miller, "Displaced Souls," 626–32.

68. See Blythe, "Sins of the Tongue," 119–42; and Linda J. Clifton, "Struggling with Will: Jangling, Sloth, and Thinking in *Piers Plowman* B," in *Suche Werkis to Werche, Essays on* Piers Plowman *in Honor of David C. Fowler*, ed. Míceál F. Vaughan (East Lansing: Colleagues Press, 1993), 29–52.

69. Tubach #1440b. The *Manuel de pechiez* does not include these introductory remarks.

ingeniously uses the convention of citing "auctoritee" not as a means to legitimate his narratives with actual authorities but as a way to transform his borrowed tales into the latest news.

Just as Mannyng manipulates "auctoritee" in order to make his narratives more immediate, so he alters the setting of these tales. When he adds narratives of his own to the collection, he emphasizes the novel and immediate rather than the distant and the authoritative. Of the seven exempla that he contributes to his text, four are set explicitly in England, with one occurring quite close to home in Lincolnshire.[70] These are tales introduced as coming not from revered "auctoritees" but from Mannyng's own experience: "yn cambrygshere yn a toune / y herd telle of a persoune" (6175–76). Even tales he borrows from appropriate authorities are altered to seem more immediate both in time and place. The tale of the wicked executors becomes the tale of the wicked Kesteven executors, as the exemplum takes place not far away, but here in the audience's very midst: "Y shal ȝow telle of a kas / Þat fyl now late yn kesteuene, / But þe name y wyl nat neuene [name]."[71] Mannyng moves his exempla from the timeless past of gospel and patristic history into the here and now of Lincolnshire. Thus the danger of backbiting he voices here becomes quite real. Yet, read against the earlier remark from the tale of the backbiting monk, this disclaimer must be understood as something more than an avoidance of sin. Just as with that earlier disclaimer, Mannyng uses this remark to generate curiosity in his audience. He offers the temptation to privy details but withholds those details, as a way of both denying the idleness of his narratives and exploiting it. Whereas the Pardoner traffics in old tales, Mannyng traffics in new ones, or at least old stories masquerading as new.

Mannyng's exemplary practice thus trades on—and inspires—his audience's desire for illicit specificity. While he never completely capitulates to

70. Fritz Kemmler lists five original exempla: the tale of Witch and the Cow-Sucking bag (line 499), the tale of Bishop Grosteste (line 4743), the tale of the Norfolk Bondman and the cattle that defile the churchyard (line 8669), the tale of the derelict midwife (line 9627), and the tale of the Bishop's corpse (line 11083). *"Exempla" in Context: A Historical and Critical Study of Robert Mannyng of Brunne's "Handlyng Synne"* (Tübingen: Gunter Narr Verlag, 1984), appendix 4, 202–4. To these, following Idelle Sullens, I add the tale of the Suffolk man (line 10403) and the tale of the Cambridgeshire Parson (line 6175). Sullens, *Handlyng Synne*, appendix 2, 381–87. These two exempla do not appear in the *Manuel de pechiez* and are listed by Tubach (#3213c and #1487, respectively) as unique occurrences.

71. Lines 6378–80. Tubach #1933. In his prologue, Mannyng identifies Kesteven as the part of Lincolnshire that includes the priory of Sempringham, his home while composing *Handlyng Synne* (lines 57–86).

that desire, he all but does so in his most elaborate exemplum, the "Dancers of Colbek." Announcing that he will tell a marvelous story that is "as soth as þe gospel" (9014), he proceeds to deliver a narrative consumed with idle talk. Yet his preoccupation with idle speech here is not, as Miller suggests, a worry about his own potentially inefficacious teaching or his sentimentalizing rhetoric, but rather a further extension of the curious tale-telling in which that teaching often engages. A narrative obsessed with naming, this exemplum provides more specific and identifying details than any other in Mannyng's collection, a fact he makes clear as he introduces the tale. Opening with a statement of "auctoritee" that would seem more appropriate for a conversational familiar than a congregation, he promises to let his audience in on what he implies is secret knowledge: "here names of alle þus fond y wrete, / And as y wote [know], now shul ʒe wete [learn]" (9027–28). In keeping with his aversion for backbiting, throughout his text, Mannyng reveals names only when they belong to holy men and Church fathers who witness, but do not commit, sin. Here, however, he tells a tale of a priest named Robert, resident of the town of Colbek during the reign of King Edward, preacher at the church of Saint Magnus and father of two children, Aʒone and Aue, who was menaced one Christmas by carolers named Gerleu, Merswynde, and Wybessyne. The tale, as Miller has shown, is as much about Robert's failings—his unprofitable admonitions, his idle and ill-advised swearing, his inability to control both his children and his temper—as it is about the carolers' sacrilege. Thus the narrative traffics in the distressing and private details of Robert's life instead of in the transgressions of an anonymous sinner. While the tale is not backbiting, since it speaks of sins already made open by other writers, it is nonetheless reliant on the illicit specificity of gossip's idle talk. Nor need such a Robert have existed for Mannyng to trade on his secrets. Rather, it is the illusion of such disclosed "pryuytee" that Mannyng uses to engage his audience. What he displays in the "Dancers of Colbek" is not a concern over idle talk but an exploitation of it.

The consequences of Mannyng's exemplary strategies become clear in the exemplum that immediately follows the "Dancers of Colbek": the story of Tutivillus. In telling this tale, Mannyng does not follow the *Manuel de pechiez*, but rather continues to develop both his theme and his method by inserting an additional narrative that resonates with his previous one. Although the tale is loosely connected to his discussion of sacrilege— "Ianglyng longeþ to sacrylage" (9258)—this exemplum seems to have more to do with the kind of speech in which he has been engaging than with this larger topic. Quite unlike the preacher of *Jacob's Well*, Mannyng highlights the narrative's humor, introducing it not as a didactic tale but as a joke, "And y shal telle as y kan, / A bourd [joke/amusing story] of an holy man" (9264–65). In his hands, the exemplum becomes a story about the fiend's embarrassment and frustration, both at being thwarted by inflexible parchment and at suffering the indignity of having his failure observed by a cleric. Mannyng repeatedly draws his audience's attention not to the jangling of a congregation, but to the antics of a buffooning devil. Relishing the comic details, he depicts a devil with a gift for dramatic flourish. This devil does not simply stretch the parchment with his teeth; he tugs and gnaws at it. And when the scroll bursts in two, he first bangs his head against the wall with such painful force that the cleric laughs, and then he takes out his frustration on the parchment, pummeling it to pieces with his fists, before storming out of the church (9288–302). The story is far more entertaining than it is persuasive, teaching his audience more about the temperament of the devil than about the dangers of idle speech. That this foregrounding of humor might compromise pastoral endeavor becomes all the more clear when we recognize that the devil's scroll—the record of the congregation's idle chatter, invoked as proof of damnation by the preacher of *Jacob's Well* and as catalyst for repentance by John Mirk—has been completely obliterated both literally and figuratively by Mannyng's narrative embellishments. His exemplary strategies—his "bourdes," marvels, and curious tales— undoubtedly succeed in holding the attention of his audience, both medieval and modern. Indeed, these strategies are precisely what make Mannyng such a popular figure in current literary anthologies. However, by overwhelming his morals with enticing narrative detail, Mannyng undermines the efficacy of the exemplum as a pastoral tool.[72]

Although their exemplary strategies are diametrically opposed, both Mannyng and the preacher of *Jacob's Well* reveal the limitations of late medieval exemplary practice when confronting idle talk. Exempla that seek to persuade against gossip either demonstrate its resistance to such tools or reveal its utility as a mode of narration, for priests as well as their audiences. More important, the strategies of these two clerics ask us to reconsider our

---

72. I am not of course suggesting that humor and entertainment are anathema to virtuous or efficacious pastoral endeavor. Rather I am pointing to the ways in which Mannyng's exemplary practice, particularly when he addresses idle talk, privileges the titillating "troteuale" of his narratives over a definitive moral conclusion.

understanding of exemplarity. For all the assertions to the contrary, by late medieval writers and contemporary medievalists alike, the exemplum seems to lack the persuasive power so often associated with it. Its "rhetorical specificity as narrative," while giving the exemplum its persuasive potential, also limits and makes problematic that potential. As narratives, exempla can be manipulated and transformed to suit the needs of individual priests and particular occasions. But as the preacher of *Jacob's Well* reveals, the more a priest enacts such manipulation, the more transparent, and thus ineffective, this pastoral tool becomes. Moreover, these narratives, celebrated for their ability to act on the memory, are retold and reinvented not just by poets and priests, but also in the minds and conversations of parishioners. The exemplum's spectacular scenes, so useful in grabbing an audience's attention, run the risk of obscuring and even erasing the moral. The nun's half-charred body borne aloft by cackling fiends is far more memorable than the constantly shifting transgression for which she was punished. And the slapstick physical comedy or disgruntled remarks of the overworked fiend inspire more laughter than fear. Finally, that illicit specificity, which Mannyng exploits in the extreme but which finds its way into exempla of all kinds, while capturing an audience's attention, draws that attention toward the specific and the personal rather than the general and the ethical.[73] That is, when it comes to idle talk, pastoral exemplarity runs the risk of setting quite a bad example.

Telling the Story of Medieval Confession

Whereas late medieval preachers attempt to silence congregations by bombarding parishioners' ears with cautionary tales, confessors labor to restrain wagging tongues by retraining parishioners in the art of appropriate speech. Yet like the exemplum, medieval confession was continually besieged by idle talk, vulnerable to gossip at almost every stage of its process. Numerous complaints are lodged against loquacious parishioners: they gossip their sins to their friends instead of recounting them to the parish priest; they treat confession as a space for gossip, telling tales of their neighbors rather than

73. As Allen argues, the complex negotiation between the particular and the general characterizes the reading of exemplary narrative. Allen, *False Fables*, esp. 4–18. Mannyng, however, acutely problematizes this general reading principle, for he not only embellishes the particulars of the narrative but also inspires in his audience the desire for ever more illicit details.

contemplating their own transgressions; and they even go so far as to gossip about the penance the priest assigns to them, trading stories of their priest's pastoral knowledge.[74] This seemingly irresistible tendency toward idle talk afflicts not just sinners but the clerics who hear their confessions. Garrulous priests shared confessional secrets, at times for the common good and at times for their personal profit, and in the process, removed the institutional barrier separating gossip and shrift. Chattering idly about the "privetee" of their parishioners, they transform confession into gossip. Yet confession's vulnerability to gossip is not simply the fault of garrulous priests and their jangling congregations, rather it is intrinsic to late medieval confession, as it was both practiced and theorized by ecclesiastical authorities.

In order to explore the ways in which gossip appropriates, contaminates, and, finally, underlies confession, I begin with a text in which idle talk itself submits to this pastoral practice: Wrath's confession in the B-text of *Piers Plowman*. Departing from standard descriptions of this deadly sin, the B-text Wrath does not commit homicide, rage, or even brawling; his transgression is gossip—the idle talk that creates unrest and inspires strife.[75] As the cook in his aunt's abbey, preparing food for prioresses and other poor ladies, Wrath

> . . . maad hem joutes of janglyng—that Dame Jone was a bastard,
> And Dame Clarice a knyghtes doughter—ac a cokewold was hir
> sire,

74. That parishioners gossip during confession is, as I discuss below, a commonplace in late medieval penitential manuals. The fact that parishioners might use gossip with a conversational intimate as a substitute for confession is a concern raised by several writers, including Robert Mannyng (lines 8320–23), and is the topic of Chapter 3, below. The seemingly excessive complaint that parishioners gossip about penance is raised not surprisingly in *Jacob's Well*. But rather than simply being the hyperbolic suggestion of a priest obsessed with his jangling congregation, it seems to have been a concern shared by other ecclesiastical authorities, who worried that such conversation would reveal the shortcomings of the clergy and thus bring scandal to the practice of confession. Caesarius of Heisterbach, for example, offers an exemplum in which a lazy priest gives the same penance to sinners who committed opposite transgressions—abstinence and incontinence—during Lent. Talking idly together, the two men discover the priest's failure and report him to his superior. Caesarius, *Dialogue on Miracles*, III. 40.

75. Blythe offers an alternative reading of Wrath's relationship to verbal transgression, arguing that Wrath addresses so many verbal transgressions because in penitential manuals the Sins of the Tongue are often discussed with the topic of Wrath. Although this is true for the *Parson's Tale*, other manuals either treat the Sins of the Tongue as a separate tract, adjacent to but not linked to Wrath, following Peyraut, or explicitly connect the Sins of the Tongue to Gluttony and the sins of the mouth, following the *Somme le Roi*. Blythe, "Sins of the Tongue," 119–42. See also note 19, above.

And Dame Pernele a preestes fyle—Prioresse worth she nevere,
For she hadde child in chirie-tyme, al oure Chapitre it wiste!
Of wikkede wordes I Wrathe hire wortes made,
Til "Thow lixt!" and "Thow lixt!" lopen out at ones
And either hitte oother under the cheke;
Hadde thei had knyves, by Crist! hir either hadde kild oother.[76]

[made them gossip stew: that Dame Joan was a bastard, and Dame Clarice a knight's daughter—but her father was a cuckold—and Dame Pernele was a priest's concubine—she'll never be prioress, for she had a child in cherry-time, our whole chapter knows it! I, Wrath, made their vegetables of wicked words, until "You lie!" and "You lie" leapt out at once and they hit one another under the cheek; had they had knives, by Christ, they would have killed one another!]

He serves up gossip stew—"joutes of jangling"—spicing his dishes with news of the nuns' transgressions: Joan is bastard, Clarice's aristocratic father is cuckold, Pernel is a priest's concubine who gave birth to his child in the spring.[77] Wrath, here, is the catalyst for rage rather than rage itself, circulating scandal until the nuns' misdeeds are common knowledge within this female community—"al our chapitre it wist." Yet Wrath's participation in idle talk is not limited to his role as the nuns' supplier; rather, he continues to gossip about them in his confession, revealing to others the illicit affairs, rampant gossip, and angry catfighting that take place behind the abbey walls.[78] In short, his confession makes these nuns infamous.

Wrath's confessional exposé, however, does more than simply engage in

76. B. V. 156–63. Unless otherwise noted, all quotations from Langland come from *The Vision of Piers Plowman, a Critical Edition of the B-Text,* ed. A. V. C. Schmidt, 2nd ed. (London: J. M. Dent and Sons, 1995).

77. Although in their editions of the poem, both Derek Pearsall and A. V. C. Schmidt have glossed "joutes of jangling" as "stews " or "soups of squabbling," jangling is not the quarrelling itself but rather its cause. The "joutes," as E. Talbot Donaldson translates, are filled with "juicy suggestions," with gossip and secret sharing. See Schmidt, *Vision of Piers; Piers Plowman by William Langland, an edition of the C-text,* ed. Derek A. Pearsall (Berkeley and Los Angeles: University of California Press, 1978); and *Will's Vision of Piers Plowman,* trans. E. Talbot Donaldson (New York: W. W. Norton, 1990).

78. The crimes committed by these nuns and their parents are, as Eileen Powers has demonstrated, the "open secret" of countless historical nuns. See Eileen Powers, *Medieval English Nunneries, c. 1275 to 1535* (Cambridge: Cambridge University Press, 1922), esp. 288–314, 436–74.

gossip by revealing the sins of these nuns. It ruminates more generally on the consequences that gossip might have for confessional practice. For as Wrath goes on to explain, the nuns are infamous, not for their sexual transgressions nor even for their angry catfighting, but for the act of divulging secrets, specifically confessional secrets:

> Seint Gregory was a good pope, and hadde a good forwit
> That no Prioresse were preest—for that he [purveiede]:
> Thei hadde thanne ben *infamis* the firste day,
> thei kan so yvele hele counseil.
> (164–66)

> [Saint Gregory was a good pope, and had good foresight that no prioress should be a priest—for he saw that they (prioresses) would have been *infamis*/infamous on the first day, they are so bad at keeping secrets.]

Nuns would make terrible priests, Wrath explains, because women can't keep secrets. If they were empowered to act as shrift-mothers, the seal of confession would be immediately broken, and the nuns would be *infamis*, both for the crime of breaking the seal and the act of defaming their parishioners.[79] The injunction to which Wrath refers appears in the *Decretals* of Gregory IX, but it was in fact Innocent III, the pope who presided over the Fourth Lateran Council and its codification of private auricular confession, who issued the decree. His *nova quaedam nuper* attempted to squelch the alarming practice undertaken by Spanish abbesses of hearing their charges' confessions.[80] Unlike Wrath's confession, however, the decree does not rely

79. *Infamia* was a well-known legal category in late medieval England, denoting any person publicly reputed to have committed a crime whether that public infamy came from judicial sentence (*infamia iuris*), the commission of a mortal sin (*infamia canonica*), or defamation (*infamia facti*). See R. H. Helmholz, *Select Cases in Defamation to 1600*, Seldon Society 101 (London: Selden Society, 1985), xx–xxiv. Not only would Wrath's nuns be rendered *infamis* for their confessional transgression: "Persons publicly reputed to have committed a crime were thereby rendered *infames*" (xxi), but also in doing so they would be the cause of another's *infamia*, one of the conditions necessary to constitute actionable defamation. In fact, throughout the passage the nuns' jangling flirts with the boundaries of English defamation law.

80. "Nova quaedam *nuper, de quibus miramur non modicum,* nostris sunt auribus intimata, quod abbatissae *videlicet, in Burgensi et in Palentinensi dioecesibus constitutae,* moniales proprias benedicunt, ipsarum quoque confessiones in criminibus audiunt, et legentes evangelium praesumunt publice praedicare. Quum igitur id absonum sit pariter et absurdum, [*nec a nobis aliquatenus sustinendum,*] discretioni vestrae per apostolica scripta mandamus, quatenus, ne id de cetero

on antifeminist rhetoric about female garrulity for its justification.[81] Instead it suggests the productive role that idle talk played for ecclesiastical authority, explaining that it was through gossip—*nostris sunt auribus intimata* (the news was intimated to our ears)—that news of this unacceptable pastoral practice reached the pope. Idle talk, it seems, was popular in papal circles as well as female monastic ones.

More than simply a humorous repetition of the antifeminist commonplace that women can't keep secrets, Wrath's depiction of these infamous nuns reveals the ways in which confession is vulnerable to idle talk. Although he attempts to restrict such confessional transgression to women by arguing that male monastic abstinence protects the community from loose tongues, his larger penitential narrative suggests that this problem of confessional rupture does not belong solely to the hypothetical prioress-priest. That is, Wrath's confession in the B-text is less about either wrath or female gossip than about confession and its vulnerability to idle talk. Corrupted confessional exchange has in fact been a constant theme of his shrift. Even the friars whom Wrath invokes in his introductory comments are concerned with confessional transgression. Although Friar Wrath concludes his remarks with the image of mendicants and beneficed priests railing against one another from the pulpit, he introduces himself through an allegorical description of confessional speech that occupies the majority of his commentary. He is an expert gardener who skillfully grafts lies onto the speech of friars until he produces the pleasing confessional discourse that blossoms in bedrooms and brings forth the bitter fruit of parishioners who would rather confess to roving friars than their parish priests (V. 135–41)—a description of idle talk's evil work wholly consistent with the rhetoric of late medieval penitential manuals. That Wrath's defining transgression lies in his corruption of confessional practice is confirmed by the poem's confessor, Repentance. Echoing the statutes governing the confessional seal, Repentance orders Wrath never to make public either by expression or by speech the confessional secrets to which he is privy—"and reherce thow nevere /

---

fiat, *auctoritate* curetis *apostolica* firmiter inhibere, quia, licet beatissima virgo Maria dignior et excellentior fuerit Apostolis universis, non tamen illi, sed istis Dominus claves regni coelorum commisit." *Corpus Iuris Canonici* (Lipsiae, ex officina Bernhardi Tauchnitz, 1881), 886–87. On the larger implications of *nova quaedam nuper* for women's ecclesiastical roles, see Claire M. Waters, *Angels and Earthly Creatures: Preaching, Performance, and Gender in the Later Middle Ages* (Philadelphia: University of Pennsylvania Press, 2004), esp. 20–27.

81. Innocent argues that since the keys of heaven were given to the apostles and not to the Virgin Mary, the exclusion of female confessors has scriptural authority.

Counseil that thow knowest, by contenaunce ne by speche" (V. 180–81). Wrath is both gossip and the gossiping priest. Positioned at the center of the sin sequence in the B-text, Wrath is, like Dante's Sloth, the fulcrum around which the other sins pivot. It is certainly the pivotal sin for Will—it is the sin to which he is the most susceptible, the one for which he weeps (V. 185). While the whole of Passus V is concerned with the limitations of late medieval confessional practice, Wrath is the turning point that signals the ultimate failure of confession in the poem—a failure that originates with idle talk.[82]

Confession's vulnerability to gossip was not merely a fourteenth-century concern about a pastoral practice in need of reform. Indeed, the document that first codified and mandated private auricular confession, the twenty-first canon of the Fourth Lateran Council ("*Omnis utriusque sexus*"), raises precisely this specter of gossip's confession rupture: "[the priest] is to give earnest heed that he does not in any wise betray the sinner by word or sign or in any other way; but if he needs more prudent advice he shall seek this cautiously without any divulging of the person, since we decree that he who shall presume to reveal a sin made known to him in the adjudication of penance, is not only to be deposed from the priestly office but also to be thrust into a strict monastery to do perpetual penance."[83] The injunction is quite straightforward and the punishment accompanying it would seem severe enough to deter loquacious confessors. Yet by assuming the necessity of a punishment for loose-tongued priests, the canon suggests not the inviolability of the confessional seal but the inevitability of its breach. Concern over the dangers posed and scandals caused by gossiping priests was already widespread before the council's decree. Almost from its inception, auricular confession was jeopardized by the idle talk of these indiscreet priests.[84] Abe-

82. This is solely a B-text phenomenon; the C-text removes all overt commentary on confessional discourse. The allegorical Friar-gardener has been replaced by a more familiar caricature of Wrath who enjoys assaulting others with stone and staff. Similarly, the prioress with the power of confession has been replaced by a gaggle of chattering laywomen, squabbling over who will make her offering first. Finally Will's own participation in the sin—his contribution to failure of confession—has been omitted.

83. John T. McNeill and Helena M. Gamer, eds., *Medieval Handbooks of Penance* (New York: Columbia University Press, 1938), 414.

84. As early as the beginning of the tenth century, Cardinal Burchard of Worms finds it necessary to prescribe the first punishment for breaking the confessional seal. The offender is to be deposed from the priestly office and sentenced thenceforth to perpetual penance. See Henry Charles Lea, *A History of Auricular Confession and Indulgences in the Latin Church*, vol. 1 (Philadelphia: Lea Brothers, 1896), 418. Thomas Tentler has quite rightly called into question Lea's validity as a source for the historical interpretation of medieval confessional practice, citing Lea's

lard laments that there are numerous such priests who render confession not simply ineffective but potentially harmful for many parishioners, and Alain of Lille advises sinners against confessing to priests who are notorious for revealing confessions.[85] The Fourth Lateran Council is thus attempting to redress this pervasive problem of priestly gossip by inextricably linking confession and its seal. But in doing so, the decree simultaneously emphasizes the central importance of the seal and the frequency with which it has been broken, suggesting the potential for future transgressions.[86]

The seal was of course designed to protect the sinner, encouraging her to reveal shameful transgressions by assuring her that those transgressions would never be made known.[87] Shrift is "goddys pryuyte," and the expert confessor would "rather die than break the seal."[88] Garrulous priests jeopardize pastoral practice and bring scandal to the Church; therefore, it is hardly surprising that medieval priests and penitential writers sought to condemn them with more vehemence than the statutes' proscriptions. Robert Mannyng, for example, suggests this grizzly punishment: "Yn erþe hys tung oghte to be out drawe / And yn helle be al to gnawe" (3675–76). The excision of and infernal gnawing upon the tongue of the gossipy priest imagined here is not unique to Mannyng; the anonymous *Book of Penance* seconds Mannyng's condemnation, amending the penalty prescribed by the Fourth Lateran Council with precisely this punishment.[89] The severity of their solu-

persistent anticlerical bias. I have therefore used Lea's *History* primarily as a reference work, drawing on his examples rather than his analysis. Thomas N. Tentler, *Sin and Confession on the Eve of the Reformation* (Princeton: Princeton University Press, 1977), xi–xiii.

85. Lea, *History of Auricular Confession*, 1:419 and 451.

86. This connection is reinforced throughout the statutes of the period. Every statute that mandates annual confession invokes the seal and reiterates the punishment for breaking it. See, among others, the statutes of Salisbury, Winchester, Worcester, Durham, Chichester, and Ely in Powicke and Cheney, *Councils and Synods II*, 1:74, 133, 173, 442, 455, and 522.

87. Tentler, *Sin and Confession*, 94–95; and Lea, *History of Auricular Confession*, I. 412–59. See also Karma Lochrie's detailed discussion of secrecy's centrality to medieval confessional practice in *Covert Operations*, 12–55.

88. *Handlyng Synne*, line 3661; Tentler, *Sin and Confession*, 102. This notion of shrift as God's secret, of confessors listening as God and therefore not revealing as men, is a commonplace in both Latin and vernacular commentary on the seal. See Lea, *History of Auricular Confession*, 1:425–28.

89. *The Book of Penance, Cursor Mundi*, ed. Richard Morris, EETS, o.s. 69 (London: Trübner, 1877), 1421. The punishment varies in the extant manuscripts. British Library MS Cotton Vespasian A. 3 suggests that the priest lose his authority, his office, and spend the rest of his life doing severe penance; Bodleian Library MS Fairfax 14 proclaims that the offending priest should spend the rest of his life in pain, have his tongue removed, and be deposed from the priestly office.

tion is perhaps justified by the gravity of the transgression. Secrecy is an essential quality in a confessor; without it, there can be no hope of successful shrift. By breaching the seal, authorities claim, the gossiping priest sins far more grievously than the original sinner.[90]

While vernacular penitential manuals offered scathing criticism of those wayward shepherds who revealed their flock's confessions, medieval scholastics speculated wildly about the sanctity of the seal. Church authorities proclaimed that there were no circumstances under which a priest would be justified in revealing confessional secrets and offered numerous hypothetical scenarios to illustrate their assertion. If a priest were to learn through confession that the chalice has been poisoned, he must still celebrate the Mass using the poisoned cup rather than risking the seal's breach. Similarly, a priest who learns through confession that his traveling companions are plotting against him must stoically face his fate rather than act on any knowledge he obtained under the seal.[91] The violation of the seal is not permissible "to save the life of the pope, or to avert the overthrow of the state, or even . . . to gain the salvation of mankind, or to prevent the conflagration of the world, or the perversion of religion, or the attempted destruction of all the sacraments."[92] Despite the support offered by scholastic speculation and the vehement disdain voiced by penitential manuals, however, for all the force that the Fourth Lateran Council's injunction had in theory, infractions against the twenty-first canon seem to have been prosecuted rarely, if at all.[93] The chances of conviction at trial were remote; as Lea explains, few penitents would have been willing to suffer either the expense of bringing such a case to trial or the shame of extending the public life of their transgression. Moreover, proof was difficult to demonstrate, especially because those who had been told unlawfully of the penitent's sins were bound by the seal and therefore not allowed to break it even to prosecute the seal's violation.[94]

Just as ecclesiastical courts offered little protection in practice, exempla on the subject of the seal designed to assuage parishioners' fears offered

90. See Tentler's discussion of the expert confessor in *Sin and Confession*, 95–104.
91. Lea, *History of Auricular Confession*, 1:433–34.
92. Ibid., 1:432.
93. The decree's punishment for violation of the seal became "the received law of the church" and on paper seems to have been in force until the eighteenth century. Lea, *History of Auricular Confession*, 1:428. The first and only successful case Lea cites dates from 1666; here the offending cleric receives a fine rather than perpetual penance in strict monastery (430).
94. Lea, *History of Auricular Confession*, 1:428–31.

them no real sense of security. Certainly there are exempla that demonstrate the power of the confessional seal. Caesarius of Heisterbach, for example, tells the tale of a sinful man saved from a violent storm at sea by the power of confession.[95] Identifying the storm as a punishment for his wickedness, he confesses all of his misdeeds to his fellow travelers, and as soon as he has poured out "so mekull horrible venom of syn" that the other passengers are pained at hearing it, the tempest subsides.[96] Once the travelers set foot on land, however, they develop a case of divinely inspired amnesia, immediately forgetting every detail of his extraordinary confession. The seal of confession is so powerful, it seems, that lay folk are unable to violate it. More surprising still is the fact that even demons are bound by the seal. Numerous exempla tell of prophetic demons who have the power to see and reveal all uncon-fessed sins.[97] In one popular version of the story, a knight, learning through town gossip that he has been cuckolded by the parish priest, takes the of-fending cleric on a trip to a village that houses one such prophetic demon. Realizing the knight's intention, the priest confesses his transgression to the knight's stablehand. Although his confession is unorthodox, his contrition, we are assured, is profound, so that the demon upon meeting him is not allowed ("non est permissus") to reveal his affair.[98]

Yet while demons and lay folk are thus bound by the seal, priests in medieval exempla are not. Exploring the protection afforded by the seal, Caesarius recounts the story of a priest who attempts to seduce his adoptive mother after she has confessed her shameful sins to him.[99] When she refuses his advances, the priest reveals all her secrets to the townspeople, but be-cause she has such a virtuous reputation, no one believes him. Even if we ignore the tale's privileging of the woman's reputation over the priest's—a notion that requires no small leap of medieval logic—and allow the narra-tive to demonstrate the power of confession to erase sin, this is hardly a ringing endorsement of either the power of the seal or the Church's ability and intention to bring its betrayers to justice. Unlike the demon or the lay travelers, the ordained priest is neither bridled nor struck with amnesia. Worse still is the exemplum in which Innocent III himself—the pope who

95. Caesarius, *Dialogue on Miracles*, III. 21. See also *Alphabet*, no. 174.
96. *Alphabet*, no. 174/5.
97. See, for example, *Jacob's Well*, 187/20–188/3; *Alphabet*, no. 177; and Caesarius, *Dialogue on Miracles*, III. 2. Tubach groups all the variants of the narrative together in entry #1202b.
98. Caesarius, *Dialogue on Miracles*, I. 112.
99. Ibid., III. 42; *Alphabet*, no. 180.

presided over the Fourth Lateran Council and its codification of the seal—licenses its violation. When presented with the case of a concerned abbot whose monastic charge confesses to celebrating the Mass without being ordained yet refuses to quit this unholy practice, the pope's learned council reaches a consensus that the seal must be preserved. Innocent, however, contradicts these advisors, ruling that the confession ought to be revealed because "so infamous a madness . . . might bring disaster upon the whole church."[100] Innocent thus establishes a loophole in the statute governing the seal. Although it is invoked for the common profit, the exception established in this exemplum is a far cry from those hypothetical scenarios that advocated drinking from a poisoned chalice to preserve the sanctity of the seal. Nor is such an exception confined to the apocryphal space of exemplary narrative. As Dyan Elliott has recently argued, confession quickly became the instrument of the Inquisition, as priests were often pressured by inquisitorial agents to report the heretics who had confessed to them.[101] Raymond of Peñaforte, one of the architects of the Fourth Lateran Council, paves the way for such breaches of the seal, arguing that heretics are not protected by it.[102] Moreover, the mendicants, whose mission was to ease the burden placed on parish priests by mandatory auricular confession, served as informants for the Inquisition and became infamous for their violations of the seal.[103] By thus blurring the distinction between sacramental and judicial confession, ecclesiastical authorities not only allowed violations of the seal but appeared to require them.

If there was no satisfactory legal recourse protecting sinners from gossiping priests, how then was a parishioner to fulfill his spiritual obligations? Penitential manuals, both Latin and vernacular, offer a practical solution, arguing that the garrulity of a priest is a valid reason for seeking an alternative confessor. Ordinarily, one had to confess all one's sins to the parish priest—a regulation established by ecclesiastical authorities in order to prevent sinners from mitigating their shame by confessing piecemeal to a variety of priests.[104] There are, however, exceptions to this rule, as the *Book of Penance* explains,

---

100. Caesarius, *Dialogue on Miracles*, III. 32; *Alphabet*, no. 179.

101. Elliott, *Proving Woman*, 31–43.

102. Ibid., 21–30.

103. Mark Gregory Pegg, *The Corruption of Angels: The Great Inquisition of 1245–46* (Princeton: Princeton University Press, 2001), 66–68.

104. Tentler, *Sin and Confession*, 104–33, esp. 109–11; Lea, *History of Auricular Confession*, 1:354–58.

Þou mai til anoþer gang,
Fra þi preist þi scrifte to tell
Quen he es bath fra-ward and fell.
And þou him haue don priue scath
Þat him to scau þou wat war wath,
Als brath, and drunkensum, and skald,
And telles in breth þat him es tald.
(26183–89)

[You may confess to another priest when your priest is hostile and
full of wrath, or if you have done him a private harm that it would
be dangerous to reveal to him because like an angry person, a
drunk or a scold, he will in anger repeat what he has been told.]

When drunk and angry, the priest here, like the monks in Wrath's confession, devolves into gossip, spilling God's secrets. He becomes in the process
a scold ("skald"), a title usually reserved for gossiping and cantankerous
women but also applied to priests who violate the confessional seal.[105] The
Book of Penance dwells on the motives, however flimsy, behind the priest's
loose tongue: that the parishioner has sinned against him, that he is drunk,
that he is enraged. While this might produce anxiety enough in the "fra-
ward" priest's congregation, even more worrying is the idea that there may
not be any mitigating factors at all—the priest may simply be an inveterate
gossip.[106] Faced with such a delinquent priest, penitents are advised to seek
a more worthy confessor. But to do so, they must acquire permission from
their gossiping priest. Admitting both that such a requirement might act as a
deterrent and that the offending priest might refuse to grant his permission,

105. Although scolding was generally a crime associated with women, court records suggest
that when a priest was so accused, it was almost always because he had violated the confessional
seal. In her thorough and insightful survey of verbal transgression in late medieval English courts,
Sandy Bardsley has recently argued that the fourteenth century saw an explosion of scolding—or
at least of its prosecution. According to Bardsley, redress for scolding, whether committed by
unruly women or talkative priests, was sought at a local level, in secular rather than ecclesiastical
courts. "Sin, Speech, and Scolding in Late Medieval England," in Fama, the Politics of Talk and
Reputation in Medieval Europe, ed. Thelma Fenster and Daniel Lord Smail (Ithaca: Cornell University Press, 2003), 145–64. I eagerly anticipate Bardsley's book, Venomous Tongues: Speech and
Gender in Late Medieval England (Philadelphia: University of Pennsylvania Press, 2006), which
had not been published when this manuscript went to press.

106. See, for example, the exception granted by Mirk, "Or ȝef he knewe by redy token / þat
hys schryfte he wolde open." Instructions for Parish Priests, ed. Gillis Kristensson, Lund Studies in
English 49 (Lund: Carl Bloms, 1974), lines 715–16.

ecclesiastical authorities offered one further antidote for the garrulous priest: if the sinner fears her confession will be revealed, she is released from her obligation to completeness and may omit those sins that she does not wish to become public knowledge.[107] Although this is certainly a practicable solution, it severely compromises the pastoral efficacy of confession.

We might be tempted to interpret these scenarios and exceptions as theoretical contingencies, designed to silence potential criticism of private auricular confession by attempting to account for its potential vulnerabilities. That is, we might assume that the punishment prescribed by the Fourth Lateran Council succeeded in deterring loquacious priests.[108] Violations of the seal, however, were not restricted to the theoretical contemplations of patristic and penitential writers. Quite the contrary, medieval parishioners across the social spectrum were vulnerable to gossiping priests. When the bishop of Gerona, confessor to James I of Aragon, revealed the king's confessional secrets, James knew better than to wait for the pope to impose the punishment enjoined by the Fourth Lateran Council. He banished the bishop himself but not before cutting out all (or at least part) of his tongue, enacting the punishment Mannyng imagines almost sixty years later. Rather than condemning the bishop for violating the confessional seal, Innocent IV excommunicated James for breaching clerical immunity, alleging that James' anger had resulted not from a violation of confessional practice but from its proper enforcement. James, he contended, was simply angry over the bishop's stern pastoral injunction that he renounce his mistress.[109] By the fourteenth century, loquacious confessors were ubiquitous. Heretics in Montaillou complained about violations of the seal performed not by friars acting on the Inquisition's behalf, but by their gossiping parish priest. Moreover, they predicated their refusal to perform the sacrament of penance on their disgust for a pastoral practice that required them to reveal their secrets to a priest who afterwards would amuse his friends with stories of their transgressions.[110]

---

107. Lea, *History of Auricular Confession,* 1:348–52.

108. Bertrand Kurtscheid adopts this position dismissing the majority of the violations of the seal alleged by Lea and others as spurious. *A History of the Seal of Confession,* trans. F. A. Marks (St. Louis: B. Herder, 1927), 303–14.

109. Lea, *History of Auricular Confession,* 1:451. For an alternative reading of this event, see Kurtscheid, *History of the Seal,* 314 n. 14.

110. "Confiteamini sacerdotibus peccata vestra, et postea ipsi facient suam delusionem de vobis, trufabunt inter se de vestris peccatis." The remark comes from the confession of Guillaume Bélibaste. *Le Registre d'inquisition de Jacques Fournier, évêque de Pamiers (1318–1324),* ed. Jean Duvernoy, 3 vols. (Toulouse: Édouard Privat, 1965), 3:229. See also Emmanuel Le Roy Ladurie's

Although suspected heretics and adulterous monarchs might have a motive for depicting their orthodox priests as untrustworthy, there is no such
bias in the 1421 indictment of John Scarle, parson of St. Leonard's in London. Arraigned on multiple charges, Scarle is accused of being a panderer, a
"baratour" (public quarreler), a scold, a "perilous Rebaude of his tungue,"
and lastly of revealing the confessions of those female parishioners who re-
jected his advances.[111] It seems that the apocryphal exemplum from Caesarius has become a historical reality in fifteenth-century London court rolls.
This is not, however, an instance of the Church prosecuting a priest for
violating the seal; these are lay folk seeking redress in civil court for the
many crimes of their corrupt priest.[112] The seal is so often associated with
its violation that by the late fifteenth century, William Dunbar is able to
employ the confessional seal as euphemism for gossip's secret sharing. In
"Tydingis hard at the Sessioun," a northern Scotsman returning home from
Edinburgh swears his neighbor to confessional secrecy—"I tell ʒow this
undir confessioun" (I tell you this under the seal of confession) (5)—before
proceeding to reveal everything he has heard at court.[113] For all ecclesiastical
polemic to the contrary, the rules designed to bridle the wagging tongues of
indiscreet confessors, it seems, are made to be broken, for the Church does
not simply fail to prosecute breaches of the seal, it licenses, and even requires, such transgressions. In the process, ecclesiastical authorities transform shrift into a kind of officially sanctioned gossip.

Whereas priests contaminate confession with idle talk by breaking Church
rules (whether in letter or in spirit), parishioners turn confession into gossip
by adhering to them, for the very guidelines designed to train the idle tongue
in the art of penitential speech encourage gossip's tale-telling. Penitential
theorists contended that a good confession must satisfy as many as sixteen
conditions, but the most universal confessional regulation was that shrift
must be complete.[114] The Fourth Lateran Council made completeness an

discussion of the Montaillou heretics' critique of confession more generally. *Montaillou, the
Promise Land of Error*, trans. Barbara Bray (New York: George Braziller, 1978), 311–13.

111. *Calendar of Plea and Memoranda Rolls, 1413–1437*, ed. A. H. Thomas (Cambridge: Cambridge University Press, 1943), 127.

112. In fact, in the following entry Scarle is indicted for passing himself off falsely as a surgeon
and killing a few "patients" in the process.

113. "Tydingis hard at the Sessioun," *The Poems of William Dunbar*, ed. James Kinsley (Oxford: Clarendon Press, 1979), 199–200.

114. Tentler, *Sin and Confession*, 106–11. As Tentler explains, popular among penitential au-

essential aspect of mandatory auricular confession, enjoining priests to in-
quire diligently into not only the sin but also its circumstances.[115] Early in
the history of auricular confession, the teasing out of these aggravating circumstances was accomplished through seemingly endless lists of questions
designed to account for all possible variations of sin.[116] But as ecclesiastical
authorities sought more practical and exportable pastoral tools, these cumbersome lists were soon replaced by a simple mnemonic verse:

> Quis, quid, vbi, per quos, quotiens, cur, quomodo, quando,
> Quilibet obseruet, animae medicamina dando.

> [Who, what, where, through whom, how many times, why, how,
> when:
> These things should be observed when applying the medicine to
> the soul.][117]

Incredibly popular in summa for confessors, the verse quickly became the
standard mechanism for exploring sin and its circumstances.[118] The questions contained in the verse, however, were not originally developed for
confessional inquiry. Derived from classical rhetorical theory, they established the "criteria for verisimilitude," serving as a tool to help orators for-
mulate credible narratives.[119] For rhetoricians from Cicero to Boethius, a
hypothesis was not viable unless it addressed these circumstances; without
authenticating detail, a *narratio* was simply not plausible. Although these

thors was a list of the sixteen conditions of a good confession. A good confession, as the mnemonic goes, must be, "simple, humble, pure, faithful, / And frequent, unadorned, discreet,
willing, ashamed, / Whole, secret, tearful, prompt, / Strong, and reproachful, and showing readi-
ness to obey" (107).

115. McNeill and Gamer, *Medieval Handbooks of Penance*, 413–14.

116. One treatise, for example, lists more than seven hundred questions that the priest should
direct toward the parishioner, while another formulates questions appropriate to every conceiv-
able profession. Lea, *History of Auricular Confession*, 1:371.

117. Raymond of Peñaforte, *Summa de poenitentia, et matrimonio* (Rome: Ioannis Tallini,
1603), 3.34.29, 463. Although this particular variation of the verse comes from Raymond of Peñaforte, this set of questions appears in numerous penitential manuals from the twelfth through
the sixteenth centuries. Tentler, *Sin and Confession*, 116–20. For a list of the variants, see D. W.
Robertson, "A Note on the Classical Origin of 'Circumstance' in the Medieval Confessional,"
Studies in Philology 43 (1946): 6–14.

118. Tentler, *Sin and Confession*, 115–16; Robertson, "Note on Classical Origin," 6–14.

119. Tentler, *Sin and Confession*, 115–16. Robertson traces the lineage of these circumstances
from the Greek rhetorician Hermagoras, through Cicero and Boethius, to twelfth- and thirteenth-
century penitential theorists. Robertson, "Note on Classical Origin," 6–14.

questions certainly have an ethical basis—they were part of the arts of prosecution and defense—they are also deeply concerned with narrative, with the practice of telling believable tales.[120] And it is precisely these narrative concerns that provide the basis for medieval confessional theory.

To argue that the structure of confessional exchange is narratively driven runs counter to scholarly assumptions about confessional practice. Given the prominent role that late medieval penitential manuals give to the species and subspecies of sin, it is hardly surprising that scholars have tended to think of confession taxonomically, as a series of topics and questions to be covered by an inquiring priest—a kind of elaborate penitential flow chart linked to a system of penitential mathematics: if you had sex in a church, and it was on a holy day, and she was a nun, then you must fast for seven years, and so on. New Historicists, heavily influenced by Foucault, have privileged surveillance and interrogation as the defining features of confession, interpreting this taxonomy as a technology for producing truth from resistant and reluctant speakers. Recently, Karma Lochrie has extended this analysis, arguing that confession is not simply a truth technology, but a technology of the secret and of the self that is constructed through the manipulation of those secrets.[121] More than simply a tool for uncovering and cataloguing illicit behavior, confession, for Lochrie, is a "technology of secrecy, interrogation, self-publication, and pleasure," utilized by penitent and priest alike.[122] Lochrie is not alone in linking confessional inquiry to the revelation and indeed construction of the self. For Lee Patterson, confession is "one of the central modes of self-representation available in late medieval England";[123] for Mary Flowers Braswell, confession's capacity for self-representation enables the development of medieval literary character.[124] While I do not wish to reject either these readings or the insight they offer into late medieval literature, I want to question their status as the exclusive paradigms for confessional practice. By recognizing confession as a kind of narrative, we discover the unintended consequences of medieval pastoral practice, for this technology designed to produce the truth is based on a technique for fabricating seeming truth.

120. Robertson, "Note on Classical Origin," 12; Tentler, *Sin and Confession*, 115–16.
121. Lochrie, *Covert Operations*, 12–55.
122. Ibid., 41.
123. Patterson, *Chaucer and the Subject of History* (Madison: University of Wisconsin Press, 1991), 386. See also his earlier essay, "Chaucerian Confession: Penitential Literature and the Pardoner," *Medievalia et Humanistica* 7 (1976): 153–73.
124. Mary Flowers Braswell, *The Medieval Sinner* (London: Associated University Presses, 1983).

The idea of confession as narrative became a defining feature of confessional practice as well as ecclesiastical theory. By the fourteenth century, the verse catalogue of circumstantial questions no longer appeared only in summa for confessors, but became a standard feature of vernacular penitential manuals, whose object was to instruct parishioners *before* they entered confession.[125] Consequently, sinners were well aware of their obligation to reveal the specific details that constituted and particularized their transgressions. Interrogation was increasingly seen as inferior to spontaneous, self-generated confession; and parishioners, rather than waiting to be questioned by the priest, were supposed to come to confession prepared with their own penitential narratives.[126] The author of *Jacob's Well* goes so far as to warn his audience that if they are aware of their sins but wait to reveal them until the priest inquires, their confession is void.[127] Even those diehard supporters of interrogation, such as Jean Gerson, acknowledged the potential use of narrative. When Gerson describes his techniques for seducing a penitent into revealing a sin, he suggests describing the transgression nonchalantly, "almost as if he is telling a story."[128] Creating an atmosphere of storytelling, it seems, will free the sinner to reveal his own penitential narrative.

The detail elicited through an accounting of sin and its circumstances is necessary for a complete confession, yet it is precisely this narrative specificity that enables unauthorized tale-telling. Under the guise of completeness,

125. See, for example, *Handlyng Synne*, lines 11511–14; *Book of Vices and Virtues*, 177/29–178/30; and *A Myrour to Lewede Men and Wymmen: A Prose Version of the Speculum Vitae*, ed. Venetia Nelson, Middle English Texts 14 (Heidelberg: Carl Winter, 1981), 125/1–12. The author of *Jacob's Well* first articulates the questions in English with accompanying examples (for example, how often have you jangled in church?) and then concludes his discussion of circumstances by calling specific attention to the Latin verse upon which he relies, ending the sermon with "versus: 'Quis, quid, vbi, per quos, quociens, cur, quomodo, quando?'" (184/6–185/4).

126. Ecclesiastical authorities routinely expressed concern about the potential dangers of interrogation. Chief among the critiques of interrogational practice were reservations about the possibility that it would introduce parishioners to new transgressions, inciting rather than purging sin. Still other pastoral writers worried that interrogation might encourage parishioners to be lax in their self-examination, relying instead on the zealous inquiry of their confessors. Tentler, *Sin and Confession*, 82–120; Lea, *History of Auricular Confession*, I: 367–78.

127. "ȝif þou knowe þe in a synne, & wylt noȝt be schreuyn þerof but þe preest aske þe þerof, & þanne þou seyst it to þe preest, be-cause þou knowyst it, & wylt noȝt tellyn it but þe preest aske þe, & þanne þou syest it; þat schrifte profyȝteth þe noȝt to þi saluacyoun" (179/33–180/4). Advising his congregation to prepare diligently for confession, he suggests "a-[forn-]recordyng, a-forn-rehersyng, a-for-syȝt, a forn-stodying, a-forn-avysement, þat þou mowe knowe þi synnes in þi mynde" (179/19–21).

128. "quasi non curans, aut fere narrans fabulam." Jean Gerson, *Oeuvres complétes*, 10 vols. (Paris: Desclée, 1971), 8:14. Jean Gerson, *Jean Gerson, Early Works*, trans. Brian Patrick McGuire (New York: Paulist Press, 1998), 372.

parishioners' narratives incorporate the transgressions of others, so that confession becomes the occasion for gossip's idle tales. This slippage between confession and commission is comically illustrated in *Piers Plowman*. For while Langland's Deadly Sins use confession as a forum for purging verbal transgressions, they also appropriate it as a venue for committing them.[129] Covetousness, for example, illustrates exactly how confession might be thus abused. The majority of his shrift documents the sins of his wife, as he praises her for weakening ale, charging exorbitant prices, and tampering with weights. Although he concludes his confession by renouncing these transgressions, since he has not admitted to committing any of them, he can rest assured that his wife will continue these lucrative business practices, as she is not the one who is confessing. We might assume that Langland is simply reflecting the fact that morally and legally Mr. and Mrs. Covetousness would be considered a single entity, and therefore Mr. Covetousness would be required to account for his wife's transgressions. Yet it is precisely this problem—confession devolving into chatter about other people—that penitential manuals address.

Not surprisingly, the preacher of *Jacob's Well*, with his congregation of inveterate gossips, is particularly anxious about confession's capacity for idle talk. Attempting to reign in his audience's penitential narratives, he repeatedly browbeats listeners with the importance of self-accusation: "breke noȝt þy schryfte in accusyng oþers synnes, as þe husbonde tellyth þe wyves defawtes [misdeeds], & þe wyf þe husbondys defawȝtes. telle þin owne synnes, & noȝt þi neyȝbouris synnes" (182/15–18).[130] He even goes so far as to mimic his parishioners' faulty confessions: it was other people's fault and not mine, my wife made me do it, my husband made me do it; my wife is more guilty than I am, others led me into temptation.[131] So vigilant is he in his campaign against idle talk that he makes self-accusation the defining feature of confession, subsuming all other manners of penitential speaking, including completeness, to it.[132] His repetitions and elaborations suggest

129. Envy backbites and lies with his adder's tongue (V. 86–132); Gluttony whispers, swears, and delights in tavern tales (V. 326; 368–78); Covetousness swears false oaths and breaks oral contracts; and Sloth is "ocupied eche day, halyday and oother, / With ydel tales at the ale and outherwhile in chirches" (403–4). See also Blythe's discussion of verbal transgression in "Sins of the Tongue," 119–42, esp. 127–28.

130. Cf. the *Book of Vices and Virtues*, 177; and *Ayenbite of Inwit*, 175.

131. *Jacob's Well*, 180/26–29.

132. Indeed, the preacher uses self-accusation to structure his discussion of shrift, so that humility, candor, completeness, and simplicity are understood as attributes not of confession generally but of self-accusation in particular. *Jacob's Well*, 180/23–183/5.

how pervasive a problem this misuse of confessional speech might have been, not simply for this particularly besieged preacher but for confessors across late medieval England. Indeed, as John Bossy has demonstrated, in rural communities, confession evolved (or rather devolved) into an "annual settlement of social accounts," a mechanism for airing community grievances and solving community disputes.[133] Although Bossy's model does not account for the situation depicted in *Jacob's Well*—the frequency with which the author chastises his chattering congregation suggests that this is not a situation that he has invited—it nonetheless reveals another unexpected way in which the Church sanctioned confession as tale-telling.

In contrast with the preacher of *Jacob's Well*, who assumes that his chattering parishioners are responsible for this corruption of confession, Robert Mannyng recognizes a more systemic problem in the easy slippage of one kind of narrative into another. He reminds confessor and penitent alike of their obligation to eschew idle talk:

> Aske aftyr noun ouþer name,
> But lestene weyl hys owne blame.
> For ȝyf þou any ouþer man namest,
> Y dar weyl seye þou hym dyffamest.
> Hyt ys gret synne to hym and þe
> To aske or telle þat shuld nat be.
> Hyt ys bakbytyng & no shryfte:
> Hyt ys a spice of euyl þryfte.
> (11639–46)

[Don't ask after any other name, but listen well to his (the confessee's) own transgressions, for if you name any other man, I dare say you defame him. It is a great sin to him and you (confessee and priest) to ask after or reveal that which should not be mentioned. It is backbiting and not shrift: it is a species of evil thrift.]

Placing the responsibility for confessional propriety on the shoulders of both penitent and confessor, he warns the priest that to ask for names constitutes defamation and advises parishioners to ignore their overly inquisitive

---

133. John Bossy, "The Social History of Confession in the Age of the Reformation," *Transactions of the Royal Historical Society* 25 (1975): 21–38, 25.

priests. As with the exemplum of the backbiting monk, for Mannyng, it is naming that crosses the boundary between proper pastoral discourse and gossip. His "don't ask, don't tell" policy on proper names, here, makes the transformation of confession into idle talk just as much the fault of the priest as the sinner. Asking for names, just like revealing them, turns confession into gossip's sinful speech; both actions are a form of backbiting.

The complaints of Mannyng and the preacher of *Jacob's Well* to the contrary, that confession becomes an occasion for gossip is not solely the result of overly inquisitive priests or parishioners who delight in talking about their neighbors. Conflicts in the rules training tongues in the art of confessional speech enable such confessional ruptures in even the most well intentioned of sinners, for the injunction to completeness is at odds with the requirement that one should speak only of oneself. Moreover, while all penitential writers assert that self-accusation is essential, they also find the need to articulate possible exceptions. Chaucer's Parson, for example, becomes tongue-tied by these conflicting requirements. He warns that "a man moot accusen hymself of his owene trespas, and nat another" (X. 1016), but adds the following caveat, getting himself embroiled in a bit of troublesome logic and providing sinning tongues with a loophole:

> But nathelees, if that another man be occasioun or enticere of his synne, or the estaat of a persone be swich thurgh which his synne is agregged, or elles that he may nat pleynly shryven hym but he telle the persone with which he hath synned, thanne may he telle it, / so that his entente ne be nat to bakbite the persone, but oonly to declaren his confessioun. (X. 1017–18)

> [But nevertheless, if another man is the occasion or enticer/instigator of his sin, or the estate of that other person is such that it makes the sin more egregious, or else if he cannot confess himself fully unless he names the person with whom he sinned, then he may name him, so long as his intention is not to backbite against the person, but only to declare his confession]

The Parson's stepping and back stepping here reveal his anxiety about the kinds of speech that this exception might unleash, as the line between backbiting and confession becomes ever thinner. The notion of an exception is not unique to the Parson, but this overtly problematic rhetoric is. Other penitential theorists offer extenuating circumstances that license the sinner to reveal his accomplices. For Raymond of Peñaforte, the preservation of the body faithful justifies the disclosure of heretics; and for Gerson, in certain cases (e.g., incest), the identity of the other person is self-evident and therefore confession is not possible without the revelation of the other parties involved.[134] Yet the Parson's exception offers no such extenuating circumstances; his concern is for the necessity of a complete confession. That is, the Parson is tongue-tied because he fears the transgressions that might be licensed by following penitential rules.[135]

The ambiguity created by the competing requirements of completeness and self-accusation constitutes only one of the ways in which confessional practice elicits idle tales. The rules of confession generate narratives that move beyond community gossip, as parishioners use confession as a space to tell tales wholly unconnected to their own transgressions. For Chaucer's Parson, these tales result from the inappropriate way in which sinners approach confession, and he warns parishioners not to rush to their priests as if they had a new tiding to tell: "Thow shalt nat eek renne to the preest sodeynly to tellen hym lightly thy synne, as whoso telleth a jape or a tale" (X. 1024). The atmosphere of urgency that the Parson condemns, however, has institutional precedent. A good confession must be performed both "hasteliche" (promptly) and "baldelye" (boldly), for confession should not be delayed nor should it be tempered by the fear of harsh penance.[136] Attempting to combat the inevitable reticence of their sinning flocks, late medieval clerics repeatedly impress upon parishioners the sense of urgency that should accompany their confession. Mirk's *Instructions for Parish Priests* illustrates both the logic and the pitfalls of this tactic. Mirk encourages the

---

134. Raymond of Peñaforte, *Summa de poenitentia*, 3.34.60, 490–91; and Gerson, "On Hearing Confession," 370.

135. This is one of the very few moments in the *Parson's Tale* in which Chaucer departs from his two major sources: Raymond of Peñaforte and Peyraut. Chaucer follows Raymond quite closely in line 1017, but line 1018—the line that voices the Parson's fear of confessional transgression—is original to the *Parson's Tale*. It is as if even in this quite straightforward treatise, there is something irresistible for Chaucer in the moment of confessional instability—where shrift meets gossip, a boundary that he blurs throughout the *Canterbury Tales*.

136. *Book of Vices and Virtues*, 174/18; and Mirk, *Instructions*, line 1202. See Tentler, *Sin and Confession*, 106–9. Middle English penitential manuals all stress the importance of a prompt confession while outlining the factors that might weaken one's confessional fortitude: *Book of Vices and Virtues*, 174/14–176/10; *A Myrour to Lewede Men and Wymmen*, 124/19–40; *Handlyng Synne*, lines 11381–408; and *Jacob's Well*, 185/5–9.

sinner to recount his transgressions boldly, quickly, and completely, yet his promptings become more frantic as the sins he probes become increasingly titillating. When he finally arrives at the sin of lechery, he abandons the stern pastoral encouragement of "þou moste say" (1218) "for nede hyt ys" (for it is required) (1226) in favor of entreaties more appropriate to a conversational familiar: "telle ȝef þou conne" (tell me if you can) (1244), "Telle me, sone, spare þow noȝt" (Tell me, son, and don't leave anything out) (1266), and "Telle me, sone, a-non ryght here" (Tell me, son, quickly, right now) (1268). Although Mirk maintains his professional distance by addressing the parishioner as his spiritual "son," the frequency of his promptings suggests an urgency that is not altogether pastoral. Moreover, the bold confession such encouragement elicits might all too easily resemble the japes and tales the Parson warns against.

Although the Parson addresses the *manner* of confession, it is clear from *Jacob's Well* that penitential jangling might easily be a matter of content as well as form. Complaining about the inappropriate stories his parishioners reveal during their confessions, the frustrated preacher chastises his congregation,

> ne telle noȝt in þi schryfte flateryng iapys & talys, ne oþere processe þat longeth noȝt to þi schryfte; . . . for summe in schryfte schal tarye þe preest wyth sleueles talys þat no-thyng longyth to schryfte. (181/12–17)

> [In your shrift, do not tell flattering jokes and tales, or other narratives that do not belong to your shrift; . . . for some in shrift detain the priest with idle tales that have nothing to do with shrift.]

Here, the parishioners are not just talking gossip-like, they are, in fact, gossiping—telling the "sleueles tales" that define idle talk.[137] For the preacher of *Jacob's Well*, these tales are not only a degradation of confession but also an imposition upon the priest's time and patience. For other confessors, however, such tales are a professional perk. The friar confessing Lady Meed in *Piers Plowman*, for instance, is rewarded for his pastoral services narratively as well as financially. After first confessing her wickedness, Meed "told him a tale and took [gave] hym a noble," conflating her shrift and her

---

137. See *Oxford English Dictionary*, s.v. "sleeveless," 2a.

gossip into a single unorthodox tale.[138] While neither Lady Meed nor the congregation of *Jacob's Well* should be held up as model penitents, their transgressions illustrate more than the misuse of confessional practice; they reveal the kinds of unofficial narratives that are licensed by ecclesiastical rules.

Officially sanctioned confession explores the circumstances of sin through a tool steeped in narrative theory; it demands of its participants a comprehensive account of all explicit (and even illicit) details; and it is administered through inquisitive priests urging hasty and bold disclosures. Built on such a foundation, late medieval confessional practice cannot help but produce gossip's unauthorized narratives, however well intentioned its participants might be. Like late medieval exemplarity, confession is everywhere susceptible to idle talk because it is itself a kind of storytelling. As a result, confession, like exemplary practice, is not simply vulnerable to gossip but dependent upon it. The most compelling proof for confession's narrativity is not the complaints lodged by frustrated clerics that parishioners are telling "sleueles tales," nor the indiscretions of priests who incorporate confessional secrets into their own idle tales, but rather the ways in which late medieval authors exploit gossip's confessional ruptures as a literary device. Far more than a means to explore character, literary confession is a vehicle for narrative and generic experimentation—experimentation made possible precisely because confessional practice is so intimately connected to idle talk. As I argue in the chapters that follow, it is gossip's ability to permeate and remake other discourses, to transform official narratives and co-opt pastoral practices, that make it such a productive literary device. While a number of late medieval writers exploit aspects of gossip's discursive transformations, no one does so more thoroughly or more inventively than Chaucer.

138. B. III. 45. The passage also appears in the C-text (III. 47). For a comic depiction of this abuse in a later text, see Ben Jonson's *Staple of News,* in which a woman purchases a "groatsworth" of news for the specific purpose of sharing it with her priest (I. iv. 10–12). Ben Jonson, *The Staple of News,* ed. Anthony Parr (Manchester, Eng.: Manchester University Press, 1988).

Figure 1. *Troilus* frontispiece, early fifteenth century. Cambridge, Corpus Christi College MS 61, frontis. Reproduced by permission of the Master and Fellows of Corpus Christi College.

CHAUCERIAN SMALL TALK

The famous portrait of Chaucer depicted in the *Troilus* frontispiece (figure 1) has long been a source for assumptions about his social, political, and poetic status. For decades critics used the frontispiece to instate Chaucer as court poet extraordinaire, claiming that this image of him standing at a pulpit before an audience of sumptuously dressed lords and ladies either records a specific historical event or attests to Chaucer's practice of reading his work aloud to the Ricardian court. Like the idea of Chaucer as a court poet, the belief that the frontispiece reflects a historical reality, has been rightly dispelled by both New Historicist and art historical criticism.[1] The illumination is in fact an amalgamation of late medieval artistic conventions. From the procession scene in the background to the appearance of individual lords and ladies, almost every detail can be traced to other manuscripts from the period.[2] Such a pas-

1. Paul Strohm's recuperation of Chaucer's primarily nonaristocratic audience conclusively dispelled the myth of Chaucer as a court poet and has since inspired a great deal of provocative scholarship on Chaucer's extratexual milieu. *Social Chaucer,* esp. 47–83. For recent work on the reception of Chaucer's poetry, see Seth Lerer, *Chaucer and His Readers* (Princeton: Princeton University Press, 1993); Allen, *False Fables;* and Stephanie Trigg, "Chaucer's Influence and Reception," in *The Yale Companion to Chaucer,* ed. Seth Lerer (New Haven: Yale University Press, 2006), 297–323.
2. In a series of articles, Derek Pearsall and Elizabeth Salter have convincingly demonstrated that the figures in the frontispiece are drawn from iconographic conventions of preaching scenes from continental manuscripts. See Derek Pearsall, "The Troilus Frontispiece and Chaucer's Audience," *Yearbook of English Studies* 7 (1977): 68–74; Elizabeth Salter and Derek Pearsall,

tiche could hardly be considered a realistic account of Chaucer's poetic per-
formances. Yet the particular conventions adopted by the illuminator resonate
with both Chaucer's aesthetic practices and his audience's interpretations of
them in the twenty-first century as well as the fifteenth.[3]

Instead of portraying Chaucer either as a writer composing his work or
as a reader narrating it—two conventions of author portraiture readily available to him—the illuminator represents the poet as a preacher, lecturing to
an audience of men and women, some of whom affirm the poet's laureate
status, paying him rapt attention, while others find their own conversations
more engaging.[4] Although Chaucer never fully becomes the besieged
preacher imagined here, that figure who speaks from the pages of numerous
late medieval penitential manuals and sermon collections, he certainly exploits this subject position for narrative purposes, not only in the *Troilus*
but throughout his poetic career in such characters as the Wife of Bath
and the Pardoner.[5] Indeed, his works are filled with remarks that reveal an
awareness of, and at times concern about, his sometimes attentive, sometimes rebellious audience; and he frequently adopts the tactics of a preacher
in order to engage with them. He appropriates the rhetorical power of the
pulpit, ventriloquizes both exemplary and unethical clergymen, borrows
pastoral forms and practices, and voices orthodox doctrine, at times in earnest, at times in game. More striking than the suggestive resonance between

---

"Pictorial Illustration of Late Medieval Poetic Texts: The Role of the Frontispiece or Prefatory
Picture," in *Medieval Iconography and Narrative: A Symposium,* ed. Flemming G. Andersen, Es-
ther Nyholm, Marianne Powell, and Flemming Talbo Stubkjer (Odense: Odense University Press,
1980), 100–123; and Elizabeth Salter, "The 'Troilus Frontispiece,'" in *Troilus and Crisyede: A
Facsimile of Corpus Christi Cambridge MS 61,* ed. M. B. Parkes and Elizabeth Salter (Cambridge:
D. S. Brewer, 1978), 15–23.

3. Several critics have offered compelling interpretations of the image as a reflection of
fifteenth-century attitudes and practices. Seth Lerer argues that the frontispiece reflects a fifteenth-century desire to elevate Chaucer to an "aureate" and "laureate" status. *Chaucer and His
Readers,* 22–24. In contrast, Laura Kendrick claims that the frontispiece suggests the possibility
of the dramatic enactment of the poem; she sees in its iconography the conventions of late
medieval *puy. Chaucerian Play: Comedy and Control in the* Canterbury Tales (Berkeley and Los
Angeles: University of California Press, 1988), 163–74.

4. Pearsall and Salter catalogue the variety of author portraits available in late medieval
manuscripts. "Pictorial Illustration of Late Medieval Poetic Texts," 115–16.

5. The *Troilus* narrator imagines and confronts his chattering audience, chastising them for
their envious gossip: "Now myghte som envious jangle thus" (II. 666). Rather than silencing
their idle talk, however, the narrator uses it both to control interpretation of and to spark further
conversation about his narrative. Inverting conventional preaching practice, the Wife of Bath is
repeatedly interrupted by the clergyman whose pulpit she has co-opted, while the Pardoner
catalogues the tactics he uses both to entertain and to maintain control of his congregation.

the scene imagined in the frontispiece and Chaucer's narrative strategies, however, is the way in which this depiction of the poet as preacher has come to dominate Chaucer scholarship. Although various Chaucers have gone in and out of scholarly fashion, this image of him at the pulpit haunts current criticism in much the same way that earlier scholarship was shaped by the vision of him as court poet.

In recent years, medievalists have shown a steadily increasing tendency to proclaim Chaucer's orthodoxy. D.W. Robertson first introduced this perspective forty years ago in *A Preface to Chaucer,* inaugurating a school of exegetical criticism that read Chaucer's poetry as moral allegory to be explicated according to Christian doctrine.[6] While the seventies and eighties saw a backlash against Robertson's methodology, as critics reinvented Chaucer as the irreverent poet who employed devilish irony for cultural critique, that backlash has itself come under fire in the last decade.[7] Just as scholars in medieval studies more generally have refocused our attention on the pervasive and indeed inescapable influence that pastoral discourse exerts on medieval literature and culture, tracing the vernacular legacy of confession, exemplarity, mysticism, *imitatio Christi,* the Sins of the Tongue, and hagiography,[8] so Chaucerians have sought to demonstrate not only the poet's indebtedness to these traditional pastoral discourses but also his dissemination of orthodox religious ideology. In this intellectual climate, he is increasingly read as "moral Chaucer," the author of the *Second Nun's Tale,* the *Retractions,* and the *Parson's Tale,* rather than the poet of "many a leccherous lay."[9] Although the resurrection of "moral Chaucer" has produced

6. D. W. Robertson, Jr., *A Preface to Chaucer: Studies in Medieval Perspectives* (Princeton: Princeton University Press, 1962).

7. Ethan Knapp provides a trenchant analysis of the history of Chaucer criticism in "Chaucer Criticism and Its Legacies," in *The Yale Companion to Chaucer,* 324–56.

8. Recent decades have produced much rich and suggestive work on the centrality of religious discourse to medieval culture. See Barbara Newman, *God and the Goddesses: Vision, Poetry, and Belief in the Middle Ages* (Philadelphia: University of Pennsylvania Press, 2003); David Aers and Lynn Staley, *The Powers of the Holy: Religion, Politics, and Gender in Late Medieval English Culture* (University Park: The Pennsylvania State University Press, 1996); Nicholas Watson, *Richard Rolle and the Invention of Authority* (Cambridge: Cambridge University Press, 1991) and "Censorship and Cultural Change"; and Craun, *Lies, Slander, and Obscenity.*

9. X. 1087. For Charles Muscatine, the "religious, almost puritanical Chaucer who emerges powerfully and suddenly at mid-century" has been a consistent critical presence since the 1960s. Charles Muscatine, "Chaucer's Religion and the Chaucer Religion," in *Chaucer Traditions: Studies in Honor of Derek Brewer,* ed. Ruth Morse and Barry Windeatt (Cambridge: Cambridge University Press, 1990), 249–62, 250. However, it is clear that in the decade and a half since Muscatine's article, there has been a dramatic increase in scholarship about "moral Chaucer." Critical attention to Chaucer's religious tales has increased exponentially: the year 2000 saw the publication of

much important and insightful work, it has also foreclosed interpretative possibilities. At the pulpit, this Chaucer's use of pastoral discourse must always conform to orthodox doctrine, his preacherly tactics must always be in service of an orthodox agenda, and the conversations of his audience must always be both troubling and transgressive.

However, as I argue in this chapter, Chaucer experiments with the power of the pulpit, deploying pastoral rhetoric as a literary technique for engaging with and manipulating both his texts and his audience. To read his pastoral appropriations solely as affirming orthodox practices is to miss the myriad and complex ways in which he deploys them. While Chaucer certainly voices conventional wisdom, that wisdom rarely speaks in uncomplicated isolation but instead is implicated in and, in fact, integral to his ongoing narrative experimentation. I take as the grounds for my argument Chaucer's appropriation and exploitation of pastoral rhetoric about idle talk. Connected as it is to the discourses of confession, exemplarity, and the Sins of the Tongue, Chaucer's use of gossip has ramifications for his preacherly tactics beyond that of mere verbal transgression.

Scholarly discussion of jangling in Chaucer's poetry has assumed his un-questioned acceptance of pastoral rhetoric that condemns this sinful speech. In fact, there is ample support for such an assumption. From his pulpit, Chaucer voices the admonition of the Parson that jangling "may nat be withouten synne" (X. 649); he illustrates the dangers of idle talk through the words of the Nun's Priest and the Manciple; and he condemns the bawdy Miller as a "janglere" (I. 560) long before he retracts Robin's sinful tale. Given this damning evidence, critics have understandably focused on the moral implications of jangling in Chaucer's poetry, arguing that while he may entertain his audience with depictions of idle talk, he ultimately renounces it as both unprofitable and dangerous.[10] Critics thus read in

---

as many articles on the *Parson's Tale* as appeared in the whole of the eighties, and the nineties witnessed more articles on the *Second Nun's Tale* (thirty-two) than the previous three decades combined. Recent critical attention to medieval ethics promises to usefully reconfigure ideas about "moral Chaucer."

10. See Craun, *Lies, Slander, and Obscenity*, 187–230; Chauncey Wood, "Speech, the Principle of Contraries, and Chaucer's Tales of the Manciple and Parson," *Mediaevalia* 6 (1980): 209–29; L. A. Westervelt, "The Mediaeval Notion of Janglery and Chaucer's *Manciple's Tale*," *Southern Review* 14 (1981): 107–15; Catherine S. Cox, "The Jangler's 'Bourde': Gender, Renunciation, and Chaucer's Manciple," *South Atlantic Review* 61, no. 4 (1996): 1–21; Stephen Manning, "Fabular Jangling and Poetic Vision in the *Nun's Priest's Tale*," *South Atlantic Review* 52, no. 1 (1987): 3–16; and Emily Jensen, 'Winkers' and 'Janglers': Teller/Listener/Reader Response in the *Monk's Tale*, the Link, and the *Nun's Priest's Tale*," *Chaucer Review* 32, no. 2 (1997): 183–95. Notable exceptions are William A. Quinn, "Chaucer's Janglerye," *Viator* 18 (1987): 309–20; and Lochrie, *Covert Oper-*

"moral Chaucer" an anxiety about the connection between his poetry and the sinful jangling it is always in danger of becoming.[11] From this perspective, the *Parson's Tale*, the text so central to the instantiation of the orthodox Chaucer, speaks the final word on idle talk, recuperating the Manciple's failed condemnation of gossip by giving it true pastoral authority and in the process putting an end to narrative as well as jangling.[12] Yet Chaucer's use of gossip is far more complicated than the conception of "moral Chaucer" will allow. Although he often begins with conventional wisdom about idle talk, he quickly moves to contradict that wisdom, exploiting gossip's most problematic attributes as a means to explore new narrative possibilities. By assuming Chaucer's "orthodoxy," we not only misconstrue his relation to and use of idle talk, but, more important, we ignore a fundamental aspect of his poetics.

In this chapter, I explore Chaucer's theory and practice of gossip, demonstrating the ways in which he takes idle talk not just as subject of his poetry but also as a method for it, a means to manipulate and transform his narratives as well as his sources. I focus my discussion on two phases of Chaucer's experimentation with gossip: his initial foray into idle talk in the early dream vision, the *House of Fame*, and his culminating venture in the *Canterbury Tales*, where gossip both serves as structuring device in the figure of the Host and appears in its most complicated and concentrated form in the Wife of Bath. Each of these phases begins with pastoral rhetoric about idle talk, begins, that is, with what appears to be an instance of Chaucer at his pulpit, yet each proceeds to subvert and exploit that rhetoric, using gossip to perform a series of narrative experiments.

My discussion begins with the *House of Fame*, because it is here that

ations, 56–92. Tracing the instances of the word "jangle" in Chaucer's poetry and reading them against the depictions of Wicked-Tongue and False-Semblant in the *Roman de la Rose*, Quinn is interested in the connections between "janglerye" and the *jangleur*—the poet as go-between, gossip as intermediary. Lochrie focuses on gossip's involvement in the gender politics at work in the *House of Fame* and the *Wife of Bath's Prologue and Tale*, investigating the role that gossip plays in the dynamic between female secrets and male ignorance, between women's speech and men's art.

11. Stephen Manning, for example, reads the Nun's Priest's jangling as Chaucer's critique of unproductive poetry. Manning, "Fabular Jangling," 3–16. Similarly, Lochrie suggests that Chaucer was anxious about the "unsettling possibility" that poetry and gossip were not "really not significantly different" from one another. Lochrie, *Covert Operations*, 80.

12. See, for example, Craun's insightful chapter on the discourse of the Sins of the Tongue as it pertains to Chaucer's Parson and Manciple. Craun, *Lies, Slander, and Obscenity*, 187–230; and Lee Patterson, "The 'Parson's Tale' and the Quitting of the Canterbury Tales," *Traditio* 34 (1978): 331–80.

Chaucer first articulates his theory of gossip—its mechanisms, its rhetoric, its transformations. His theorization relies on the terms and assumptions of pastoral discourse about idle talk, yet it recuperates as narratively productive precisely those traits deemed most problematic by ecclesiastical authorities. Moving from Chaucer's theory about gossip to his practice of it, I turn to the *Canterbury Tales* and in particular, to the Host, Harry Bailly, that figure caught somewhere between a character in the poem and a narrator of it. Well aware of gossip's reputation, Harry preaches to his fellow pilgrims about the dangers of idle talk. Even as he does so, however, he acts as the agent of this transgressive speech. Commenting on the tales of his fellow pilgrims and stirring up an atmosphere of speaking everything with his repeated injunctions to "spare it nat" (III. 1763), he enables verbal exchanges which seem to reproduce actual gossip. That gossip in turn makes possible the generic alchemy in which Chaucer engages throughout the poem. I conclude the chapter with the Wife of Bath, a character and a text that mark the culmination of Chaucer's experimentation with idle talk. Standing at a pulpit of her own, she articulates and embodies the pastoral commonplace that a jangler is almost always a jangleress. Yet her mastery of gossip is less about the inability of women to keep secrets than about gossip's potential as narrative device, for it is through the Wife of Bath's idle talk that Chaucer enacts some of his most radical narrative transformations.

"Fild ful of tydynges": Gossip and the *House of Fame*

At first glance, the *House of Fame* appears to be an exemplum on the dangers of idle talk. The poem begins its dream vision contemplations with Dido and her sullied reputation as it spreads rapidly on countless tongues, and it concludes with a cacophony of questionable tidings that conflate truth and falsehood. Critics have understandably drawn the conclusion that the poem condemns idle talk, arguing that it demonstrates the inherent unreliability of speech,[13] that it "attacks oral transmission,"[14] and more specifically, that it

13. Sheila Delany argues that Chaucer's critique of tidings is a further instance of the skepticism that he articulates throughout the poem, revealing that worldly experience is no more reliable than traditional authorities. *Chaucer's House of Fame: The Poetics of Skeptical Fideism* (Chicago: University of Chicago Press, 1972), esp. 110–12. John Fyler offers a similar argument about the "uncertain truth value" of the both the poem's tidings and the literary authorities it describes and incorporates. Fyler, *Chaucer and Ovid* (New Haven: Yale University Press, 1979), 23–64, 61.

14. Britton J. Harwood, "Building Class and Gender into Chaucer's *Hous*," in *Class and Gender in Early English Literature: Intersections*, ed. Britton J. Harwood and Gillian R. Overing (Bloomington: Indiana University Press, 1994), 95–111, 98.

is Chaucer's "anxious exclusion of gossip from the domain of art."[15] Indeed, Geffrey's narration of the Dido legend in Book I foregrounds gossip's destructive potential, articulating the conventional wisdom voiced by late medieval penitential manuals.[16] However, while Chaucer acknowledges pastoral rhetoric about gossip throughout the poem, calling attention to gossip's idleness, its capacity for unchecked proliferation, and its tendency toward distortion, he does so in order to appropriate those characteristics for his poem. The *House of Fame* voraciously pursues gossip, dwelling not on how destructive it is but on how productive it might be both socially and narratively. Although critics generally agree that the poem is Chaucer's attempt to articulate an *ars poetica,* because gossip is always assumed to have a negative valence, its instrumental role in the construction of this *ars poetica* has been largely ignored.[17] Chaucer does not exclude idle talk from the domain of poetry; rather he embraces it as fundamental. Gossip both provides him with new subject matter—what Sheila Delany calls the "raw material of tradition" circulating in the House of Rumor[18]—and, more important, affords him a new method for handling his old sources. That is, gossip becomes the means by which the poet renegotiates his relationship to traditional literary authority.

Gossip is almost universally condemned as idle, as the trivial and unproductive speech that performs no socially or morally acceptable labor. Even contemporary theorists who attempt to rehabilitate gossip's social and psychological work define it as idle, as insisting on "its own frivolity."[19] This

15. Lochrie, *Covert Operations,* 83. Although Lochrie acknowledges that in the poem, "art is everywhere revealed to be no more than gossip," she assumes that Chaucer attempts to avoid gossip rather than actively appropriating its methods.

16. In this moment, Geffrey depicts gossip as a problematic but essential instrument of social control, policing communal morality by punishing transgressions against that morality. The model of gossip as an agent of social control, first articulated by Max Gluckman, has long been a staple of contemporary gossip theory. Gluckman, "Gossip and Scandal."

17. Jesse M. Gellrich, *The Idea of the Book in the Middle Ages: Language, Theory, Mythology, and Fiction* (Ithaca: Cornell University Press, 1985), 169–200; Fyler, *Chaucer and Ovid,* 23–64; Katherine H. Terrell, "Reallocation of Hermeneutic Authority in Chaucer's *House of Fame,*" *Chaucer Review* 31, no. 3 (1997): 279–89; Piero Boitani, *Chaucer and the Imaginary World of Fame* (Cambridge: D. S. Brewer, 1984), 189–216; and J. A. W. Bennett, *Chaucer's Book of Fame* (Oxford: Oxford University Press, 1986). Notable exceptions are Frank Grady and Vance Smith who see in the poem's depiction of tidings Chaucer's exploration of the ethics of poetry. Frank Grady, "Chaucer Reading Langland: *The House of Fame,*" *Studies in the Age of Chaucer* 18 (1996): 3–23; and D. Vance Smith, "Chaucer as an English Writer," in *Yale Companion to Chaucer,* 87–121.

18. Delany, *Chaucer's House of Fame,* 106. David Wallace sees this depiction of tidings as the "raw material of storytelling" as indicating Chaucer's awareness of the "commercial aspects of fiction writing." David Wallace, *Chaucerian Polity: Absolutist Lineages and Associational Forms in England and Italy* (Stanford: Stanford University Press, 1997), 205.

19. Spacks, *Gossip,* 6.

idleness would seem by nature a difficult trait to recuperate as productive, yet the *House of Fame* embraces gossip's triviality as socially and intellectually useful. Rather than advocating a work ethic, the poem celebrates an ethic of idleness. The image of the poet poring over his books, that scene of intellectual labor which opens so many of Chaucer's dream visions, here serves as a source of ridicule.[20] The scene is invoked not by the narrator as a means to frame the poem's speculations, but by the eagle who describes Geffrey's labor less as a virtue than as an affliction:

> For when thy labour doon al ys,
> And hast mad alle thy rekenynges,
> In stede of reste and newe thynges
> Thou goost hom to thy hous anoon,
> And, also domb as any stoon,
> Thou sittest at another book
> Tyl fully daswed ys thy look;
> And lyvest thus as an heremyte.
>
> (652–59)

According to the eagle, Geffrey lives as a recluse, absenting himself from society's talk in order to read in silence. In choosing continued intellectual labor over idleness and news—"reste and new thynges"—Geffrey does the socially astonishing instead of the socially expected. His labor is represented as problematic rather than laudable; the eagle calls explicit attention both to Geffrey's conversational shortcomings—"thou hast no tydynges" (644)— and to the egregiousness of their scope:

> And noght oonly fro fer contree
> That ther no tydynge cometh to thee,
> But of thy verray neyghebores,
> That duellen almost at thy dores,
> Thou herist neyther that ne this.
>
> (647–51)

20. In the *Book of the Duchess*, the scene of reading is represented as the result of and remedy for the narrator's insomnia; the meditation over Ovid's *Metamorphoses* both enables him to sleep and provides the framework for the dream vision that ensues (44–290). The profitability of such intellectual labor is made explicit in the *Parliament of Fowls*; the narrator, seeking "a certeyn thing to lerne" (20), explains that "out of olde bokes, in good feyth, / Cometh al this newe science" (24–25). According to John Fyler, this use of the scene of reading as the "occasion and provocation for a dream" is Chaucer's innovation. *Riverside Chaucer*, 347.

Geffrey does not simply miss news from around the world; he fails to engage in the gossip of those neighbors talking idly at his very doorstep. Condemnation of gossip is wholly lacking from the eagle's explanation. Although he links gossip to idleness, to the time spent after (and as an alternative to continued) labor, he presents that idleness as both preferable to and more acceptable than Geffrey's reclusive habits. Similarly, he equates gossip with the trivial, with the "this and that" which somehow both signifies nothing and accounts for everything, yet he renders the trivial necessary. Gossip's "this and that" constitutes the most basic of social bonds; it prevents one from becoming a hermit.

While the eagle's remarks on Geffrey's conversational lack are clearly an instance of Chaucer's self-deprecating humor, complementing quips about his amorous shortcomings and portly physique, they also introduce into the poem the notion that idleness is productive. Gossip is both the reward for Geffrey's reclusive poetic labor and the means to continue it. Idle talk, in all its triviality, is repeatedly presented as educational, as providing Geffrey with the opportunity to learn something useful (1088; 1998–99). We might be tempted, influenced by pastoral rhetoric on triviality, to assume that gossip is not the real source of instruction, locating it instead in the various lessons the poem offers on sound, astronomy, Fame's palace, and literary history. But although Geffrey tries to hide his curiosity to know the latest news under the guise of higher intellectual pursuits, he makes clear that he has no interest in these other phenomena, for they are neither the knowledge nor the news he seeks. In fact, when the eagle attempts to teach him about astronomy, Geffrey announces that he wishes to learn "ryght naught" (994) of the stars, blaming his old age for his intellectual incapacity for such topics but betraying his complete lack of interest. Moreover, after having learned all of what would seem to be the poem's legitimate lessons, Geffrey exits the House of Fame declaring his frustration at not yet having acquired the education he was promised: "But these be no suche tydynges / As I mene of" (1894–95). Tidings are the object of his (and the poem's) quest; they are the source its education: "The cause why I stonde here: / Some newe tydynges for to lere" (1885–86). Through Geffrey's comically insistent pursuit of the latest news, tidings themselves as well as the individual pieces of news they carry become the proper subjects of poetry. The poem thus represents gossip as an idle amusement that is narratively productive.

* * *

While Chaucer's exploration of gossip's idleness suggests a new source for poetry, his theorization of gossip's capacity to proliferate produces a new narrative method. The fear that "gossip will not be suppressed," that it will "spill over" the boundaries of one intimate exchange spreading further and further into the conversations of other people, is, as Patricia Spacks argues, the central reason behind gossip's negative reputation.[21] Medieval penitential manuals offer similar admonitions about idle talk's propensity to create unrest through the "efter telleres" who repeat its tidings.[22] Yet it is precisely gossip's capacity to multiply that Chaucer both embraces and appropriates. The idea of "multiplicacioun" (784) pervades the poem.[23] It is a defining feature—a "kynde thynge" (1292)—of Fame, both the goddess and the discourse over which she presides. Chaucer offers a detailed account of how gossip's proliferation takes place, tracing a rumor's journey to and from Fame's palace and demonstrating its multiplication at every stage, so that it "woxen more on every tonge / that ever hit was" (2082–83). Fame herself is ever expanding, seeming at first glance to be no more than a "cubite" and then appearing to reach the heavens. Even the gemstone from which her palace is constructed—beryl—functions to magnify.[24]

More than simply a descriptive category for Fame and her temple, however, multiplication becomes the poem's narrative strategy. At first, that technique is applied only to the characters, as the eagle piques Geffrey's interest by claiming that Fame's palace will contain more forms of gossip than he could possibly imagine: more tidings, more stories of love, more jealousies, more discords, more jokes, and more deceptions than anywhere

---

21. Spacks, *Gossip*, 263 and 3.

22. *Ayenbite of Inwit*, 58. Cf. *Book of Vices and Virtues*, 58/32–36.

23. According to both the *Oxford English Dictionary* and the *Middle English Dictionary*, Chaucer's use of the word, "multiplication," in the *House of Fame* is the first in English. His only other use comes in the *Canon's Yeoman's Tale*, where multiplication denotes the Canon's unholy (and wholly unsuccessful) alchemy (VIII. 849). *Oxford English Dictionary*, s.v. "multiplication"; and *Middle English Dictionary*, s.v. "multiplicacioun."

24. In the poem, beryl "made wel more than hit was / To semen every thinge, ywis" (1290–91). According to the descriptions provided by late medieval lapidaries, beryl is a particularly appropriate stone for the *House of Fame*. It nourishes the love between a man and a woman (enabling the poem's love-tidings) and may have been used to make medieval spectacles, hence its ability to magnify. See Marbode of Rennes, *De Lapidibus*, ed. and trans. John M. Riddle (Wiesbaden: Franz Steiner, 1977), 49; and Joan Evans and Mary S. Serjeantson, eds., *English Mediaeval Lapidaries*, EETS, o.s. 190 (London: Kegan Paul, Trench, Trübner, 1933), 28, 47–48, 72–73, and 125. For a further exploration of beryl's possible meanings in the *House of Fame*, see Howard R. Patch, "Precious Stones in the *House of Fame*," *Modern Language Notes* 50 (1935): 312–17.

on earth.[25] Geffrey, however, quickly adopts the maneuver for himself, re-peatedly enticing his audience with a sense of surplus. In Fame's palace, he claims to see more poets, minstrels, instruments, and heralds than he can possibly describe. Similarly, outside the House of Rumor, he offers a prolif-erating and seemingly endless list of all the possible subjects of the tidings he will hear—marriages, peace, war, idleness, work, and good governance, to name a few (1959–76). From a pastoral perspective, Chaucer's interest in multiplying here is troubling in and of itself, quite apart from its connection to gossip. If multiplying is not explicitly connected to matters pastoral, to the procreative increase of "God bade us for to wax and multiply," or to the penitential mathematics through which God's mercy, one's possessions, or one's sins are multiplied, then it is allied with the swindling practiced by figures like the Canon and the Pardoner.[26] Yet Chaucer does not legitimize multiplication by associating it with pastoral discourse; rather he appro-priates it as a kind of narrative confidence game, for he uses gossip's capacity to multiply to produce the *promise* of surplus rather than surplus itself.[27]

This promise of multiplicity is the source of the poem's narrative tension, as readers are everywhere led to anticipate the fulfillment of that promise. Surplus is continually invoked but never realized because the rhetoric of multiplication operates in tandem with the trope of *occupatio*, withholding multiplicity even as it pretends to reveal it.[28] *Occupatio*, or rather *occultatio*, as it is more properly named, is a figure of occlusion, a figure that simulta-neously divulges and withholds.[29] Tracing its lineage through Geoffrey of

25. In the eagle's twenty-six-line advertisement (674–99), the adjective "more" recurs with greater frequency than in any other of Chaucer's poems, including the whole of the *Troilus*.

26. See the *Middle English Dictionary*, s.v. "multiplien"; and the *Oxford English Dictionary*, s.v. "multiply," 2. The Wife of Bath stands at the intersection between pastoral rhetoric and discursive swindling, as she twists the logic of "wax and multiply," increasing not mankind but both the number of her husbands and the sources of "auctoritee."

27. Laura Ruffolo makes the related claim that lists in the poem are often wholly without content. Laura Ruffolo, "Literary Authority and the Lists of Chaucer's *House of Fame*: Destruc-tion and Definition Through Proliferation," *Chaucer Review* 27, no. 4 (1993): 325–41.

28. As part of his argument about movement in the poem, Steven Kruger similarly observes that "the consistent promise of revelation is consistently undermined." For Kruger, the poem's movement outward toward external phenomena and upward toward "a transcendent realm of abstract and universal ideas" continually collapses back into self-exploration. Steven Kruger, "Imagination and the Complex Movement of Chaucer's *House of Fame*," *Chaucer Review* 28, no. 2 (1993): 117–34; quotations on 124 and 117.

29. *Occultatio* is the Latin translation for the Greek term, *paralipsis*. As H. A. Kelly explains, the Occupatio/occultatio confusion is due to a ninth-century translation error in the *Rhetorica ad Herennium*. H. A. Kelly, "*Occupatio* as Negative Narration: A Mistake for *Occultatio/Praeteritio*," *Modern Philology* 74 (1977): 311–15. Because all manuscripts of the *Rhetorica* from the ninth cen-

Vinsauf back to the anonymous *Rhetorica ad Herennium, occupatio* "occurs when we say that we are passing by, or do not know, or refuse to say that which precisely now we are saying."[30] The figure was originally used in the courtroom, for instances when suggestion might be preferable to and indeed more powerful than explicit statement, since one could imply a transgression without needing to prove it. As such, it straddles the border between truth and falsehood, the liminal space where gossip thrives. *Occupatio,* in this original context, is gossip's trope and this is precisely how Chaucer uses it in the *House of Fame.* Elsewhere in his poetry, he follows the prescriptions of medieval rhetorical authorities, employing *occupatio* as a technique for abbreviating his sources.[31] While he certainly adopts this conventional approach to the figure in the *House of Fame*—repeatedly deploying it in Book I so as to avoid telling a version of the Dido legend wholly faithful to either Ovid or Virgil—he also does something more, emphasizing occlusion over abbreviation.[32]

---

tury forward contain the mistake, medieval rhetoricians as well as their Renaissance successors, adopt the name "occupatio." Consequently, it is the term of choice among medievalists, despite the scholarly consensus in the classics community that the medieval translation is erroneous.

30. "Occultatio est cum dicimus nos praeterire aut non scire aut nolle dicere id quod nunc maxime dicimus" (IV.xxvii.37). *Rhetorica ad Herennium,* ed. and trans. Harry Caplan (Cambridge: Harvard University Press, 1954), 320–21. Geoffrey of Vinsauf, *Poetria Nova,* trans. Margaret F. Nims (Toronto: Pontifical Institute of Medieval Studies, 1967), lines 1158–62. See also James J. Murphy, *Three Medieval Rhetorical Arts* (Berkeley and Los Angeles: University of California Press, 1971) and *Rhetoric in the Middle Ages: A History of Rhetorical Theory from Saint Augustine to the Renaissance* (Tempe: Arizona Center for Medieval and Renaissance Studies, 2001).

31. Both classical and medieval rhetoricians categorize *occupatio* as a trope of abbreviation. Chaucer's most infamous example comes in the *Knight's Tale* in the description of Arcite's funeral. Here, in the longest sentence in the Chaucer cannon, the Knight explicitly details the scene he pretends not to describe, painstakingly cataloguing, for example, each species of tree used to build the funeral pyre even as he laments that to do so would occupy too much time (I. 2919–62). While scholars have discussed the use of *occupatio* in Chaucer's poetry, they have tended to focus on the *Knight's Tale* and have largely ignored its role in the *House of Fame.* See Stephen Knight, *Rymyng Craftily: Meaning in Chaucer's Poetry* (Atlantic Highlands, N.J.: Humanities International Press, 1973), 98–160; A. C. Spearing, ed., *The Knight's Tale* (Cambridge: Cambridge University Press, 1966), 33–38; and J. M. Manly, "Chaucer and the Rhetoricians," *Proceedings of the British Academy* 12 (1926), 95–113. A notable exception is Thomas Kennedy, who argues that the trope makes the reader continually aware of time's passage, in order to express the limitations both of the human condition and of language to express that condition. Thomas C. Kennedy, "Rhetoric and Meaning in the *House of Fame,*" *Studia Neophilologica* 68 (1996): 9–23.

32. Fyler reveals the ways in which Chaucer combines Virgil and Ovid by adopting Ovid's perspective on Virgil's narrative and in the process creating a version of the legend that calls both into question. For Fyler, the use of *occupatio* enables Chaucer to suture together the two versions. Fyler, *Chaucer and Ovid,* 30–41.

Chaucer adopts this trope, with its capacity for simultaneous disclosure and concealment, in order to propel the narrative forward, creating the sense that there is something more important toward which the poem is trying to tend. While this sense of forward momentum is introduced early on in Geffrey's coy refusal to describe the illicit love affair between Dido and Aeneas, it reaches its height in Book III as the poem nears its conclusion.[33] When Geffrey arrives at Fame's palace, instances of *occupatio* occur with increasing frequency as he warns his audience at least eight times about the dangers of wasting time.[34] The more frequent the *occupatio*, the greater the anticipation for the love-tidings that have been repeatedly deferred, promised, and multiplied. Inside Rumor's house the building of suspense intensifies, as Geffrey teases his audience with what sounds like gossip but turns out to be all appearance and no content:

> And than he tolde hym this and that,
> And swor therto that hit was soth—
> "Thus hath he sayd," and "Thus he doth,"
> "Thus shal hit be," "Thus herde y seye,"
> "That shal be founde," "That dar I leye."
> (2050–54)

To avoid sharing the tidings he overhears, he first teaches his audience how to identify gossip by providing the speech tags of idle talk, and then hides

33. By refusing to narrate the affair—"Hyt were a long proces to telle, / And over-long for yow to dwelle" (251–52)—Geffrey occludes from the Dido narrative the love-tidings that become his poetic reward and therefore the topic of the rest of the poem. Concealing that which would be most enticing, he then promises to tell a new version of it in expanded detail. That is, he promises to use his poem to multiply the love tidings, or alternatively to use tidings to multiply his poem.

34. See, for example, Geffrey's description of the "castel-yate" (1294):

> Hyt nedeth noght yow more to tellen,
> To make yow to longe duellen,
> Of this yates florisshinges,
> Ne of the compasses, ne of kervynges,
> Ne how they hatte in masoneries,
> As corbetz, ful of ymageries.
> (1299–1304)

Cf. 1252–58, 1282–85, 1354–55, 1415–18, 1451–55, 1503–6, and 1513–19. While not all of these examples on the dangers of wasting time are formally *occupatio*, they nonetheless contribute both to the poem's forward momentum and to the atmosphere of concealment.

behind another *occupatio,* claiming that he cannot possibly describe the wondrous things he hears.[35] It is not the case that Geffrey cannot hear the tidings—that he only hears the tags because he is an outsider.[36] Quite the contrary, he hears them and then purposefully withholds them, keeping his audience on the outside. His building of anticipation is relentless, each time coming closer to, without ever actually telling, a tiding. Assuring the audience of his diligence in learning the latest news as he hurries about the whirling House of Rumor, he hints at news he has heard "of som contre" (2135), but quickly disclaims that it "shal not now be told" by him (2136). Still *occupatio* is used to build anticipation, still it gives the sense that there is something more important toward which this poem is tending. And when we hear the "gret noyse" (2141) coming from the corner where men tell love tidings, when we witness the stampede in which men are leaping one on top of the other to hear this new tiding that no one knows, when we catch sight of the "man of gret auctorite" (2158), when we assume, that is, that the long-awaited tiding has finally arrived, the poem ends without a word, without ever telling us "this or that."

The poem's unfinished conclusion is its ultimate concealment, the culmination of the multiplying and withholding in which it has continually engaged. That the poem is unfinished is essential to both its method and its theorizations.[37] Rather than lamenting the failure of language or denouncing the unreliability of idle talk,[38] the poem's ending, as with the instances of *occupatio* that enable it, makes manifest gossip's unlimited potential: to oc-

---

35. As Kennedy argues, the figure of *occupatio* is often linked to the inexpressibility topos. "Rhetoric and Meaning," 14–16.

36. Reading this moment as a further instance of the male ignorance she describes and condemns, Lochrie argues that "tags of gossip . . . are all that Geffrey actually hears." Lochrie, *Covert Operations,* 89.

37. While earlier critics blamed the poem's abrupt ending on a poor manuscript tradition, more recently scholars have argued that the poem breaks off as a deliberate fragment. See, for example, Larry Benson's suggestion that the ending is a courtly in-joke, alluding to the news arriving from the Italian court that the wedding of Richard II and Caterina Visconti was off and poking fun at the messenger who delivered it by derisively referring to him as a "man of gret auctorite." Larry D. Benson, "The 'Love-Tydynges' in Chaucer's *House of Fame,*" in *Chaucer in the Eighties,* ed. Julian N. Wasserman and Robert J. Blanch (Syracuse: Syracuse University Press, 1986), 3–22.

38. Kennedy argues that the ending underscores the limitations of human language in that "what has been omitted cannot be expressed in words." Kennedy, "Rhetoric and Meaning," 16. Cf. Donald Fry's assertion that the ending humorously demonstrates the "unreliability of transmitted secular knowledge." Donald Fry, "The Ending of the *House of Fame,*" *Chaucer at Albany,* ed. Rossell Hope Robbins (New York: Burt Franklin, 1975), 27–40, esp. 27–28.

clude, abbreviate, amplify, and multiply. Only as we find ourselves at the top of the pile, waiting to hear the news, listening for the words of the "man of gret auctoritee" do we recognize the process to which we have been subjected; only in that moment do we fully appreciate that gossip has become the poem's narrative method. Idle talk's capacity to "penetrate method" has been established by gossip theorists working on the novel. As Spacks argues, "novelistic narrators often arouse in readers the kind of intense interest in personal detail that gossip generates, and they may attempt to establish with their readers a kind of relationship approximating that of gossip."[39] Yet Geffrey's machinations in the *House of Fame* supersede the novelistic approximations Spacks describes. Gossip is not used to create an intimacy with the reader in order to convey another narrative more immediately; gossip *is* the story.

The story of gossip as method, however, does not end with multiplication and occlusion, does not end, that is, with a narrative strategy for generating interest. Idle talk distorts as it proliferates, becoming that "malicious" gossip characterized by misrepresentation and falsehood and providing Chaucer with a new method for transforming his sources.[40] As penitential manuals are fond of warning, gossip's truth-content is uncertain and those who traffic in it are often considered fools and liars because of the "newe tydynges" they tell.[41] Echoing pastoral wisdom, the goings-on inside both Fame's palace and the House of Rumor frequently involve some manner of distortion. Fame's arbitrary judgment tarnishes the most pristine reputations with infamy and attributes heroic deeds to idle men. The inhabitants of Rumor's whirling house add "more encres" (2074) to every tiding they tell, without concern for veracity. Chaucer even goes so far as to allegorize gossip's capacity to distort by depicting the moment in which a lie and a sober truth meet on a window ledge inside the House of Rumor. Since neither has precedence, the two decide to become sworn brothers, promising never to leave each other's side, and thus, truth and falsehood are forever conflated in one tiding: "fals and soth compouned / Togeder fle for oo tydynge" (2108–9).

What appears to be an exemplum of gossip's inherent unreliability in fact serves as an emblem of poetic practice. As Vance Smith has argued, the scene of "fals and soth compouned" illustrates the "work of poetry."[42] Yet

---

39. Spacks, *Gossip*, 10.
40. Ibid., 8.
41. *Book of Vices and Virtues*, 55/33–36. Cf. *Ayenbite of Inwyt*, 58; and *Jacob's Well*, 148/25–27.
42. Smith, "Chaucer as an English Writer," 111.

rather than an anxious depiction of poetry's capacity for deception, the scene reveals gossip's potential for poetic invention. Just as the poem turns idle talk's "this and that" into narrative, so it turns literary tradition into "this and that," transforming the wisdom of literary "auctoritees" into the he said/he said of gossip:

> Betwex hem was a litil envye.
> Oon seyde that Omer made lyes,
> Feynynge in hys poetries,
> And was to Grekes favorable;
> Therfor held he hyt but fable.
> (1476–80)

Not only are Homer's texts made akin to the tidings that combine truth and falsehood, but also the literary criticism of later authorities is rendered nothing more than jealous and idle chatter. As John Fyler has demonstrated, Chaucer refers here to an actual literary dispute of some magnitude about the relative reliability of different poetic accounts of the Trojan War, yet surrounded by so much idle talk, that debate becomes just another kind of news.[43] And it is in this conflation that Chaucer appropriates as a technique gossip's capacity for distortion, for like the tidings invoked elsewhere, this gossip—the idle talk of old sources and revered authorities—can be abbreviated, expanded, and conjoined. In fact, throughout the poem, Chaucer has been transforming his sources in much the same way that the House of Rumor's residents alter the tidings they hear. Even (or perhaps especially) in those moments in which he proclaims his originality—"Non other auctour alegge I" (314)—Chaucer combines and amends the texts of Ovid and Virgil so that the two accounts become both inextricably bound and radically altered.[44] That is, his poetic practice mimics gossip's combinatory talent of presenting "fals and soth compouned." Gossip's distortion, like its capacity for proliferation, becomes linked to the creative process of the poem as Chaucer's authorial strategies—augmenting, conflating, concealing, and multiplying his old sources to make them new—are everywhere made analogous to the idle talk he describes.

43. Fyler, *Chaucer and Ovid*, 30–32.
44. For a detailed discussion of Chaucer's appropriations of Ovid and Virgil, see Fyler, *Chaucer and Ovid*, 23–64. Virgil and Ovid are the central but not the only sources that are combined and transformed in the poem.

Tidings and the *Tales*

In the *House of Fame*, Chaucer's theory of gossip is thus intertwined with his theory of poetry, as the exploration of idle talk's characteristics leads to the discovery of new literary techniques. Represented as the source for the raw material of poetry, a method for creating narrative momentum, and a means to transform old sources into new tales, gossip is both the vehicle of Chaucer's *ars poetica* and one of its central tenets. Although the poem does experiment with idle talk's capacities, its interest in gossip remains for the most part at this theoretical level, suggesting but not enacting gossip's myriad narrative possibilities. However, the tales told by the House of Rumor's inhabitants—those shipmen, pardoners, and pilgrims who provide the cast of characters for the *Canterbury Tales*—put that theory into practice, making explicit the connections between idle talk and formal narrative everywhere implied in the *House of Fame*. Whereas the early dream vision details gossip's characteristics, analyzing and exploiting pastoral rhetoric about deviant speech as a means to develop narrative strategies, the *Canterbury Tales* foregrounds and repeatedly implements those strategies. Gossip's capacity for narrative transformation is no longer a theoretical possibility but a favorite device. Moving beyond the conflation, abbreviation, and amplification of literary "auctoritees" that constitute the model of source transformation sketched in the *House of Fame*, idle talk in the *Canterbury Tales* performs the discursive and generic alchemy so central to Chaucer's poetic experimentation.[45]

Chaucer reveals gossip's centrality to his poetic practice early in the *Canterbury Tales* in the literary musings of the Man of Law. Faced with the frustrating reality that Chaucer has told all the "thrifty" (II. 46) tales there

---

45. For Derek Pearsall, generic experimentation is a defining feature of the *Canterbury Tales:* "In taking over the different genres of narrative that were traditionally current in the Middle Ages, [Chaucer] is able, through the fiction of the tale-telling, to exploit, challenge and often defy the expectations that they carry of the relationship between fiction and reality. Instead of contenting his readers with replications of kinds of literary experience that they are used to, he constantly creates questions and disturbances, so that readers are jolted into re-examining their customary assumptions." Derek Pearsall, *The Canterbury Tales* (London: Unwin Hyman, 1985), xiii. See also David Benson's compelling argument that the stylistic "drama" of the *Canterbury Tales* inheres in its generic play and more recently, Caroline Eckhardt's reading of the *Canterbury Tales* as an "anthology of genres." C. David Benson, *Chaucer's Drama of Style: Poetic Variety and Contrast in the Canterbury Tales* (Chapel Hill: University of North Carolina Press, 1986); and Caroline D. Eckhardt, "Genre," in *A Companion to Chaucer*, ed. Peter Brown (Oxford: Blackwell, 2000), 180–94, 186.

are to tell, the Man of Law is at a loss for a narrative and must therefore seek a new source for his story. As if taking a cue from the *House of Fame,* he argues that the whisperings of the House of Rumor might offer the only remaining untapped source of storytelling inspiration, for he would be "of tales desolaat" were it not for news-trafficking merchants—those "fadres of tidynges / And tales" (II. 129–30) who provide him with the story of Constance. In the Man of Law's account of his narrative's origins, tidings and tales become one and the same, as news supplants traditional literary sources. Through his unorthodox attribution of literary authority, tidings are established both as an appropriate source for narrative and, more important, as a means to make old tales new. Indeed, the fiction of the Man of Law's merchants enables Chaucer to transform an incredibly popular tale, familiar to readers from its frequent medieval retellings, into news.[46] That news, moreover, has the power to generate its own stories, for in addition to providing the Man of Law with his tale, merchants' tidings initiate the story's action.[47] The news of Constance and her virtues circulates throughout Rome until it reaches the ears of the Syrian merchants who then bring it to the Sultan—a man who craves tidings almost as much as the reclusive Geffrey. So enthralled is the Sultan by the talk of Constance that he renounces his faith in order to marry her, setting the tale's events into motion.

Chaucerian gossip, however, does more than provide titillating sources for the Canterbury narratives, more, that is, than transform old stories into the new *Tales.* As productive as the merchants' tidings are, they provide only a superficial sense of gossip's poetic inspiration. Long before the Man of

---

46. No doubt this fiction functions in part as an inside joke between Chaucer and his contemporaries. Although Chaucer's primary source is Nicholas Trivet, Gower would have been the most recent trafficker in the tale's tidings, and thus comically linked to the Man of Law's newsmongering merchants. The joke is made all the more humorous by the fact that Gower seems not to be interested in tidings at all. Gower's Sultan, curious about the religious constancy of his subjects rather than news from around the world, is converted not by tidings about Constance but by her faith—a faith that has already converted his merchants. The tale's popularity as well as its numerous late medieval retellings have been amply documented by Patricia Eberle in her notes to the *Riverside Chaucer.* For the most recent discussion of Chaucer's departure from his sources as well as their larger cultural significance, see Kathy Lavezzo's provocative essay, "Beyond Rome: Mapping Gender and Justice in the *Man of Law's Tale,*" *Studies in the Age of Chaucer* 24 (2002): 139–80.

47. Both Wallace and Smith have recently discussed the tale's privileging of the merchants' tidings; Wallace sees them as emblematic of the role merchants played in medieval England, whereas Smith interprets them as evidence of Chaucer's literary "Englishness." Wallace, *Chaucerian Polity,* 182–211; and Smith, "Chaucer as an English Writer," esp. 112–18.

Law takes recourse in his news-mongering sources, he introduces a theory of gossip that makes idle talk integral to both the production and reception of poetry. In the *Introduction* to his tale, the Man of Law catalogues Chaucer's poetic corpus as proof of the dearth of narratives available to him—his grumbling that Chaucer has told more stories than Ovid quickly becoming a list of Chaucer's many Ovidian borrowings.[48] To tell any story, he complains, is to risk being considered nothing but a poor imitation:

> But of my tale how shal I doon this day?
> Me were looth be likned, doutelees,
> To Muses that men clepe Pierides—
> *Methamorphosios* woot what I mene
> (II. 90–93)

Demonstrating that he too can appropriate classical narrative, the Man of Law invokes a well-known tale of literary pretension from the *Metamorphoses*, that text from which Chaucer does so much of his own poetic pilfering.[49] The temptation to savor this invocation as a brilliant literary joke—the culmination of a series of poetic quips made throughout the *Introduction*—is almost irresistible. The passage comically calls into question Chaucer's own status as a poetic imitator by invoking the text he so frequently imitates. At the same time, it pokes fun at the Man of Law's claims to be a learned reader, for he muddles the details of Ovid's story, confusing the Muses themselves—called Pierides from their birthplace, Pieria—with the nine daughters of King Pierus who challenged their divine rivals to a singing

48. The Man of Law's listing is infamously selective, consisting primarily of the tales told in the *Legend of Good Women*. Scholars have understandably taken a keen interest in this selective cataloguing, interpreting it variously as "moral" Chaucer's repudiation of his secular poetry in favor of a poetry of Christian "truth," as a complaint about his public reputation as a poet of love, and as a literary conservatism, "a tyranny of orthodox authority" that will be overthrown by the Wife of Bath's narrative of experience. V. A. Kolve, *Chaucer and the Imagery of Narrative: The First Five Canterbury Tales* (Stanford: Stanford University Press, 1984), 293–96; Alfred David, "The Man of Law vs. Chaucer: A Case in Poetics," *PMLA* 82, no. 2 (1967): 217–25, and *The Strumpet Muse: Arts and Morals in Chaucer's Poetry* (Bloomington: Indiana University Press, 1976); and Lee Patterson, " 'For the Wyves Love of Bathe': Feminine Rhetoric and Poetic Resolution in the *Roman de la Rose* and the *Canterbury Tales*," *Speculum* 58, no. 3 (1983): 656–95, 693. On the *Legend*'s indebtedness to Ovid, see Fyler, *Chaucer and Ovid*, 96–123.

49. As John Fyler argues, most of the material that Chaucer directly borrows from Ovid comes from the *Metamorphoses*. Fyler, *Chaucer and Ovid*, 17.

competition.[50] Yet much more is at stake in both the reference and the conflation it foregrounds than self-deprecating humor.

The Man of Law's Ovidian invocation, with the conflation it performs,
articulates the relationship between gossip and poetic practice. In Ovid's
narrative, the Pierides, presumptuous sisters whose unproductive verses
were neither tuneful nor well narrated, lost the singing contest and were
punished by being transformed into magpies—those gossiping birds whose
idle chatter echoes throughout Chaucer's poetry.[51] Magpies are the telltales
of the aviary community; they are Fame's informants; and they are the
"wikked tongues" whose ears Pandarus's stratagems are designed to avoid.[52]
That is, they represent idle talk—the unproductive language that for Ovid
compares so poorly to the poetry of the Muses. Rather than functioning as
an exemplum about the dangers of idle talk, however, the allusion serves as
an illustration of gossip's generative possibilities. For the Man of Law (and
for Chaucer behind him), both magpie and muse go by the same name. By
conflating the two sets of sisters, he makes idle chatter and poetic performance one and the same.[53] What is more, according to the Man of Law, Ovid's
poem is in on the joke: "the *Methamorphosios* woot what I mene." In the
phrasing of implied intimacy, the wink and the nudge of the inside joke
practiced by Pandarus and the Miller, and made infamous by the Wife of
Bath, the Man of Law transforms Ovid's *Metamorphoses* into a conversational companion.[54] Ovid's text is figured as the Man of Law's *confidante*

50. This line has caused a great deal of editorial consternation. Scholars have tended to focus
on either the Muses or their rivals, noting the Man of Law's self-effacement or his flattering
elevation of Chaucer, and have not attempted to deal with the conflation of the two. In her notes
to the *Riverside Chaucer*, Eberle acknowledges the confusion but does not attempt to account for
it (854). Notable exceptions are Kevin Harty, who sees the reference as signaling both the Man of
Law's awareness of the storytelling competition and his desire to win it, and more recently, James
Simpson, who sees the conflation as deliberate and authorial. Kevin J. Harty, "Chaucer's Man of
Law and the 'Muses That Men Clepe Pierides,'" *Studies in Short Fiction* 18, no. 1 (1981): 75–77;
and James Simpson, "Chaucer as a European Writer," in *Yale Companion*, 78–79.

51. Ovid, *Metamorphoses*, ed. Frank Justice Miller, 3rd ed. (Cambridge: Harvard University
Press, 1977–84), 5.293–678.

52. The *Squire's Tale*, V. 650, the *House of Fame*, 703, and *Troilus and Criseyde*, III. 527.

53. Simpson makes the compelling argument that this conflation offers a "model of Chaucer
as literary magpie," illustrating the dissolution of "Chaucer's claims to originary status as an
author." Simpson, "Chaucer as a European Writer," 79.

54. While knowing (or not knowing) what someone means is a question raised throughout
Chaucer's work, the joking, "*you* know what I mean," occurs only four times; and only in the
Man of Law's Introduction is a text said to be in the know. Cf. *Miller's Tale*, I. 3371, *Wife of Bath's
Prologue*, III. 200, and *Troilus and Criseyde*, III. 256.

with whom he chatters about the characters and tales contained within it. Just as tidings can become tales, so tales can also become tidings. In the process, reading is reimagined as intimate conversation, that is, as gossip's idle talk. Ovid and Chaucer, muses and magpies, the Man of Law and the *Metamorphoses* become mutually implicated in poetic production, literary reception, and gossip. For the Man of Law, both muse and magpie are problematic, but for Chaucer, this moment of clever wordplay, equating the work of a classical "auctor" with idle talk and revealing his poetry's dependence on both, outlines a new methodology—a mixing of news and narrative that becomes fundamental to the structure of the *Canterbury Tales.*

Chaucer uses the Man of Law to introduce into the *Canterbury Tales* his expanded theory of gossip's narrative utility, but it is through the Host, Harry Bailly—the pilgrim who figures most prominently and gossips most egregiously in the poem's framework—that he puts theory into practice. As a character, Harry's attitude toward gossip is deeply conflicted. He speaks as both an avid participant and a vehement critic, simultaneously encouraging the blurring of tidings and tales and demanding their strict segregation. Even as he delights in gossiping about the transgressions and shortcomings of his fellow pilgrims—the Cook's dodgy culinary practices, the Monk's extracurricular activities, and the Canon's shady financial situation, to name a few—the Host preaches against idle talk for the benefit of his traveling companions. He reminds the Friar that such speech is unbecoming in a man of his social standing and warns the Manciple that the slighted Cook might well gossip about his habitual larceny, a lesson the Manciple transforms into the fifty-line *moralitas* of his tale. He even represents the storytelling competition—the model that provides the framework of the *Tales*—as a means to recuperate the unproductive idle talk in which the pilgrims would engage were it not for his timely intervention:

> And wel I woot, as ye goon by the weye,
> Ye shapen yow to talen and to pleye;
> For trewely, confort ne myrthe is noon
> To ride by the weye doumb as a stoon;
> And therfore wol I maken yow disport,
> As I seyde erst, and doon yow som confort.
>
> (I. 771–76)

According to Harry, pilgrims have a well-known propensity to gossip ("talen").[55] Conversation, he implies, is as natural state of affairs for a pilgrimage as it was for Geffrey's neighbors, and any form of entertainment ("pleye") must necessarily involve such idle talk. Thus, by proposing a tale-telling competition, he is attempting to substitute one kind of talk for another more profitable one, using his authorized telling of old tales, of "aventures that whilom han bifalle" (I. 795), to replace the new tales, the tidings, the gossip about which the pilgrims would ordinarily "talen." While it is certainly true that in performing this substitution he has in mind not the "common profit" invoked by the penitential manuals but the lining of his own purse, he nonetheless acts as the arbiter of conversational morality, offering, as Cynthia Richardson argues, "a better way, a more moral way, to pass time."[56]

The Host's frequent attempts to elevate the conversations of his companions make him the persistent if hypocritical voice of conventional wisdom about idle talk—a man who worries about wasted time and wasted words, for all that he enjoys gossiping.[57] Indeed, as a preacher, he has something of the Pardoner in him, as he practices what he preaches against, even going so far as to use his sermons as an opportunity to indulge in his vice. Warning the Manciple about the dangers of jangling enables him to jangle about the Manciple's embezzling. More flagrantly, he uses the pastoral wisdom that idle talk is a female vice as an excuse to gossip about his wife. Indeed, his gossip about Goodelief is a narrative he delivers in installments throughout the poem, a narrative he specifically identifies as his "tale" (IV. 2440), his contribution to the storytelling competition he established to supplant just

55. Although editors have tended to gloss "talen" as "to tell tales," implying that the pilgrims would naturally tell stories on the road to Canterbury, elsewhere in Chaucer's poetry, "talen" encompasses the "jangling" in church that the Parson condemns (X. 378) and the scheming gossip in which Pandarus and Troilus engage (III. 231). Cf. *Oxford English Dictionary*, s.v. "tale," II.6: "To discourse, talk, gossip."

56. Cynthia C. Richardson, "The Function of the Host in *The Canterbury Tales*," *Texas Studies in Literature and Language* 12 (1970–71): 325–44, 343.

57. As numerous critics have observed, Harry is preoccupied with time, repeatedly rebuking his fellow pilgrims for their "ydelnesse" (II. 32) by reminding them that "tyme wasteth" (II. 20). See among others, Barbara Page, "Concerning the Host," *Chaucer Review* 4 (1969): 1–13; Walter Scheps, "'Up Roos our Hoost, and Was our Aller Cok': Harry Bailly's Tale-telling Competition," *Chaucer Review* 10, no. 2 (1975): 113–28; Richardson, "Function of the Host"; and most recently, John Plummer, "'Be Fructuous and That in Litel Space': The Engendering of Harry Bailly," in *New Readings of Chaucer's Poetry*, ed. Robert G. Benson and Susan J. Ridyard (Cambridge: D. S. Brewer, 2003), 107–18.

this kind of talk.[58] By blurring tidings and tales here, Harry obscures the distinction between his preaching and his gossip, a discursive conflation that will come to define his speech in the poem. The "tale" of Harry's gossip, however, is not simply the story of a husband who gossips about his wife while claiming that idle talk is women's work, a secular version of the hypocritical clerics the Wife of Bath derides. That is, his attitude toward idle talk is not just another of his myriad inconsistencies—a further manifestation of his flawed character—for his idle talk has structural as well as dramatic ramifications, influencing the tales framed by his gossip as much as the development of his character.[59]

Critics have tended to separate the Host's structural role from his transgressive speech. Exploring the character, they have noted his love of jokes, jangling, and ribald tales;[60] discussing his structural function, they have agreed that he is a "unifying feature of the whole pilgrimage fiction," linking the potentially disparate narratives into a unified whole.[61] Beyond the claim that Harry and his inappropriate speech provide the continuity between the tales, scholars have ignored the connections between these two aspects of his character. Harry's gossip, however, is fundamental to the structure of the *Canterbury Tales;* it is the medium through which the tales are told and

58. As I discuss below, Harry's "tale" has two episodes. He introduces his narrative in the *Epilogue to the Merchant's Tale* and unfolds it details in the *Prologue to the Monk's Tale.*

59. Critics have long noted Harry's various hypocrisies, documenting his inconsistent attitude toward "sentence and solaas," his contradictory self-presentation on the topics of idleness, literary merit, and virility; the contradictions inherent in his representation of "bourgeois masculinity," and his ever-shifting notions of governance. S. S. Hussey, "Chaucer's Host," *Medieval English Studies Presented to George Kane,* ed. Edward Donald Kennedy, Ronald Waldron, and Joseph S. Wittig (Wolfboro, N.H.: D. S. Brewer, 1988), 153–61; Page, "Concerning the Host"; Mark Allen, "Mirth and Bourgeois Masculinity in Chaucer's Host," in *Masculinities in Chaucer: Approaches to Maleness in the Canterbury Tales and Troilus and Criseyde,* ed. Peter G. Beidler (Cambridge: D. S. Brewer, 1998), 9–21; David R. Pichaske and Laura Sweetland, "Chaucer on the Medieval Monarchy: Harry Bailly in the *Canterbury Tales,*" *Chaucer Review* 11 (1977): 179–200.

60. See among others, R. M. Lumiansky, *Of Sondry Folk: The Dramatic Principle in the Canterbury Tales* (Austin: University of Texas Press, 1955); and Page, "Concerning the Host," esp. 1–5.

61. Hussey, "Chaucer's Host," 155. First articulated by Ralph Baldwin, the Host's function as a unifying device has been explored by many critics. See, among others, Ralph Baldwin, *The Unity of the Canterbury Tales* (Copenhagen: Rosenkilde and Bagger, 1955), esp. 67–79; Lumiansky, *Of Sondry Folk;* Donald R. Howard, *The Idea of the Canterbury Tales* (Berkeley and Los Angeles: University of California Press, 1976); Pichaske and Sweetland, "Chaucer on the Medieval Monarchy"; and most recently, Thomas C. Richardson, "Harry Bailly: Chaucer's Innkeeper," in *Chaucer's Pilgrims: An Historical Guide to the Pilgrims in the Canterbury Tales,* ed. Laura C. Lambdin and Robert T. Lambdin (Westport, Conn.: Greenwood Press, 1996), 324–39.

the mechanism through which they are interpreted.[62] Despite his im-
promptu preaching against it, Harry's avid participation in idle talk creates
an atmosphere of speaking everything that pervades the poem. Repeatedly
encouraging his fellow pilgrims to "spareth nat" (III. 1337), he facilitates the
blurring of tidings and tales, eroding the distinction between the personal
and the literary, and along with it, the boundary between prologues and
tales. These structural shifts are in turn accompanied by generic transformations, as the tell-all atmosphere the Host creates enables the slippage between fabliau and exemplum—between amoral wit and pastoral wisdom. If
Harry serves as a muse to his fellow pilgrims, he also acts as magpie, chattering about their tales. While his small talk catalyzes the gossip of others, his
gossiping commentary accomplishes generic transformations of its own. His
persistent moralizing reframes all narratives as exempla, further muddying
the distinction between idle talk and pastoral wisdom. Using his gossip to
interpret as well as inspire, Harry functions as reader for his fellow pilgrims'
tales. Although his readings are comically unconventional, they nonetheless
call into question orthodox hermeneutics, serving as a mechanism through
which Chaucer continually troubles the rules of interpretation. To dismiss
Harry's gossip as a unifying theme, a humorous but incidental feature of the
Canterbury Tales, is to miss its centrality to the two of the most prominent
and consistent aspects of Chaucer's Canterbury poetics, for Harry's idle talk
is a favorite tool that Chaucer deploys both to experiment with narrative
forms and to complicate his audience's reception of them.

"Spareth nat": Catalyzing Gossip in the Friar, Summoner, and Canon's Yeoman

A ubiquitous feature of the *Canterbury Tales*' dramatic framework, Harry's
idle talk influences the tales of his fellow pilgrims. In his role as "governour"

---

62. By claiming that gossip structures the *Tales*, I am not suggesting that idle talk is at issue
in each of the poem's individual narratives. Rather, I want to demonstrate the ways in which
gossip inheres in the poem's frame in the links between tales and the prologues that accompany
them, for it is in this framework that Chaucer employs idle talk as a technique for both shaping
his tales and transforming his sources. As James Andreas has argued, the links, the "dialogical"
spaces between the narratives, are "literally the *means* by which new tales are generated miracu-
lously out of old materials." James R. Andreas, " 'Wordes Betwene': The Rhetoric of the Canterbury Links," *Chaucer Review* 29, no. 1 (1994): 45–64, 60. Recognizing the uncertain status of some
of the links, I have limited my discussion to texts of established authority: prologues to tales,
links between tales within the same fragment, and links that scholarly convention has accepted
as authorial.

(I. 814), Harry relies on gossip as a tactic of negotiation, as he attempts to ensure that the tale-telling competition proceeds in an orderly fashion. Embracing the idle talk he claims to abhor, he deploys gossip to silence disputes, to channel personal animus into narrative invention, and to persuade reluctant speakers to disclose their tales. His handling of the contestation between the Friar and the Summoner is an amusing case in point. While the Host initially chastises the Friar for jangling, he quickly becomes the incendiary go-between, encouraging a no-holds-barred verbal melée with jeers like "Now telleth forth, thogh that the Somonour gale; / Ne spareth nat, myn owene maister deere" (III. 1336–37) and "Tel forth thy tale, and spare it nat at al" (III. 1763).

The consequences of the Host's incitement to gossip are immediately obvious in the narratives that result from it. Prologues and tales collide as the matter of fiction quickly becomes the matter of gossip. For the Friar, the distinction between his rival and the character in his tale is so fine as to be nonexistent:

> For though this Somonour wood were as an hare,
> To tell his harlotrye I wol nat spare;
> For we been out of his correccioun.
> (III. 1327–29)

Although he begins his tale with "Whilom" and the safe, fictional distance of "aventure," the ambiguity of his pronouns here erases that distance, as "this" Summoner becomes both the one on the pilgrimage and the one in the tale, and *his* "harlotrye" belongs to both. Such ad hominem narrative retaliation is one of the defining features of the *Canterbury Tales*, the means, as numerous critics have argued, by which Chaucer transforms what could be a static collection of familiar stories into a dynamic, seemingly self-generating narrative.[63] The Host's rallying cry of "spare it nat" certainly participates in this narrative rejuvenation, making a popular exemplum read like a late-breaking exposé on the corruption of summoners and turning com-

---

63. Kittredge's landmark study of the dramatic framework has been amplified and complicated by numerous critics, most notably, Lumiansky, Ganim, and Andreas. George Lyman Kittredge, *Chaucer and His Poetry* (Cambridge: Harvard University Press, 1915), esp. 146–218; John M. Ganim, *Chaucerian Theatricality* (Princeton: Princeton University Press, 1990); Lumiansky, *Of Sondry Folk*; and Andreas, "Wordes Betwene."

monplaces about clerical misconduct into the latest news.[64] But it would be a mistake to limit the effect of Harry's gossip to this revitalization of old tales—a mistake, that is, to dismiss his incitement to gossip as merely a device for facilitating the narrative competition between rival pilgrims.

More than making familiar stories seem new, the permissive atmosphere created by the Host catalyzes the generic experimentation that takes place in the tales of the Friar and the Summoner. Both tales are characterized by their troubling of generic boundaries, mixing exemplary truth with fabliau justice. Although the *Friar's Tale* and the *Summoner's Tale* that follows it have sermon exempla as sources and analogues, critics have long been troubled by the two tales' generic aberrations.[65] Scanlon makes a compelling case for reading both narratives as exempla, citing their shared thematic concern with exemplarity as well as their exemplary sources. Even as Scanlon argues for their status as exemplary narratives, however, he acknowledges their tendency toward generic instability, noting that as a pairing the two tales modulate from exemplum to fabliau.[66] In fact, despite their emphasis on exemplarity, these two narratives borrow extensively from fabliau tradition: both draw heavily on fabliau imagery;[67] both operate "according to the assumptions and systems of values appropriate" to the fabliau;[68] and both have fabliaux as analogues.[69] Attesting to the tales' generic hybridity, Larry Benson and Theodore Andersson provide a selection of analogues for them in a volume devoted to Chaucer's fabliaux but are compelled to offer the disclaimer that the tales do not strictly belong to this genre, classifying them

64. Citing more than three dozen extant analogues, Peter Nicholson provides a comprehensive account of the variety and popularity of this exemplum, particularly in England. Peter Nicholson, "The Friar's Tale," in *Sources and Analogues of the Canterbury Tales*, vol. 1, ed. Robert M. Correale and Mary Hamel (Cambridge: D. S. Brewer, 2002), 87–99. On the historical accuracy of the Friar's indictment of summoners, see Thomas Hahn and Richard W. Kaeuper, "Text and Context: Chaucer's *Friar's Tale*," *Studies in the Age of Chaucer* 5 (1983): 67–101.

65. Scanlon offers a detailed discussion of both tales' relation to their exemplary sources and analogues, as well as introducing a new analogue for the *Summoner's Tale*. Scanlon, *Narrative, Authority, and Power*, 147–75. See also Nicholson, "Friar's Tale," 87–99; Walter Morris Hart, "The Summoner's Tale," *Sources and Analogues of Chaucer's Canterbury Tales*, ed. W. F. Bryan and Germaine Dempster (Chicago: University of Chicago Press, 1941), 275–87; and Larry D. Benson and Theodore M. Andersson, eds., *The Literary Context of Chaucer's Fabliuax* (Indianapolis: Bobbs-Merrill, 1971), 339–65.

66. Scanlon, *Narrative, Authority, and Power*, 160–63.

67. Janette Richardson, *Blameth Nat Me: A Study of Imagery in Chaucer's Fabliaux* (The Hague: Mouton, 1970), 73–85 and 147–58.

68. Pearsall, *Canterbury Tales*, 217.

69. Nicholson, "Friar's Tale"; Hart, "Summoner's Tale"; and Benson and Andersson, *Literary Context*, 339–65.

with the catch-all designation "other tales."[70] Similarly, for Derek Pearsall, the genre-bending of these two tales defies available categories, necessitating the creation of new subgenre, the "satirical anecdote," which weds the comic with the exemplary.[71] As scholars' frustrated attempts to classify these stories reveal, generic transformations and conflations are taking place within the individual tales themselves as well as in the modulation between them.

Under the influence of the Host's blurring of tidings and tales, the Friar's exemplum adopts the characteristics of a fabliau, as the Friar takes a narrative that properly belongs in a sermon and delivers it as a joke dependent on fabliau justice for its humor. Indeed, it is the fictional summoner's stupidity—his failure to recognize that his traveling companion is the devil— rather than his professional corruption that effects his punishment.[72] In the process, the ecclesiastical authority usually embodied in the exemplum comes to sound uncomfortably similar to gossip, with its not so subtle commentary about the affairs of other people.[73] Even the Friar's half-hearted attempt to recuperate his exemplary practice with a concluding moral returns to the specific transgressions of his rival pilgrim: "prayeth that thise somonours hem repente / Of hir mysdedes, er that the feend hem hente!" (III. 1663–64). The merging of exemplum with fabliau, with its attendant equating of pastoral rhetoric with idle talk, becomes all but explicit in the *Summoner's Prologue*. An inversion of an exemplum from Caesarius of Heisterbach, the Summoner's narrative about the final resting place of wicked friars is told not with the reverence appropriate to orthodox exemplarity but as a bawdy joke at his rival's expense.[74] Moreover, the Summoner's proclamation of the tale's authority—"pardee, ye han ofte tyme herd telle" (III. 1675)—sounds more like the set up for a gag or a preface for the latest news than a citation of ecclesiastical "authoritee." By the time the Summoner begins his tale proper, exemplarity has become completely im-

---

70. Benson and Andersson, *Literary Context*, 339–65.

71. Pearsall, *Canterbury Tales*, 166 and 217.

72. As Pearsall argues, the "point of the attacks is not that the victims are wicked but that they are stupid." Pearsall, *Canterbury Tales*, 217.

73. The ideologically motivated shifting of critique from lay worldliness to clerical abuse that Scanlon observes in Chaucer's amplification of his sources is accompanied and perhaps even overshadowed by a generic shift that critiques exemplary practice as a form of clerical abuse. Scanlon, *Narrative, Authority, and Power*, 147–75.

74. John Fleming discusses Chaucer's inversions of Caesarius. John V. Flemming, "The Summoner's Prologue: An Iconographic Adjustment," *Chaucer Review* 2 (1967): 95–107.

plicated in both fabliau sensibility and idle talk. Delivered in an atmosphere of "sparing nat," these exempla are freed from both generic and ideological constraints, becoming new tidings that can be manipulated and transformed. And it is in this narrative exchange between the Friar and this Summoner that we can begin to see how gossip might serve as a useful poetic device. Idle talk, here, is a technique that faciliates the conflation of ideologically opposed genres, enabling Chaucer to appropriate exemplary narratives without having to submit to exemplary authority.

Given the retaliatory context of these two narratives, we might assume that this blurring of tidings and tales and the generic transformations that accompany it are dependent upon rival pilgrims who tell tales about one another rather than upon the Host's gossip. However, these discursive and generic conflations transcend the setting of adversarial exchange. The Canon's Yeoman, who has no connection to the pilgrim band and no ready-made rivalry in which to become embroiled, is nonetheless swept up in both the atmosphere of speaking everything and the generic alchemy it licenses. In fact, his membership in the community of pilgrims is predicated on his willingness to talk, and of course it is the Host who brokers that membership. First Harry asks the Yeoman if his master can tell a tale—the price of admission to this group of travelers—and then repeatedly importunes him to deliver his own tell-all narrative. What was well-timed encouragement earlier in the poem here becomes a perpetual siege, as Harry relentlessly solicits the Canon's secrets. The Host's dialogue with the Yeoman, his longest sustained conversation in the *Tales,* is littered with phrases that betray his curiosity. He tries everything from polite encouragement, "Telle me that, and that I thee biseche" (VIII. 639), to feigned concern for the Canon's secrets, "Where dwelle ye, if it to telle be?" (VIII. 656); from forced intimacy, "yit lat me talk to the" (VIII. 663), to the promise of safe haven, "telle on, what so bityde. / Of al his thretyng rekke nat a myte!" (VIII. 697–98). More than a comic illumination of his perpetual interest in gossip, Harry's aggressive curiosity provokes a narrative equally aggressive in its conflations—structural, rhetorical, and generic.

The structural instability of "prologue" and "tale" is more pronounced in the Canon's Yeoman's narrative than at any other point in the *Canterbury Tales.* Prefacing his *Tale* with a promise of full disclosure heavily influenced by the Host's rhetoric—"I wol nat spare; / Swich thyng as that I knowe, I wol declare" (VIII. 718–19)—the Yeoman introduces not one narrative, but two. In the first, he recounts the failed alchemical endeavors of his employer and mentor, the Canon; in the second, he depicts a morally bankrupt canon and his infamous swindling of innocent layfolk and gullible clergymen. The two potentially distinct narratives, however, compose the singular *Canon's Yeoman's Tale*. What would be autobiographical prologue for another pilgrim is for the Canon's Yeoman the first part of his tale, while the tale proper, the "pars secunda" as it is commonly called, begins without any formal marker to distinguish it from what has preceded.[75] The Canon's Yeoman does not offer the "My tale I wol bigyne" (VI. 462) of the Pardoner or the Wife of Bath (III. 828) but instead refers to both parts as his "tale."[76] And while modern editors insist on the separation of the two parts, inserting the rubric "pars secunda," medieval readers were unwilling or unable to make that distinction: the manuscripts that preserve the tale fail to offer a consistent division between its two halves.[77] Without editorial intervention, the separation between autobiography and fiction collapses, as the audience is left to wonder whether Yeoman's Canon and the wicked canon of the second part are one and the same—left to wonder, that is, where gossip ends and narrative begins.

The blurring of the personal and the fictional that takes place in the *Canon's Yeoman's Tale* is more than an incidental structural conflation owing to the absence of formal divisions between the tale's component

75. Samuel McCracken demonstrates the structural parallels between this tale and others in the *Canterbury Tales*, most notably those of the Pardoner and the Wife of Bath. Samuel McCracken, "Confessional Prologue and the Topography of the Canon's Yeoman," *Modern Philology* 68, no. 3 (1971): 289–91.

76. The Canon's Yeoman concludes both narratives with a similar formulation, ending the first with "By that I of my tale have maad an ende" (971) and the second with "And there a poynt, for ended is my tale" (1480). The Wife of Bath similarly refers to both prologue and tale as her "tale"; exclamations like "Now wol I telle forth my tale" (III. 193) and "A ha! By God, I have my tale ageyn" (III. 586) both refer to her *Prologue*. Yet the beginning of the *Wife of Bath's Tale* is clearly marked by both the Wife's own remarks, "Now wol I seye my tale, if ye wol heere" (III. 828), and the Friar's frustrated recognition that the initial "tale" was merely a "preamble" (III. 831).

77. Of the extant manuscripts, twenty-nine indicate no division whatsoever at line 972 (the point at which the "pars secunda" conventionally begins); ten mark this line with a capital; a further three use marginal notation to call attention it; and only Ellesmere offers the Latin rubric adopted by the *Riverside Chaucer*, "Explicit prima pars, Et sequitur pars secunda." As I discuss below, three other manuscripts mark the beginning of the tale at line 1012. John M. Manly and Edith Rickert, *The Text of the Canterbury Tales*, 8 vols. (Chicago: University of Chicago Press, 1940), 3:535. For a detailed discussion of the manuscripts and the consequences of their inconsistent divisions, see Albert E. Hartung, "'Pars Secunda' and the Development of the *Canon's Yeoman's Tale*," *Chaucer Review* 12, no. 2 (1977): 111–28.

parts; it is a defining feature of the narrative's rhetoric. Caught up in the Host's atmosphere of speaking everything, the Canon's Yeoman is at constant pains to ensure his audience both that his "tale" will disclose closely held secrets—"Now he is goon, I dar seyn boldely" (VIII. 902)—and that this narrative "shal tellen more" (VIII. 1167), titillating his audience with the promise of his unexpurgated and illicit gossip.[78] What is more, when he moves from the first tale to the second, he continues to represent his narrative as gossip, insisting on the actual rather than merely fictive presence of his tale's canon—"Ther is a chanoun of religioun / Amonges us" (VIII. 972–73).[79] Forgoing the fictional distance of "whilom," he proceeds to tell in the present tense a story of a canon who lives among us now, who beguiles today, who practices his mischief perhaps at this very moment. Here, in the Yeoman's rather unorthodox use of the present tense, gossip commandeers conventional narrative rhetoric, so that the "tale" continues to sound like idle talk, implicating ever more narratives and characters in its proliferating conversation.[80]

So clear is gossip's capacity for discursive appropriation that the Yeoman makes numerous disclaimers attempting to proscribe the limits of his speech. He not only informs his audience that he is no longer discussing his former employer, but also reassures the potential canons in his audience that the trickery he describes pertains only to this particular "shrewe" (995). Taken as awkward and intrusive, both remarks have been interpreted as evidence that Chaucer has not adequately adapted to the Canterbury Tales a narrative originally written for another context.[81] Far from incongruous, however, the Yeoman's remarks, understood as disclaimers, make perfect sense in relation both to the Prologue and to the Canterbury Tales more generally. That these disclaimers constitute an abrupt shift in the Yeoman's usual mode of address, turning from the audience as a collective to specific individuals within it, need not be taken as proof of the tale's disunity. Al-

78. In just over 900 lines, the Canon's Yeoman's Prologue and Tale uses the verb, 'to tell,' thirty-three times, more than any other text in the Canterbury Tales with the exception of the much longer offerings of the Man of Law and the Wife of Bath.

79. For an alternative reading of the Canon's Yeoman's inability to separate fiction from reality, as appropriate both to the Yeoman's complicated self-examination and to alchemical science more generally, see Pearsall, Canterbury Tales, 109–10.

80. For a more conservative reading of Chaucer's use of the present tense here, see Hartung, "'Pars Secunda,'" 119.

81. Hartung, following Manly and others, has argued that in combination, the two remarks indicate the ambiguous state of Chaucer's draft (O¹). Hartung, "'Pars Secunda,'" 113–15; John Matthews Manly, Some New Light on Chaucer (New York: Henry Holt, 1926), 235–52.

though it is true that elsewhere in the "pars secunda," the narrator refers to his audience with the plural "sires," his singling out of the Host is far from arbitrary:

> This chanon was my lord, ye wolden weene?
> Sire hoost, in feith, and by the hevenes queene,
> It was another chanoun, and nat hee,
> That kan an hundred foold moore subtiltee.
>
> (VIII. 1088–91)

Given the Host's aggressive interest in the Canon's affairs, it is perfectly understandable that the Yeoman would specifically address the potential misconceptions of the overcurious Host, the character most likely to assume ("weene") and indeed hope that the tale is a further exposé.[82] Similarly, the reassurances offered to the "worshipful Chanons religious" reflect the Yeoman's concern over the offensive and proliferating potential of his speech.[83]

In fact, the Yeoman is so disconcerted by the ever-expanding implications of his narrative gossip that immediately following his apology to the canons, he retreats into the safety of the fictional past: the canon who used to be among us, now tricks a priest who *was* in London. That the shift is significant rather than accidental, that it denotes not a seam between unassimilated texts but a transition to the past tense of fiction, is evidenced by the fact that it occurs in all of the manuscripts containing the tale and remains in effect for the duration of the narrative. Indeed, several of Chaucer's early

---

82. I am not disputing that the tale may have been written for another context; rather I am arguing that this remark is not a sign of Chaucer's careless revision. It is wholly consistent with the atmosphere created by the Host in the prologue to the tale as well as in the *Tales* more generally.

83. Numerous critics have taken these lines as conclusive proof that the tale was not originally written for the *Canterbury Tales*. Manly, for example, used them to speculate that Chaucer performed the tale before the canons of King's Chapel at Windsor. *Some New Light*, esp. 247–50. Scholars who recuperate the lines have done so on the grounds of both rhetorical consistency and dramatic realism. F. N. Robinson notes that Chaucer uses the device of rhetorical apostrophe throughout the *Tales*, including an instance of just this length and detail in the *Physician's Tale* (VI. 72–92). Judith Herz contends that the Yeoman has misidentified one of the religious on the pilgrimage as a canon, while Pearsall proposes the less contentious argument that in these lines the Yeoman "reveals his consciousness of the possibility of causing offence." Pearsall, *Canterbury Tales*, 110; Judith Scherer Herz, *"The Canon's Yeoman's Prologue and Tale," Modern Philology* 58, no. 4 (1961): 231–37; and F. N. Robinson, ed. *The Works of Geoffrey Chaucer*, 2nd ed. (Boston: Houghton Mifflin, 1957), 761.

readers acknowledged the significance of the shift, identifying the Yeoman's adoption of the past tense as the beginning of the "tale."[84] Even as the Canon's Yeoman attempts to distance himself from the blurring of gossip and fiction he has created here, explicitly rejecting the present tense of idle talk, he continues to demonstrate gossip's potential as a poetic device. Despite his pretense to fictional distance, his idle talk remains the tale's narrative mode.

Accompanying and indeed superseding gossip's rhetorical appropriations and structural conflations is its generic alchemy, as idle talk in the Canon's Yeoman's narrative enables a seemingly endless series of generic experiments. What begins as an individual confession, in which the Yeoman reveals how destitute alchemical inquiry has made him personally—"Al that I hadde I have lost therby" (VIII. 722)—quickly becomes a tell-all exposé of his infamous profession, "I wol speke of oure werk" (VIII. 749), as the atmosphere of speaking everything draws professional secrets into the conversation. Under the guise of both, the Yeoman delivers an alchemical treatise, an amalgamation of scientific lore drawn from a variety of authorities.[85] The genre shifting here is not superficial: the "tale" did in fact pass for a legitimate scientific treatise; late medieval readers identified Chaucer as an alchemical authority on the basis of this tale.[86] However, the Canon's

84. Three manuscripts of different textual traditions make this claim: Holkham Hall MS 667 opens line 1012 with a large capital; Fitzwilliam Museum MS McClean 181 offers the heading, "The Chanons Yeman"; and most striking of all, Harley 7334 uses a marginal "Narrat" to declare the tale begins at 1012. Manly and Rickert, *Text*, 3:535. While none of these manuscripts is considered "authoritative," they nonetheless give evidence that fifteen-century readers recognized the past tense as a marker of the fictional.

85. Although the precise identity of Chaucer's alchemical sources remains uncertain, several scholars have shown his borrowings from particular texts. Pauline Aiken argues that he relies exclusively on Vincent of Beauvais's *Speculum naturale,* while Edgar Duncan demonstrates Chaucer's indebtedness to late medieval alchemical texts, such as the *book Senior,* Geber's *Sum of Perfection,* and the works of Arnaldus of Villanova. Pauline Aiken, "Vincent of Beauvais and Chaucer's Knowledge of Alchemy," *Studies in Philology* 41 (1944): 371–89; and Edgar H. Duncan, "The Literature of Alchemy and Chaucer's Canon's Yeoman's Tale: Framework, Theme, and Characters," *Speculum* 43, no. 4 (1968): 633–46.

86. As George Kaiser has recently demonstrated, late medieval and early modern alchemy enthusiasts "regarded Chaucer as a fellow-student of the art (or science)." George Kaiser, "The Conclusion of the *Canon's Yeoman's Tale*: Readings and (Mis)readings," *Chaucer Review* 35, no. 1 (2000): 1–21, 2. Kaiser provides a detailed and insightful discussion of the tale's reception history. Two citations form the basis for the scholarly consensus about Chaucer's status as alchemical authority: Thomas Norton's 1477 reference to the tale in the *Ordinal of Alchemy* and Elias Ashmole's inclusion of the tale in his 1652 alchemical compendium, *Theatrum Chemicum Britannicum.*

Yeoman's narrative does not read like the Parson's penitential manual, in which the text stands *as* treatise. Instead, by presenting lists of substances, equipment, and techniques as disclosed secrets, Chaucer uses gossip to translate treatise into "tale."[87]

The generic alchemy of the *Canon's Yeoman's Tale* serves both to enliven scientific discourse and to lend legitimacy to this unconventional narrative.[88] Concluding the first part of his tale with a moral, the Yeoman combines confession, exposé, and treatise to create an exemplum: "he that semeth the wiseste, by Jhesus, / Is moost fool, whan it cometh to the preef; / And he that semeth trewest is a theef" (VIII. 967–69). Couched as a disclosure about his alchemical community—"Right so, lo, fareth it amonges us" (VIII. 966)—the moral is both a continuation of the Yeoman's idle talk and his attempt to recuperate it as instructive. This recuperative maneuver is repeated in the "pars secunda," where generic alchemy consists not in the translation of treatise into exposé, but in the fusing of generic opposites, as fabliau trickery compounds with sober exemplarity.[89] Just as in the hybrid offerings of the Friar and the Summoner, Chaucer tests the permeability of the boundaries between these two genres, but here the reaction runs in reverse. Rather than an exemplum operating under fabliau rules, the "pars secunda" is a fabliau about alchemical trickery transmuted into a moral tale. Not only does the tale end with the lesson that Christ is the source of true alchemy (VIII. 1472–81), but throughout the narrative the Yeoman encourages his audience to condemn rather than laugh at the false canon's trickery. He does so, however, through a series of exclamatory asides, which, in the

87. As Kaiser has demonstrated, it was Chaucer's narrative alchemy, as much as his alchemical acumen, which early readers of the tale celebrated: "one must acknowledge that these scribes and their readers looked upon Chaucer as the poet who discovered how to make vernacular poetry from the language of alchemy." Kaiser, "Conclusion," 16–17.

88. In his rich and suggestive essay on the *Canterbury Tales,* Seth Lerer offers a much more pessimistic interpretation of the Canon's Yeoman's narrative alchemy, reading his efforts as offering dross rather than gold. Lerer, *"The Canterbury Tales,"* in *Yale Companion to Chaucer,* 283–86.

89. The tale's straddling of the two genres is reflected in the variety of sources and analogues scholars have proposed for it. Although no exact source for the tale has been found, several analogues have been proposed, both fabliaux and exempla. Willa Folch-Pi connects the tricks in the "tale" to a story by Ramón Llull. Willa Babcock Folch-Pi, "Ramon Llull's Felix and Chaucer's Canon's Yeoman's Tale," *Notes and Queries* 212 (1967): 10–11. Spargo suggests that a similar trick occurs in the *Novelle* of Sercambi. John W. Spargo, "The Canon's Yeoman's Tale," in *Sources and Analogues,* ed. Bryan and Dempster, 685–95. Reyes has recently argued that Chaucer was influenced by Exemplum 20 of Don Juan Manuel's "El Conde Lucanor." Jesus L. Serrano Reyes, *Didactismo y moralismo en Geoffrey Chaucer y Don Juan Manuel* (Córdoba: Universidad de Córdoba, 1996), 251–368.

context of his previous gossip, establish conversational intimacy rather than exemplary distance. Declarations like "the foule feend hym fecche!" (VIII. 1159) and "yvele moot he cheeve!" (VIII. 1225) cannot help but resonate with his earlier complaints about his master, "the foule feend hym quelle!" (VIII. 705). Perpetually anxious that his "tale" not be taken as gossip, the Yeoman insists that he takes no pleasure in revealing the Canon's trickery, claiming that he only offers it as a public service:

> It weerieth me to telle of his falsnesse,
> And nathelees yet wol I it expresse,
> To th'entente that men may be war therby,
> And for noon oother cause, trewely.
> (VIII. 1304–7)

Although he insists that his intent is virtuous, what comes across most clearly in the Yeoman's disclaimer is not his weariness at having to expose such behavior, but his willingness to disclose yet more details about it. That is, he protests too much, implying the very motive he pretends to eschew. For the Canon's Yeoman, the turn to exemplum, like the retreat into the past tense of fiction, is an attempt to distance himself from the proliferating dangers of idle talk. Yet it is in precisely these moments of abjuration that the Yeoman reveals the unlimited potential of gossip as a poetic technique, for his tactics of renunciation are themselves wholly dependent on idle talk. Here as in the *House of Fame*, Chaucer uses an acknowledgment of conventional wisdom about idle talk to explore its potential, recuperating as narratively productive those aspects of gossip deemed most problematic.

"I dar wel sayn": Reinterpreting the Merchant, the *Melibee*, and the Physician

The generic, structural, and rhetorical conflations embodied in the tales of the Friar, Summoner, and Canon's Yeoman arise from narrators who respond to Harry Bailly's atmosphere of speaking everything by engaging in gossip of their own. Harry is their muse, inspiring their hybrid narratives as well as their idle talk. Yet Harry functions as more than a catalyst for gossip's various transformations; he also acts as gossip's agent, using his trademark idle talk to evaluate the other pilgrims' narratives. Poking fun at the Host's "lewed" pronouncements has been a favorite critical pastime. Analyzing his role as judge, scholars have approached his remarks as assessments of the tales based on literary merit. Whether they identify him as a "horseback editor," a literary critic, or an "ordinary" reader, they are unanimous in their assertion that his judgments are fundamentally flawed.[90] In this context, the Host's devastating review of the *Monk's Tale* has been a popular case in point, revealing, as Emily Jensen has argued, that he is tone deaf, unable to appreciate subtle variations on literary themes.[91] But in the rush to condemn Harry's aesthetic judgment, to distinguish his lack of interpretative subtlety from the more nuanced readings of the poet and his ideal readers and critics, scholars have overlooked an important aspect of Harry's commentary. As much as the Host delights in providing stylistic evaluations of the pilgrim narrators—the Monk's monotonous repetition and Chaucer's "drasty rymyng" (VII. 930)—he spends most of his time analyzing the narratives' characters and their behavior. Pontificating about virtuous conduct, adulterous tactics, exemplary heroines, and wicked villains alike, the Host attaches his own morals to the tales of his fellow pilgrims.

Harry acts as a ribald and bourgeois St. Paul who uses idle talk to interpret everything according to his doctrine. His gossip shifts the interpretative framework of the tales, suggesting that any narrative might be read as an exemplum. Indeed, the Host has a penchant for converting fabliaux into exempla, as his moralizing commentary offers a further demonstration of the permeability between these polar generic opposites. Like the Canon's Yeoman, Harry uses idle talk to turn amoral trickery into instructional narrative. But he does so in order to school his audience in his unique moral philosophy, rather than to proscribe the limits of his transgressive speech. At times his moralizing commentary comes in the form of bawdy anticlerical humor turned into practical advice, as in his comical remarks at the end of the *Shipman's Tale*. Swearing "by Seint Austyn" (VII. 441) for full ironic effect and gossiping gleefully about the humiliation suffered by the husband and wife at the hands of the wily monk, the Host interprets the Shipman's

90. Alan T. Gaylord, "*Sentence* and *Solaas* in Fragment VII of the *Canterbury Tales*: Harry Bailly as Horseback Editor," *PMLA* 82, no. 2 (1967): 226–35; Lumiansky, *Of Sondry Folk*, 94 and passim; and Richardson, "Function of the Host," 333. See also L. M. Leitch, "Sentence and Solaas: The Function of the Hosts in the *Canterbury Tales*," *Chaucer Review* 17, no. 1 (1982): 5–20.

91. Jenson, "'Winkers' and 'Janglers,'" 183–95. Illuminating the tale's variations on the theme of tragic changes in fortune, Jensen compares the reactions of the Host and the Knight to earlier scholarly assessments of the *Monk's Tale*'s shortcomings.

complex exploration of the relationship between kinship and language as an exemplum about the dangers of lodging clerical houseguests: "Felawes, beth ware of swich a jape . . . / Draweth no monkes moore unto youre in" (VII. 439–42).[92]

Although clerics are occasionally the subject of the Host's moralizing, more often than not he deploys his exemplary readings as a vehicle for his gender politics, reading the fabliau as an indictment of women's deceitful nature. When he adds a moral to the already genre-troubled *Merchant's Tale*, this tactic appears in its clearest form:

> Now swich a wyf I pray God kepe me fro!
> Lo, whiche sleightes and subtilitees
> In wommen been! For ay as bisy as bees
> Been they, us sely men for to deceyve,
> And from the soothe evere wol they weyve;
> By this Marchauntes tale it preveth weel.
>
> (IV. 2420–25)

Just as with the *Shipman's Tale*, Harry's lesson is couched in gossip about the narrative's characters; but unlike that brief quip, his more substantial commentary on the *Merchant's Tale* consists of a several interrelated arguments: women are crafty by nature, they are as busy as bees to deceive men, and they will always deviate from the truth. More important, Harry specifically identifies his commentary *as* a moral—"By this Marchauntes tale it preveth weel." His moral arises from the specifics of the tale, from May's trickery (her "sleightes and subtilitees"), and then modulates through the inevitability of antifeminist logic into a critique of women more generally. The moral's content resonates with the battle of orthodox "auctoritees" waged by Persephone and Pluto toward the tale's conclusion. Its modulation from specific detail to general principle mirrors the structure of orthodox exemplarity as the tale's events are made to give rise to a moral lesson.[93] What is more, like a preacher linking related exempla together in a single sermon, the Host uses the moral he derives from the *Merchant's Tale* to preface an exemplum of his own. Of course, Harry's exemplarity is comi-

---

92. The connection between kinship and idle talk in the *Shipman's Tale* is the subject of Chapter 3, below.

93. On the structural patterns of late medieval exemplary practice, see Scanlon, *Narrative, Authority, and Power*; and Allen, *False Fables*, as well as Chapter 1, above.

cally self-interested. The cautionary tale he introduces is a reckoning of his wife's vices; he gossips about Goodelief to his fellow pilgrims in strictest confidence—"in conseil be it said" (IV. 2431)—but then quickly abandons his "tale" for fear that some female member of the company (i.e., the Wife of Bath) will report his gossiping to her.[94] Despite its self-interestedness, however, the Host's moralizing gossip with its modulations and its linkages nonetheless resembles more conventional exemplary reading, suggesting the parallels between idle talk and exemplary practice.

When the Host explicates fabliaux through his gossip he troubles the distinction between amoral wit and exemplary wisdom, implicating orthodox moralizing in his idle talk; but when he deploys his gossip to interpret exempla, he calls into question the practice of exemplary reading itself, suggesting that the paradigm of drawing univocal morals from complex narratives might be inherently flawed. Chaucer's *Tale of Melibee* provides Harry with the opportunity to bring the tale of his wife's transgressions to fruition, as Prudence's virtue compels him to testify about his wife's vice. Taking advantage of the fact that Chaucer does not offer his own moral to the tale, the Host instructs his fellow pilgrims on the true meaning of this lengthy "tretys" (VII. 957). According to Harry, this "moral tale vertuous" (VII. 940)—critically acclaimed as an exploration of the complexity of household politics, the relationship between benevolent governance and good counsel, the necessity of prudence in the face of provocation, and the utility of appropriative reading—is in fact a positive exemplum of wifely patience so convincing that it could affect his intractable wife.[95] Here, as in the *Epilogue to the Merchant's Tale,* Harry links related narratives; demonstrating a bit of

---

94. "It sholde reported be / And toold to hire of somme of this meynee—/ Of whom, it nedeth nat for to declare, / Syn wommen konnen outen swich chaffare" (IV. 2435–38). Harry's theory that idle talk unites all women, even those who have never met, is shared by the author of the *Tale of Beryn,* who imagines the Wife of Bath, the Canterbury host's wife, and the Prioress as gossips: "madam ! wol ye stalk / Pryuely in-to þe garden, to se the herbis grow? / And aftir, with our hostis wyff, in hir parlour rowe, / I woll gyve ʒewe the wyne, & yee shull me also" (282–85). Sharing secrets in the garden and wine in the parlor, the nun, the tapster, and the *femme sole* become kindred spirits. *The Tale of Beryn,* ed. F. J. Furnivall and W. G. Stone, EETS, e.s. 105 (London: Kegan Paul, Trench, Trübner, 1909).

95. In the last decade, critics have recuperated the *Melibee* from scholarly oblivion, offering a range of provocative readings demonstrating the tale's larger cultural significance. See, among others, Wallace, *Chaucerian Polity,* 212–46; Strohm, *Social Chaucer,* esp. 161–63; Scanlon, *Narrative, Authority and Power,* 206–15; Lerer, "Canterbury Tales," esp. 278–79; and Karla Taylor, "Social Aesthetics and the Emergence of Civic Discourse from the *Shipman's Tale* to *Melibee,*" *Chaucer Review* 39, no. 3 (2005): 298–322.

pedagogical ingenuity, he yokes opposing pastoral strategies by coupling the *Melibee* with a negative exemplum about his wife's imprudent and destructive wrath. Harry understands that a tale must be "wel reported" (VII. 2804) in order to be pastorally successful, as he will soon remind the Monk, and his storytelling does not disappoint. His exemplum is vivid in its detail, unfolding the scene of Goodelief's war-mongering and recording her colorful calls for violence: "Sle the dogges everichoon" (1899). He depicts her as a medieval caricature of Lady Macbeth; Goodelief urges her husband to bloody deeds first by placing weapons in his hands—"She bryngeth me forth the grete clobbed staves" (VII. 1898)—and then by impugning his masculinity, calling him a "milksop" (VII. 1910) and suggesting that he is better suited to women's work: "have my distaf and go spynne!" (VII. 1907). To underscore his didactic intent, Harry closes his entertaining narrative with a moral, teaching his fellow pilgrims about the consequences of such misconduct. If Prudence's wise words bring about the peaceful resolution of a volatile situation, then Goodelief's fist-shaking is sure to result in homicide: "I woot well she wol do me slee som day/ Som neighebor" (VII. 1917–18). In terms of either its pastoral instruction or its interpretative insight, Harry's "tale" is far from exemplary. As a reading of the *Melibee*, it offers gross oversimplification; as a teaching tool, it sounds more like the gossip of a hen-pecked husband than pastoral wisdom. But this is precisely the point. Harry appropriates pastoral techniques to interpret everything according to his husbandly doctrine. In doing so, he suggests the possibility that all such single-minded readings might be similarly flawed. That is, Harry's compromised exemplarity serves as a device for critiquing orthodox interpretative practice.

If the Host's response to the *Melibee* suggests the potential flaws inherent in exemplary hermeneutics, then his infamous gossip about the *Physican's Tale* makes those flaws explicit. Nowhere in the *Canterbury Tales* does he offer more animated or more extensive moralizing commentary. In the previous examples, Harry's exemplarity has been deeply self-interested, using the narratives of other pilgrims as an occasion for gossiping about his wife's temper and deceit; in his response to the *Physician's Tale*, he abandons this self-serving agenda, making possible a more sustained critique of exemplary practice. Playing his dual role of judge and "reportour" (I. 814), Harry does not merely evaluate the tale; he re-tells it, inflecting it with his own sensibilities.[96] Despite the fact that the good doctor has already concluded with a

96. Editors have had great difficulty glossing the word, "reportour." The description of

moral of his own, the Host finds the urge to comment almost irresistible, swearing madly in his rush to pass judgment on and express pity for the tale's characters:

> Oure Hooste gan to swere as he were wood;
> "Harrow!" quod he, "by nayles and by blood!
> This was a fals cherl and a fals justise.
> As shameful deeth as herte may devyse
> Come to thise juges and hire advocatz!
> Algate this sely mayde is slayn, allas!
> Allas, to deere boughte she beautee!
> Wherefore I seye al day that men may see
> That yiftes of Fortune and of Nature
> Been cause of deeth to many a creature.
> Hire beautee was hire deth, I dar wel sayn.
> Allas, so pitously as she was slayn!
> Of both yiftes that I speke of now
> Men han ful ofte moore for harm than prow."
>
> (VI. 287–300)

His visceral reaction to the tale calls explicit attention to itself as both preaching and idle talk. His method—wishing the most shameful death imaginable for Appius and his henchman, repeatedly sighing for poor Virginia ("allas! / Allas, . . . Allas"), and speculating about the real cause of the events (I dare say it was her beauty that killed her)—exhibits all the hallmarks of gossip: reporting behavior, evaluating reputations, and revealing contradictions.[97] His phrasing—"I dar wel seyn"—echoes the speech tags of idle talk that circulated in the House of Rumor.

This concentrated version of Chaucerian small talk functions as an alter-

---

Harry's duties constitutes Chaucer's only use of it. The *Riverside Chaucer* offers the neutral and official sounding, "record keeper." The *Middle English Dictionary* identifies the Host as a judge or umpire (s.v. "reportour," b), while the *Oxford English Dictionary* declares Harry to be a "narrator" (s.v. "reporter," 1a), a suggestion that Hussey takes up in his argument that the Host, rather than Chaucer the Pilgrim, originally functioned as the poem's narrator. Hussey, "Chaucer's Host," 155–56. Yet Harry is neither simply a judge nor is he only a narrator. Rather, he is a "talebearer," a gossip, who retells and reinterprets the tales of others, a signification licensed by an alternative definition given in the *Middle English Dictionary* (s.v. "reportour," a).

97. Luise White, "Between Gluckman and Foucault." Gossip theorists across disciplines agree that gossip is above all evaluative. See Max Gluckman, "Gossip and Scandal"; Sally Engle Merry, "Rethinking Gossip and Scandal"; and Spacks, *Gossip*, 13.

native moral for the tale. Following the paradigm he established in the *Merchant's Tale*, Harry delivers a multifaceted and cumulative lesson, which begins with an assessment of Virginia's specific plight and then modulates to more general commentary on the danger of fortune's gifts. Whereas his reaction to May's deceit followed antifeminist logic, his commentary on Virginia's plight, as Mark Allen has demonstrated, operates according to the language and logic of commerce. For Harry, "beauty and chastity become like riches and lordship, possessions that can cost one dearly and, when not worked for, often bring more harm than good."[98] Despite its governing logic, Harry's moral misses the point of the Physician's narrative, as decades of critical derision make clear.[99] The concerns of economy and class he invokes have nothing to do with Virginia's tale as the Physician tells it. His outpouring of pity appears comically excessive and his distillation of the tale's wisdom into a warning about beauty is at best literal-minded.

Like his one-dimensional interpretation of Prudence's virtue, the Host's misreading of Virginia's plight is far more than a joke about his lack of interpretative acumen, for his misguided moralizing throws into relief the similarly ill-fitting conclusion posed by the Physician. Whereas the Host is prone to the overly specific, the good doctor errs in the opposite direction, offering a moral that is general to the point of irrelevance: "Heere may men seen how synne hath his merite" (VI. 277). For all that it is grounded in conventional pastoral rhetoric, his string of moral commonplaces about the rewards of sin, the unpredictability of death, and the "worm of conscience" (VI. 280) that gnaws incessantly upon sinful souls, is inappropriate if not wholly unconnected to the tale.[100] This questionable moral is the last in a series of changes Chaucer has made to this popular narrative to test its generic limits. Both his predecessors and his contemporaries make the pastoral intent of their tales perfectly clear, framing the narrative variously as a posi-

98. Allen, "Mirth and Bourgeois Masculinity," 17–18.

99. Notable exceptions are Elizabeth Allen, who makes a compelling case for the Host's response being "exactly what the *Physician's Tale* calls for," filling the tale's "logical and moral gaps" with emotion, and Anne Middleton, who argues that the Host's takes his cue from "the tale Chaucer wrote, not the one the Physician seems to think he just concluded." Allen, *False Fables*, 98; and Anne Middleton, "The *Physician's Tale* and Love's Martyrs: 'Ensamples Mo than Ten' as a Method in the *Canterbury Tales*," *Chaucer Review* 8, no. 1 (1973): 9–32, 13.

100. For a provocative recuperation of the tale's moral, see Angus Fletcher, "The Sentence of Virginia in the *Physician's Tale*," *Chaucer Review* 34, no. 3 (2000): 300–308, 306. On the moral's applicability to Appius, see Patricia M. Kean, *Chaucer and the Making of English Poetry*, vol. 2: *The Art of Narrative* (London: Routledge and Kegan Paul, 1972), 179–85; and Lee Ramsey, "'The Sentence of It Sooth Is,'" *Chaucer Review* 6 (1972): 198–97, 195–96.

tive exemplum extolling the virtues of either Virginia or her father, a negative exemplum castigating the unjust Appius, or a public exemplum
depicting the consequences of political corruption.[101] The *Physician's Tale*,
however, troubles these categories, eluding all of them, at the level of plot,
characterization, and narration.[102] Attached to this ambiguous narrative, the
Physician's overly general moral offers his audience little interpretative guid-
ance. The Physician is thus no more successful at explicating his narrative
than the Host; the morals of both men operate according to a consistent
logic, but that logic has no real connection to the tale itself.[103] By depicting
the two characters' morals as equally inappropriate, Chaucer grants them
equal authority, a fact made all the more astonishing when we consider that
the Physician's concluding "auctoritee" is no less than Innocent III.[104] While
the juxtaposition of the two morals does not translate Harry's gossip into
orthodox authority, it does transform orthodox authority into idle talk.

The double failure of exemplarity in the *Physician's Tale* casts a larger
doubt about the possibility of satisfactorily explicating any narrative though
a single moral lesson. This is, of course, a question that Chaucer raises
throughout the *Canterbury Tales*. The proliferating morals of the *Nun's
Priest's Tale* suggest that the "fruyt" (VII. 3443) of narrative might not be
the moral attached to it. The Manciple's endless *moralitas* loses track of its
narrative altogether. The Friar and the Summoner use morals for revenge
rather than elucidation. And even the devout Clerk offers a series of alternative readings for his tale. What is more, numerous pilgrims and their charac-

101. As Sheila Delany has argued, while Chaucer's primary source is the *Roman de la Rose*, he
supplemented this version with Livy's history of Rome and was likely familiar with the versions of
both Boccaccio and Gower. Delany offers a persuasive reading of the ways in which these other
versions function as public exemplum, private exemplum, or some combination of the two.
Sheila Delany, "Politics and the Paralysis of Poetic Imagination in *The Physician's Tale*," *Studies
in the Age of Chaucer* 3 (1981): 47–60. See also Allen, *False Fables*, 84–99; and Middleton, "*Physician's Tale*."

102. For Delany, "Chaucer systematically obliterates the traditional social content of the leg-
end"; for Pearsall, he strips the characters of both agency and motivation; and for Allen, the
Physician's "stylistic variety . . . undermines the creation of significance." Delany, "Politics and
Paralysis," 51; Pearsall, *Canterbury Tales*, 278; and Allen, *False Fables*, 96.

103. Andrew Welsh makes a similar claim about the insufficiency of both morals as part of
his discussion of proverbs, fables, exempla, and the making of narrative meaning in the *Canterbury Tales*. Andrew Welsh, "Story and Wisdom in Chaucer: *The Physician's Tale* and *The Manciple's Tale*," in *Manuscript, Narrative, Lexicon: Essays on Literary and Cultural Transmission in
Honor of Whitney F. Bolton*, ed. Robert Boenig and Kathleen Davis (Lewisburg, Pa.: Bucknell
University Press, 2000), 76–95, esp. 77–79.

104. Cf. Innocent III, *De miseria condicionis humane*, ed. Robert E. Lewis (Athens: University
of Georgia Press, 1978), 3.2.

ters challenge the interpretation of various "auctoritees," pitting one against another, as Chaucer advocates multiplicity over singularity. To suggest that Chaucer troubles exemplary practice is not to argue that he denies poetry's moral capacity. Quite the contrary, Chaucer's poetry, as much rich scholarship has shown, is deeply invested in the interrogation of moral principals. His comic depiction of Harry Bailly as St. Paul stands not as a rejection of Pauline hermeneutic, but as a caution to those who would apply it unthinkingly. If we dismiss Harry's moralizing gossip as a joke about bad reading or as lively but incidental narrative detail, we not only overlook a device through which Chaucer questions exemplary interpretation, we miss the fact that this suspicion of exemplarity is fundamental to the structure of the *Canterbury Tales.*

"Amonges othere thynges smale": The Wife of Bath as Arch-gossip

As a structural device, the Host's idle talk enables a multitude of narrative transformations. The atmosphere of "sparing nat" that he creates makes possible the metamorphosis from old source to new tale and catalyzes the generic alchemy in which Chaucer engages throughout the poem. Harry's role as reporter, retelling the tales of his fellow pilgrims by gossiping about them, further facilitates that alchemy, providing a mechanism through which to test generic limits and question conventional hermeneutics. Although Chaucer uses the Host as a favorite tool for experimenting with gossip's transformative possibilities, it is the Wife of Bath who stands as the apotheosis of Chaucerian small talk. Alisoun is an arch-gossip; instead of pretending to condemn idle talk, she openly embraces it—as subject, pastime, discursive mode, and narrative device. Her storytelling strategies and the discursive appropriations that accompany them are everywhere indebted to idle talk. Created by gossip and negotiating the world through it, the Wife of Bath demonstrates both gossip's utility as a rhetorical technique and its centrality to Chaucer's poetic practice, for she stands as the embodiment of idle talk and its myriad narrative possibilities.

It is a favorite commonplace of both pastoral rhetoric and antifeminist discourse that idle talk is women's work. The image of female garrulity is ubiquitous in medieval culture. In stained-glass windows, wall paintings, and sermon exempla, Tutivillus, the demon whose task it is to record gossip in church, sits on specifically female shoulders.[105] In the imaginary taverns of carols and ballads, gossips meet to drink ale and talk about their husbands' wares.[106] Countless antifeminist tracts and riddles caution potential husbands about the horrors of a chattering wife, while penitential manuals direct warnings about the dangers of idle talk to wives, widows, and virgins alike.[107] According to conventional wisdom, a jangler is almost always a "jangleresse."

Perhaps no character embodies this cultural assumption more clearly than the Wife of Bath. Like Geffrey, she stands before her audience to gossip. But where Geffrey was gossip's neophyte, the overexperienced Alisoun is as ever an authority. She does not simply acknowledge the orthodox consensus about women's speech, she seeks to reinforce it: giving herself the title of "jangleresse" (III. 638), parroting antifeminist arguments about female garrulity, and delivering a series of her own exempla about women's idle talk. Demonstrating both the proliferating capacity of women's gossip and its detrimental effect on male society, she tells the story of her husband's secrets as they pass through the wifely rumor mill, spreading to her "gossyb dame Alys," her beloved niece, and many "another worthy wyf" (III. 536). To her husband's deep mortification, she confesses his transgressions to an ever-widening circle of women, exposing him to public scorn and potential retribution. In her tale, she implicates both her own speech community and that of all women, adapting from Ovid's *Metamorphoses* an exemplum on women's inability to keep secrets. She hints at the sexual consequences of idle talk when she confronts her husband's suspicion about her male gossip (III. 243–45) and reveals the connection between gossips and gadabouts, unruly tongues and unruly women, as she wanders about town to hear the latest news (III. 544–53). Most telling of all, her idle talk provokes a male cleric to cast aspersions on her loquacity; the Friar complains that her *Prologue* "is a long preamble of a tale" (III. 831). From her pulpit, the Wife of

---

105. Tutivillus appears on women's shoulders in the stained glass window at St. Nicholas Church, Stanford on Avon, Northamptonshire; and in wall paintings at Peakirk, Seething and Little Melton, Melbourne, and Colton. See Anderson, *Drama and Imagery*, 173–77; Alexander and Binski, *Age of Chivalry*, 444–46; and Rouse, *Medieval Wall Paintings*, 68–69. As I discuss in Chapter 1, above, the exemplum appears in a large number of medieval sermon collections and penitential manuals.

106. See, among others, the *Good Gossips* in *The Early English Carols*, ed. Richard Leighton Greene, 2nd ed. (Oxford: Clarendon, 1977), 249–53; and *A Talk of Ten Wives on Their Husbands' Ware*, in *Jyl of Breyntford's Testament*, ed. F. J. Furnivall (London, 1871), 29–33.

107. See the warning to virgins in *Myrour to Lewede Men and Wymmen*, 169; and to young widows in *Book of Vices and Virtues*, 256.

Bath both preaches orthodox doctrine about women's idle talk and embodies it, serving as an exemplum of gossip in the way that the Parson serves as
an "ensample" (I. 496) of virtue.[108]

Given the pervasiveness of the assumption that gossip is always women's
work in both late medieval culture and the Wife's own text, it is understandable that contemporary scholars have followed suit, interpreting the Wife's
words as transgressive female speech that confronts authoritative male discourse. As the rich body of Chaucer criticism reveals, Alisoun ventriloquizes
the rhetoric of clerical glossators, challenging orthodox interpretation by
asserting the authority of the female text.[109] She co-opts pastoral practice,
exploiting the confessional mandate to speak everything in order to recuperate the silenced female body.[110] And she appropriates the power of the pulpit, delivering a dilating and digressive *sermon joyeux*.[111] The Wife's idle talk
structures and enables these rhetorical appropriations. As Lochrie has recently argued, gossip is the "discursive mode that frames, interprets, and
even authorizes" Alisoun's experience.[112] Describing the Wife's gossip as an
"insurrectionary discourse on the part of women as a marginalized medieval
community," Lochrie, like the vast majority of scholars, explicitly identifies
Alisoun's appropriative talk as female speech—language intimately connected, as the Wife herself insists, to the female body.[113] Alisoun's gossip,
however, has other tales to tell, for while idle talk provides the Wife of Bath
with a strategy for resistance, it enables Chaucer to transform antifeminist
stereotype into a character so vivid that for scholars her strategies often
overshadow his.

Although it would be absurd to deny that gender is a central issue in both

108. See Scanlon's suggestive reading of the Parson as exemplum. Scanlon, *Narrative, Authority, and Power*, 3–26.

109. Carolyn Dinshaw, *Chaucer's Sexual Poetics* (Madison: University of Wisconsin Press,
1989), 120. See also Carherine S. Cox, "Holy Erotica and the Virgin Word: Promiscuous Glossing
in the *Wife of Bath's Prologue*," *Exemplaria* 5, no. 1 (1993): 207–37.

110. Jerry Root, "'Space to Speke': The Wife of Bath and the Discourse of Confession,"
Chaucer Review 28, no. 3 (1994): 252–74.

111. Patterson, "For the Wyves Love," esp. 669–80. Andrew Galloway further explores the
preaching enacted in the *Wife of Bath's Prologue,* tracing the text's relation to a variety of sermon
subgenres. Andrew Galloway, "Marriage Sermons, Polemical Sermons, and *The Wife of Bath's
Prologue:* A Generic Excursus," *Studies in the Age of Chaucer* 14 (1991): 3–30.

112. Lochrie, *Covert Operations,* 57.

113. Ibid. This is equally true of those earlier arguments that interpreted the Wife's use of
pastoral discourse as corruption rather than appropriation. See, for example, Robertson's description of the Wife's exegesis as "hopelessly carnal and literal." Robertson, *Preface to Chaucer,*
317–31, 317.

the Wife of Bath's texts and the speech that defines her (her opening lines establish the opposition between female speech and male textual authority), to interpret her idle talk only through this lens is to overlook the complicated use Chaucer makes of it. Indeed, to do so is to dismiss gossip as merely female talk, however subversive that speech might be. As I have argued throughout this chapter, Chaucer acknowledges conventional wisdom about idle talk in order to exploit it, and the notion that gossip is women's work is no exception. That he appropriates rather than defers to the commonplaces about women's speech is evidenced by the fact that those who engage in Chaucerian gossip are usually men: Geffrey, the House of Rumor's inhabitants, the Miller, the Manciple's crow, the Friar's summoner, Chaunticleer, sultans, messengers, classical poets, and above all, the loquacious Host. Only in the context of these other explorations of idle talk can we fully understand the ways in which gossip defines both the Wife of Bath and her texts. The gendering of idle talk is not the end of the *Wife of Bath's Prologue and Tale,* but its means, for despite all her explicit statements to contrary, the Wife's mastery of gossip is less about the inability of women to keep secrets than about idle talk's potential for narrative transformation. For Chaucer, the connection between women's gossip and storytelling is not an "unsettling possibility" but an irresistible opportunity.[114]

In her *Prologue,* the Wife of Bath performs the myriad functions of Chaucerian gossip. Like Harry Bailly, she uses idle talk to multiply conversation: her *Prologue* contains more interruptions than any other text in the *Canterbury Tales.* In fact, her loquacity triggers the dispute between the Friar and Summoner that Harry later co-opts. Not one to be outdone, the Wife of Bath improves upon Harry's strategies. Generating both conversation about and interest in her marital "privitee," the Wife uses idle talk to transform her audience into her conversational familiars. Early in her *Prologue,* she attempts to draw male and female listeners alike into her company of "us wyves" (III. 144), elbowing her audience knowingly with such phrases as "Ye woot wel what I meene of this, pardee!" (III. 200) and "Ye wise wyves, that kan understonde" (III. 225). As readers, or as fellow pilgrims, we, like her "gossyb dame Alys," accompany the Wife as she walks from house to house to "heere sondry tales" (III. 547). We, too, know her "herte, and eek [her] privetee" (III. 531)—or at least she leads us to believe that we do.[115] We,

114. Lochrie, *Covert Operations,* 80.
115. See Karma Lochrie's discussion of the Wife of Bath's lack of disclosure. Ibid., 58–59.

too, are privy to her husbands' secrets; that is, we become complicit in her gossip.

The Wife of Bath deploys idle talk to transform her texts as well as her audience. Her infamous glossing resembles nothing so much as gossip in the *House of Fame*. Whether it be her discussion of "octagamye" (III. 33) or her reinterpretation of the biblical mandate to "wexe and multiplye" (III. 28), she uses idle talk to amplify, abbreviate, distort, and multiply both biblical texts and patristic authorities.[116] Blurring news and narrative in her *Prologue*, she repeatedly refers to her confessional tidings as her "tale," a digressive narrative that incorporates a series of embedded stories. She performs the generic alchemy of the Canon's Yeoman, translating treatise into tale by gossiping antifeminist tracts as the story of a marital spat. Indeed, this antifeminist rhetoric undergoes a double transformation. Inviting her audience to overhear her marital dispute—"herkneth how I sayde" (III. 234)—the Wife first presents antifeminist commonplaces as her husband's drunken preaching, "Thow seyst that droppyng houses, and eek smoke, / And chidyng wyves maken men to flee / Out of hir owene houses" (III. 278–80). After ventriloquizing an endless litany of "Thou seist . . . Thou seyst . . . Thow seyst . . . Thus seistow" (III. 248–302), she then lets us in on the bigger secret that she fabricated his entire tirade—"And al was fals" (III. 382). Engaging in audience manipulation, textual transformation, generic alchemy, and the blurring of tidings and tales, the Wife of Bath embodies Chaucerian "small talk" in all its splendor. Moreover, it is through the Wife's embodiment of gossip that Chaucer is able to transform a text composed almost entirely of antifeminist stereotypes into a larger-than-life character.

In the *Wife of Bath's Prologue*, Chaucer recapitulates his earlier demonstrations of gossip's potential; in the *Tale*, he brings his experiment to fruition, making explicit the connection between idle talk and poetic practice. Here, too, gossip is both a topic and a mode of narration. The digressions and

---

116. On the subject of the Wife of Bath's glossing practices and her debate with patristic authorities, see among others, Dinshaw, *Chaucer's Sexual Poetics*, 113–31; Ralph Hanna, "*Compilatio* and the Wife of Bath: Latin Backgrounds, Ricardian Texts," in *Latin and Vernacular: Studies in Late-Medieval Texts and Manuscripts*, ed. Alastair J. Minnis (Cambridge: D. S. Brewer, 1989), 1–11; Warren S. Smith, "The Wife of Bath Debates Jerome," *Chaucer Review* 32, no. 2 (1997): 129–45; and Susan Signe Morrison, "Don't Ask, Don't Tell: The Wife of Bath and Vernacular Translations," *Exemplaria* 8, no. 1 (1996): 97–123.

dilations that characterized the Wife's idle talk in the *Prologue* continue through her tale as she interpolates several other narratives into her romance. In fact, the *Tale* begins with a digression: the Wife of Bath comments on the disappearance of fairies in order to gossip about the sexual exploits of friars and thereby retaliate against the male cleric who criticized her loquacity. But by far the most infamous of the Wife's narrative interpolations comes when she digresses into the topic of idle talk itself. When she gossips with her audience about what women most desire, only one suggestion inspires both ridicule and disbelief, compelling Alisoun to take up her pulpit once again:[117]

> And somme seyn that greet delit han we
> For to been holden stable, and eek secree,
> And in o purpos stedefastly to dwelle,
> And nat biwreye thyng that men us telle.
> But that tale is nat worth a rake-stele.
> Pardee, we wommen konne no thyng hele;
> Witnesse on Myda—wol ye heere the tale?
>
> (III. 945–51)

As if delivering a sermon on women's idle talk, she first proclaims the truth of the antifeminist commonplace that women can't keep secrets—"Pardee, we wommen konne no thyng hele"—and then proceeds to deliver an exemplum, drawn from Ovid, to prove her point. Of course, the Wife of Bath does not tell the whole truth of the Ovid tale.[118] Rather, she glosses it, altering details to suit her rhetorical purposes and using only the part of the narrative that proves her point. Under the influence of the Wife of Bath's abbreviating and distorting gossip, Ovid's text undergoes a metamorphosis of its own, as a story about a male servant's betrayal is transformed into a tale about a wife's inability to keep her husband's secrets.

Rather than indicting women's gossip, the Wife's antifeminist revision of

---

117. The Wife's commentary on the answers the knight receives is unique to Chaucer's version of the narrative.

118. On the Wife's narrative machinations here, see Patterson, "For the Wyves love," 656–58; Dinshaw, *Chaucer's Sexual Poetics*, 126–29; Judson Boyce Allen and Patrick Gallacher, "Alisoun Through the Looking Glass: Or Every Man His Own Midas," *Chaucer Review* 4 (1970): 99–105; and Richard L. Hoffman, "Ovid and the Wife of Bath's Tale of Midas," *Notes and Queries* 211 (1966): 48–50, and *Ovid and the Canterbury Tales* (Philadephia: University of Pennsylvania Press, 1966), 145–49.

the Midas story recuperates this speech as productive. What is more, in a brilliant twist of Chaucerian irony, the Wife's narrative strategies implicate antifeminist rhetoric and pastoral practice in the recuperation. For as the Wife turns a tale that had nothing to do with women's speech into an exemplum about women's idle talk, she calls explicit attention to her textual manipulation, inviting readers to consult the narrative she has so radically changed: "The remenant of the tale if ye wol heere, / Redeth Ovyde, and ther ye may it leere" (III. 981–82).[119] By simultaneously altering and invoking Ovid's original, she exposes not the dangers of women's talk, but the process of textual transformation in which she (and Chaucer behind her) is so heavily engaged.[120]

That Chaucer uses the Midas story to make explicit the connection between idle talk and tale-telling practice is evidenced by the fact that the Wife of Bath alters Ovid's status as literary "auctoritee" as well as the content of his narrative. Rather than introducing the Midas story as a revered text, Alisoun translates Ovid's *Metamorphoses* into "small talk":

> Ovyde, amonges othere thynges smale,
> Seyde Myda hadde, under his longe heres,
> Growynge upon his heed two asses eres.
>
> (III. 952–54)

In late medieval England, "small things" was often a euphemism for salacious matters. The Wife of Bath refers to male and female genitalia as "oure bothe thynges smale" (III. 121), and Gower describes the stealing of a woman's virginity as the theft "of some othre smale thinges."[121] To speak of such small things is to gossip. Among their talk of "this and that," Pandarus and Crisyede engage "in speche of thynges smale" about their neighbors (II.

---

119. Here, as in the *Physician's Tale,* Chaucer uses the exemplum not as a vehicle for orthodox doctrine but as a means both to experiment with narrative technique and to raise questions about exemplary practice.

120. For an alternative reading, see Patterson, "For the Wyves Love," 656–58. For Patterson, the Wife of Bath's version of the Midas story indicts not female speakers but male listeners who "prefer the immediate self-gratifications of antifeminism to the severer pleasures of self-knowledge" (658). While I do not disagree with Patterson's analysis, I think he overlooks the larger implications that the Wife's textual transformations have for Chaucer's narrative practice.

121. In the tale of Neptune and Cornix, Gower suggests that Neptune does not want rings or broaches, but other treasures, other "smale thinges." John Gower, *Confessio Amantis,* ed. G. C. Macaulay, EETS, e.s. 81–82 (London: Kegan Paul, Trench, Trübner, 1900–1901), V. 6174.

1191). The Host, well versed in gossip's euphemisms, warns the Manciple that the Cook will speak "smale thynges" about his shady business dealings (IX. 73). Moreover, the *Secret of Secrets* condemns gossip's triviality by proclaiming that great men do not marvel at the "smale thynges that thay hyryth."[122] Combining the bodily, the idle, and the excessive, the talk of small things would seem to embody all the traits ascribed to women's gossip by both medieval authorities and contemporary critics. Yet for Chaucer, "small talk" refers not to the Wife of Bath's gossip but to male textual authority. Just as the Man of Law turned Ovid's *Metamorphoses* into a conversational companion sharing the latest tidings, so the Wife of Bath turns it into idle talk, tales meant to be multiplied and transformed as she gossips with her audience of conversational familiars.[123]

This double transformation of the *Metamorphoses* into both exemplum and small talk is the most egregious but certainly not the only textual manipulation that the *Wife of Bath's Tale* performs. Quite the contrary, the larger romance in which the Midas story is embedded consistently engages in and ruminates over deliberate transformations, both textual and thematic.[124] Through the Wife of Bath, Chaucer tells the tale of disenchantment of the "Loathly Lady," a popular folktale that appeared in many versions throughout the Middle Ages.[125] Although several sources have been proposed for the majority of the *Tale*, there are details that find no parallel in any extant version, including those Middle English analogues deemed closest to Chaucer's text.[126] That is, Chaucer has used the Wife of Bath to make

122. *Three Prose Versions of the Secreta Secretorum,* ed. Robert Steele, EETS, e.s. 74 (London: Kegan Paul, Trench, Trübner, 1898), 172/1–2.

123. The connection between gossip and the *Metamorphoses* is something of a Chaucerian refrain; the *Book of the Duchess* also suggests that this Ovidian text engages in idle talk by speaking of "other thinges smale" (59).

124. Lerer links the shape-shifting of the *Wife of Bath's Tale* to poetic composition, "authorship and tale telling are a kind of magic." Lerer, "*Canterbury Tales,*" 258. See also Susanna Greer Fein's exploration of the larger implication of "faery" in the Wife's tale. Fein, "Other Thought-Worlds," in *A Companion to Chaucer,* ed. Peter Brown (Oxford: Blackwell, 2000), 332–48, esp. 336–41.

125. For a comprehensive account of the tale's multiple versions, see George H. Maynadier, *The Wife of Bath's Tale: Its Sources and Analogues* (London: D. Nutt, 1901); and Sigmund Eisner, *A Tale of Wonder: A Source Study of the Wife of Bath's Tale* (Wexford, Eng.: J. English, 1957).

126. The three Middle English analogues, which like the *Wife of Bath's Tale,* combine the "Loathly Lady" with the motif of the man whose life depends on the correct answer to a question, are a ballad entitled the "Marriage of Sir Gawaine," the metrical romance, the *Weddynge of Sir Gawen and Dame Ragnell,* and Gower's "Tale of Florent." These analogues have been edited by Bartlett J. Whiting, "The Wife of Bath's Tale," in *Sources and Analogues,* ed. Bryan and Dempster, 223–68. For the most recent discussion of the *Tale*'s sources, see Susan Carter, "Coupling the

several changes to what critics refer to as the "normal" version of the tale.[127] These alterations would have been particularly legible to Chaucer's audience since Gower had recently published a more conventional version of the narrative in his "Tale of Florent," a text that the Wife's *Tale* explicitly echoes.[128]

Just as in her *Prologue*, the Wife employs the technique of her glossing gossip to reconfigure her texts. Multiplying narratives, in addition to the Midas story, she interpolates into her *Tale* the Old Hag's sermon on poverty and *gentillesse*, itself an embodiment of the Wife's glossing practices.[129] Through the medium of the Wife's idle talk, a virtuous knight, who in some versions is King Arthur himself, has been metamorphosed into a rapist, whose promises and decisions leave him wholly at the mercy of the "Loathly Lady." Whereas Florent and Arthur understand the repercussions of the promises they are making (to marry the old woman or to marry Gawain to her), the knight in the *Wife of Bath's Tale* promises only to do whatever she asks and is therefore left without recourse when the Old Hag announces the marriage to the court. Similarly, the decision the knight faces at the tale's conclusion, instead of being a choice between private pleasure and public reputation (fair by night and foul by day or foul by night and fair by day), becomes the impossible dilemma, informed by antifeminist rhetoric, that his wife will either be ugly and faithful or beautiful and promiscuous.[130] The logical consistency of these changes has led critics to interpret the *Tale* as an extension of the *Prologue*, indeed as an exemplum of Alisoun's doctrine of Wife Supremacy.[131] But while it is true that these changes are in keeping

---

Beastly Bride and the Hunter Hunted: What Lies Beneath Chaucer's *Wife of Bath's Tale*," *Chaucer Review* 37, no. 4 (2004): 329–45.

127. Pearsall, *Canterbury Tales*, 87. Scholars have proposed sources for most of Chaucer's changes, but none of those sources contain the tale of the "Loathly Lady." See Joseph P. Roppolo, "The Converted Knight in Chaucer's 'Wife of Bath's Tale,'" *College English* 12, no. 5 (1951): 263–69; Margaret Schlauch, "The Marital Dilemma in the Wife of Bath's Tale," *PMLA* 61, no. 2 (1946): 416–30; George R. Coffman, "Another Analogue for the Violation of the Maiden in the 'Wife of Bath's Tale,'" *Modern Language Notes* 59, no. 4 (1944): 271–74; and Robert P. Miller, "The Wife of Bath's Tale and Mediaeval Exempla," *ELH* 32, no. 4 (1965): 442–56.

128. Among other scenes, Chaucer borrows the detail that the newly married knight hides himself "as an owle" (III. 1081) from the *Confessio* (I. 1727–31).

129. While the sermon has sources in Dante, Boethius, Seneca, and John of Salisbury, among other "auctoritees," it is never found in conjunction with the tale of the "Loathly Lady." For a discussion of the sermon's sources, see Christine Ryan Hillary's notes to the *Riverside Chaucer*, 872–75.

130. Cf. III. 253–56 and 265–68. Margaret Schlauch has uncovered the rhetorical tradition behind the knight's dilemma. Schlauch, "Marital Dilemma," 416–30.

131. On the Wife's *Tale* as a reflection of her personal politics, see among others, Mary Carruthers, "The Wife of Bath and the Painting of Lions," *PMLA* 94, no. 2 (1979): 209–22;

with the Wife's rhetoric, the *Tale*'s final scene suggests that more is at stake than marital sovereignty.

From the gossip about Midas to idle talk about a rapist-knight, the changes enacted in the *Wife of Bath's Tale* have foregrounded the Wife's narrative revisions, and the final scene serves as the culmination of that process. The *Tale*'s raison d'être—the disenchantment of the "Loathly Lady"—is both the physical metamorphosis of the Old Hag into a young and beautiful wife and, more important, the Wife's final textual manipulation. Transforming the folktale's conventional motif, the Wife of Bath allows her protagonist to shape-shift at will. In other versions of the narrative, the metamorphosis comes about because a spell has been broken: the "Loathly Lady," "shapen by nygramancy . . . and by enchauntement," is freed by the knight's granting of sovereignty.[132] For the Wife of Bath, however, as well as for the poet behind her, the transformation is not a foregone conclusion imposed by an external source, whether magical or literary. It is a deliberate decision, a self-generating metamorphosis. The Old Hag speaks her transformation, declaring herself young again. And it is in this nexus of thematic and textual metamorphoses that the utility of the Wife of Bath's idle talk as a narrative technique is fully realized. The self-imposed disenchantment of the "Loathly Lady," as the Wife gossips it, is more than an emblem of female "maistrie" (III. 1040); it is a model for Chaucer's relationship to his sources. Borrowing from but not beholden to literary "auctoritees," he transforms them at will, using the idle talk of his characters to amplify, distort, conflate, abbreviate, and multiply his inherited tales. That is, Chaucer uses gossip to speak his narrative transformations.

Dinshaw, *Chaucer Sexual Poetics*; David Aers, *Community, Gender, and Individual Identity: English Writing, 1360–1430* (London: Routledge, 1988); Martin Puhvel, "The Wife of Bath's Tale: Mirror of her Mind," *Neuphilologische Mitteilungen* 100, no. 3 (1999): 291–300; and Lochrie, *Covert Operations*, esp. 56–60.

132. *The Wedding of Sir Gawen and Dame Ragnell, Sources and Analogues*, ed. Bryan and Dempster, 260, lines 691–93. The stepmother is traditionally the source of the spell. Cf. the "Tale of Florent": "my Stepmoder for an hate, / Which toward me sche hath begonne, / Forschop me" (*Confessio*, I. 1844–46); and "the Marriage of Sir Gawaine": "Shee witched me." *Sources and Analogues*, ed. Bryan and Dempster, 240. The fact that the enchantment is caused by another has an additional narrative side effect: the answer to the question of what women most desire is kept as a jealously guarded secret and the revelation of that secret is considered treasonous. In the "Tale of Florent," for example, the Loathly Lady is described as betraying the sisterhood of women: "Ha treson, wo thee be. / That hast thus told the privite, / Which alle wommen most desire!"(*Confessio*, I. 1659–61). Chaucer deletes all reference to this covert community of women and its secret knowledge, focusing instead on overt transformations, as he once again abjures conventional wisdom about idle talk.

Chaucer employs the Wife's of Bath's idle talk to tell the tale of his own poetic practice. In her appropriative gossip he makes transparent his own techniques for reimagining and reinventing his sources. Rather than merely serving as an exemplum of women's idle talk, Alisoun acts as the allegorical embodiment of both gossip and poetic invention, that is, of gossip as poetic invention. Her jangling is everywhere tied to her discursive appropriations, as her idle talk revises biblical text, patristic authority, Ovidian narrative, and pastoral practice. Those moments that would most condemn female loquacity, either explicitly or implicitly, function to further reveal the transformative capacity of this transgressive speech. Even Alisoun's exemplum about the secret sharing of her female community serves to show how idle talk can appropriate pastoral practice, for Alisoun uses her co-optation of orthodox exemplarity to suggest that gossip might substitute for and indeed remake confessional practice. Combining all of his other experiments, Chaucer transforms pastoral ideas about gossip into a character who both embodies the negative characteristics ascribed to this sinful speech and recuperates them as narratively and socially productive. What was introduced as a possibility in the envious jangling of literary authorities in the *House of Fame* comes to fruition in the Wife of Bath's conversational manipulation, as the blurring of tidings and tales makes all texts, sacred and profane, susceptible to gossip's transformations. The Wife of Bath serves as the apotheosis of Chaucerian small talk precisely because she is female. Making gossip a woman, and thereby exploiting the foregone conclusions of pastoral rhetoric, allows Chaucer to test the limits of idle talk's possibilities. Only by representing gossip in its full orthodox regalia—as idle, proliferating, distorting, and female—can he harness its full poetic potential. Yet we should not confuse this clever ploy with the idea that he represents gossip as women's work.

Unlike medieval priests and penitential writers, Chaucer does not stand at the pulpit preaching against the dangers of idle talk, browbeating his audience for their jangling. Rather he embraces that jangling variously as the subject of his poetry, the characters who people it, the sources for their tales, the device that structures them, and the mode through which they are narrated. Thus, while Chaucer acknowledges and indeed deploys pastoral rhetoric, he does so in order to test new narrative theories rather than to exert social control by enforcing community morals. What is at stake in Chaucer's experimentation with gossip is both the discovery of a multifaceted literary technique and the articulation of an alternative rhetoric about idle talk that endows it with functions and capacities unsanctioned by pastoral authority. No longer simply the idle talk that disrupts sermons and threatens confession, gossip has productive value, creating new stories out of old texts and forging alliances between narrators and those who listen to them. Gossip's capacity for manipulating both texts and audiences suggests other transformative possibilities—possibilities Chaucer raises briefly in the relationship between the Wife of Bath and her gossip Dame Alys but ultimately subsumes into his exploration of idle talk's narrative potential. Although Chaucer does not pursue this avenue in the *Wife of Bath's Tale*, the Wife's gossip with Alys has a literary legacy nonetheless. As I demonstrate in the remaining two chapters of this book, the gossips who jangle in late medieval carols, ballads, and narrative poems resurrect the Wife of Bath's transforming talk. And while these gossips' songs represent idle talk as women's work, to be both mocked and condemned accordingly, they also illustrate its capacity to alter not only texts but also pastoral practices and social and familial relationships. Far from idle, these women's talk does all manner of cultural work.

"SISTERIS IN SCHRIFT":
GOSSIP'S CONFESSIONAL KINSHIP

She knew myn herte, and eek my privetee,
Bet than oure parisshe preest, so moot I thee!
To hire biwreyed I my conseil al.[1]

When the Wife of Bath describes the intimate conversations shared with her "gossyb dame Alys," she identifies their idle talk as confession. Rather than revealing her "privetee" to the parish priest, the Wife divulges her secrets to her female companion, replacing her shrift-father with a more accommodating surrogate. Granting to Alys the access usually reserved for only the most skilled confessor, the Wife reveals her "herte" as well as her secrets, disclosing not just her actions but also her dispositions and intentions to her "gossyb." That is, the Wife claims to speak more openly—to perform a more perfect shrift—with her gossip than with her official confessor. Given the Wife's persistent attack on the tools of the clerical trade, it is hardly surprising that she would disparage orthodox confession. Yet the Wife does not reject confessional practice; she reinvents it, recuperating its functions for conversational exchange. Substituting the "biwreying" of "counseil" for the acknowledgment of sins, the Wife outlines a more comprehensive model of secret-sharing, in which she can unburden her tongue as well as her "herte." The consequences of her confessional appropriations inhere in the word "biwreye," for while the revelation of secrets is fundamental to orthodox shrift, "biwreying" describes transgressive speech. Elsewhere in the Wife's narrative, "biwreying conseil" involves betrayal, signifying the act of

---

1. *Wife of Bath's Prologue*, III. 531–33.

divulging the secrets with which one has been entrusted. The Wife's proclamation that women cannot keep secrets invokes this term, as does the Midas
story she tells to illustrate her point.[2] In fact, throughout the *Canterbury
Tales*, to "biwrey conseil" is to betray someone by divulging their secrets.[3]
And the Wife of Bath's confessional conversations with Alys are no exception. As the Wife makes clear, when she "biwreyed" her "conseil al," it was
her husband's secrets she was betraying and not her own.[4] What the Wife
imagines in her brief remarks about Alys is an appropriation of pastoral
practice that both exploits and betrays confessional speaking.

Given that the confessional appropriations enacted by the Wife of Bath
and her "gossyb dame Alys" play such a minor role in the *Wife of Bath's
Prologue* and *Tale*, scholars have understandably ignored its larger implications. Interpreting the conversational intimacy of these two women as short-
hand for their close female friendship, scholars have overlooked the literary
precedent set by their confessional gossip. But as I argue throughout this
chapter, late medieval writers repeatedly depict women's idle talk as confessional exchange, exploring the ways in which female characters remake pastoral practice through their gossip. Even writers whose depictions of
women's conversations draw heavily on antifeminist stereotype, representing shrewish and promiscuous wives who malign their husbands' sexual
prowess, frame these conversations in terms of confessional practice. Following in the Wife of Bath's footsteps, female characters throughout the
period "biwreye conseil," revealing secrets and confiding troubles, not to
the sanctioned ears of the parish priest but to their friends and neighbors.
As these intimate confessional exchanges co-opt pastoral practice, they
transform relationships, for the characters who engage in them forge kinship
through conversation, claiming one another as sisters and cousins. This con-

2. *Wife of Bath's Tale*, III. 948 and 974. Indeed, her account of Midas's wife demonstrates
both the betrayal at work in "biwreying conseil" and the catharsis such speech enables: Midas's
wife is so oppressed by the secret she keeps that it causes her physical pain—"it swal so soore
aboute hir herte" (III. 967)—and the only way to unburden her heart, and thus cure her affliction, is to "biwreye" the secret: "nedely som word hire moste asterte" (III. 968).

3. Prudence delivers a long lecture on the importance of not "biwreiyng" either one's own
secrets or those of others (VII. 338–48). The Man of Law chastises messengers for revealing
secrets and thus betraying their masters (II. 773). For the Monk, such disclosures have tragic
repercussions (VII. 2029); and for the Parson, the "biwreying of conseil" is a Sin of the Tongue
that leads to defamation (X. 645).

4. In the very next line, the Wife elucidates the topic of her "confession" to Alys: "For
hadde my housbonde pissed on a wal, / Or doon a thyng that sholde han coste his lyf / To hire
. . . / I wolde han toold his conseil every deel" (III. 534–35, 538).

versational kinship, like the confession that accompanies it, is structured by betrayal; women swear alliance to one another at the expense of loyalty to their husbands.

My discussion of gossip's confessional appropriations focuses on two texts: Chaucer's *Shipman's Tale* and Dunbar's *Tretis of the Tua Mariit Wemen and the Wedo*. These poems draw explicit attention to the ways in which women's supposedly idle talk alters relationships and co-opts pastoral practice. Both texts reveal the connections and dependencies among conversation, kinship, and confession; yet in doing so, each explores one aspect of gossip's dual transformation—one focusing on kinship, the other on the confession it enables. Embracing "cosynage" as its subject, Chaucer's *Shipman's Tale* illustrates the mechanisms through which conversational kinship is constructed, revealing the consequences that such a kinship might have and suggesting the co-optations it licenses. Dunbar's *Tretis*, by contrast, ruminates over the pastoral appropriations of its three female characters, depicting in vivid and venomous detail their co-optation and corruption of confessional practice. The difference in emphasis between the two texts is apparent in the first words the women speak. While the wife of the *Shipman's Tale* enters the narrative by calling on her "cosyn," the Wedo hails her sisters with a call to confess.[5]

In order to recognize the betrayals inherent in the confessional appropriations of these texts, we need first to consider briefly confession in its idealized form. Private auricular confession as it was mandated by the Fourth Lateran Council had a twofold purpose: to absolve parishioners of their sins and to teach them the basic tenets of the faith.[6] A forum for both spiritual healing and pastoral instruction, confession provided the Church with an annual method for assessing the spiritual well-being of its extensive congregation. As part of the Fourth Lateran Council's pastoral mission, parish priests were obligated to examine their parishioners on the most basic pastoral syllabus, making sure that they knew the Pater Noster, Ave Maria, the Creed, the articles of the faith, the Ten Commandments, and the seven

---

5. *Shipman's Tale*, VII. 98; *Tretis of the Tua Mariit Wemen and the Wedo, Poems of William Dunbar*, line 41.

6. Lee Patterson speaks of "the double use of the confessional as a place of instruction as well as penance" in his discussion of the *Parson's Tale* and its relationship to penitential manuals from the period. "'Parson's Tale,'" 337. See also Tentler, *Sin and Confession*, 57–133.

deadly sins.[7] That is, annual confession provided the priest (and behind him, the Church) with both an opportunity and a method for ensuring that members of the Catholic congregation shared a common set of religious knowledge. Confession's pastoral and penitential functions worked in tandem; priests used their examinations of parishioners' religious knowledge to structure their inquiries about sin.

For members of the congregation, however, confession involved more than religious instruction and the enjoining of penance; it enabled spiritual catharsis. In its idealized form, shrift provided a mechanism through which parishioners could unburden their souls of sin. Sinners approached confession encumbered, "heuy, / And cumbred ful of þoȝt and drede" and left it feeling "wundyr lyȝt."[8] Aided by the questions of a discreet and knowledgeable shrift-father, parishioners freed themselves of their transgressions by speaking them aloud. In order to achieve this curative effect, the model confessional utterance was speech at its most transparent: "simple, humble, pure, faithful, and . . . unadorned."[9] Unlike the "curious" and "sotel" talk in which members of the congregation typically engaged, penitential speech was supposed to be straightforward—unembellished words that acknowledge sin without reveling in it, that catalogue rather than narrate. The exemplary penitent humbly admitted her failings rather than engaging in self-aggrandizement—either by boasting about her transgressions or by recounting them as entertainment. She had no ulterior motives; in laying bare her own sins, she did not talk about other people's affairs, blame her transgressions on others, curry the priest's favor, or distract him with irrelevant tales. Above all, her confessional speech was truthful: she did not misrepresent small sins as grievous acts, attempt to disguise serious vices as trifles, or falsely admit to nonexistent crimes.[10] That is, in a model confession, the sinner's heart and tongue accorded together; they were not "double in thynkyng oon, and tellyng an-oþer."[11]

7. For an example of such an examination, see Mirk, *Instructions for Parish Priests*, lines 805–972.

8. Mannyng, *Handlyng Synne*, lines 11962–63 and 11967.

9. Tentler, *Sin and Confession*, 106–7. My discussion of the model confession is deeply indebted to Tentler's insightful and exhaustive chapter on the practice of auricular confession. See esp. 82–133.

10. Middle English penitential manuals repeatedly stress the importance of both truthful and proportionate confessions. See, for example, *Jacob's Well*, 182/3–12; and *Handlyng Synne*, lines 11705–10.

11. *Jacob's Well*, 181/9–10.

For the priest who presided over this idealized shrift, confessional speaking functioned not as a source of entertainment but as a diagnostic tool. The confessor served as a spiritual physician who endeavored to cure the wounds caused by sin. Probative rather than prurient, his questions attempted to find the true cause of the sinner's spiritual infirmity, helping to recover forgotten sins so that he could prescribe the most effective remedy. Like the exemplary penitent, the conscientious priest's motives were pure. He studiously avoided impropriety, refraining from looking directly at female penitents lest his gaze elicit shame or inspire lust and taking care not to introduce naive parishioners to new transgression through overzealous questioning. He struck a delicate balance between encouragement and instruction, coaxing confessions out of reluctant speakers while warning them about the dangers of sin, never overtly expressing the disapproval that might shame sinners into silence. Even as he worked to put his parishioners at ease, however, he avoided being overly familiar with them, maintaining his professional distance as the spiritual father to his flock.

In their reinvention of this idealized confessional practice, the women in Chaucer's *Shipman's Tale* and Dunbar's *Tretis* do not eschew shrift's pastoral and medicinal functions, rather they appropriate them, using their confessional gossip to unburden their "hertes" and instruct their conversational kin. Yet as they confess, these female characters do not offer humble and transparent declarations of their transgressions; rather they boldly recount "legendes" of their lives, relishing in the details of their (and their husbands') secrets and crafting their penitential narratives for personal gain. What is more, their confessional gossip collapses the structural distance between the speaker and her penitential guide, transforming the relationship between the shrift-father and his spiritual child into the intimate alliances of conversational kin. By "biwreying counseil," these female characters betray not just their husbands' secrets and the kinship bonds sanctioned by secular and ecclesiastical authority, but confessional speaking. That is, their betrayals occur both at the level of plot and at the level of language.

Confessing Cousins

That the *Shipman's Tale* is preoccupied with questions of kinship is evident from the remarkable frequency with which the words "cosyn" and "cosynage" recur throughout the text.[12] That this kinship is constructed through language, the Shipman makes clear early in his tale. Based on familiarity rather than familial ties, "cosynage" is a kinship established by verbal proclamation: "The monk hym claymeth as for cosynage, / And he agayn; he seith nat ones nay" (VII. 36–37). For the monk and the merchant, mutual spoken acceptance of their "eterne alliaunce" (VII. 40) of "bretherhede" (VII. 42) is the only necessary condition of their kinship. It is solely the act of calling each other "cosyn" which makes them so. Yet the question of what it might mean to call someone "cosyn"—that is, what is implied by that verbally constructed relationship—is a concern over which the text continues to ruminate. The tale's frequent reiteration of the word "cosyn" has made the signification of this term of address a scholarly preoccupation as well, as numerous critics have speculated about Chaucer's punning conflation of "cozen" (as a verb, to dupe; as a noun, a strumpet) and "cousin" (kinsman).[13] Although "cozen" does not appear in English until long after Chaucer's poem,[14] when the merchant's wife speaks of "cosynage" at the tale's conclusion, the word cannot be without the added valences of duping, cuckolding, and manipulation that have taken place in its name. Moreover, this manipulation, betrayal, and deceit are not only licensed by claimed "cosynage," but inherent in it. That is, in this tale, "cosyn" itself is a term of

12. The word "cosyn" appears almost as many times in this brief tale (thirteen instances) as in the rest of Chaucerian corpus put together (fifteen instances). "Cosynage," which occurs only in the *Shipman's Tale,* appears three times.

13. While noting the philological evidence to the contrary, numerous critics have argued for the existence of the pun, basing their claims on analogous examples from French literary texts. See Ruth M. Fisher, "'Cosyn' and 'Cosynage': Complicated Punning in Chaucer's 'Shipman's Tale,'" *Notes and Queries* 210 (1965): 168–70; David H. Abraham, "*Cosyn* and *Cosynage*: Pun and Structure in the *Shipman's Tale,*" *Chaucer Review* 11, no. 4 (1977): 319–27; Roy J. Pearcy, "Punning on 'Cosyn' and 'Cosynage' in Chaucer's *Shipman's Tale,*" *American Notes and Queries* 17, no. 5 (1979): 70–71; and Lee Patterson, *Chaucer and the Subject of History,* 351 n. 72. Gerhard Joseph calls for the unequivocal acceptance of the pun, though he allows that "not all of Chaucer's audience would have 'gotten' it." Joseph, "Chaucer's Coinage: Foreign Exchange and the Puns of the *Shipman's Tale,*" *Chaucer Review* 17, no. 4 (1983): 341–57, 352. More recently, Karla Taylor has made the provocative argument that even if this English pun did not yet exist, Chaucer's bilingual readers would have recognized Chaucer's punning on the French word, *coçonage,* which referred to "often shady" business dealings. Taylor, "Social Aesthetics and the Emergence of Civic Discourse," 308. For counterarguments, see Richard Firth Green, "Chaucer's *Shipman's Tale,* lines 138–41," *Chaucer Review* 26, no. 1 (1991): 95–99, 98 n. 5; and J. A. Burrow and V. J. Scattergood in their notes to the *Riverside Chaucer,* 910–13.

14. According to the *Oxford English Dictionary,* the word first appears in 1573: s.v. "cozen" and "cozenage."

deception, denoting a claimed, and therefore feigned, kinship—a relationship that can be established only through a series of conversational manipulations.[15]

The Shipman alerts his audience both to the deceptions inherent in this kinship and to the discursive maneuvers that construct it when he introduces the monk as "my lord daun John, / Oure deere cosyn, ful of curteisye" (VII. 68–69). His use of the "domestic 'our'" here confers upon Daun John a sense of intimate familiarity, not only in terms of the merchant and his household but also, more generally, for the narrator and his audience. By using this pronoun as he directly addresses the audience, the Shipman is attempting to make the monk *our* "cosyn" as well. As John Tatlock explains, the "domestic 'our'" "is an extension of an ordinary possessive to cases where it involves taking the point of view of the person addressed, and finally becomes stereotyped, especially in 'our dog,' 'our cat,' and in 'our sire' and 'our dame' for the goodman and the good wife of the household implied. Suggesting the intimacy of the household or parish, the Domestic 'Our' has a curious racy savor of the narrow community life of the middle ages."[16] If "oure deere cosyn" were the only use of the "domestic 'our'" in the *Shipman's Tale,* then we might treat it simply as a case in which the narrator, adopting the point of view of the merchant couple, invites his audience to share the intimacy of their household, producing what Pearsall describes as a "familiar, homely and quite friendly" effect.[17]

The use of this pronoun, however, is "unusually frequent" in the tale,[18] and its occurrences have an even more "racy savor" than Tatlock suggests.

15. This notion that claimed "cosynage" is synonymous with deception recurs in numerous later texts in which "cosyn" is a euphemism for a potential lover. The warning given in *A Prohemy of a Mariage betwix an Olde man and a Yonge Wife* sounds almost proverbial: "be wel ware of feyned cosynage, / And gossiprede" for these are the means through which a wife will have her pleasure. John Lydgate, *A Selection from the Minor Poems of Dan John Lydgate,* ed. J. O. Halliwell, Percy Society 4 (London: Percy Society, 1840), 36. Similarly, the author of the *Fyftene Joyes of Maryage* (STC 15258) makes countless references to a man whom the not-so-model wife claims as her "cosyn." This man, the poet explains with heavy sarcasm, "is as nyghe kynne vnto me / As vnto her." Wynkyn de Worde (London, 1509), fol. C2v.

16. John S. P. Tatlock, "The Source of *the Legend,* and other Chauceriana," *Studies in Philology* 18 (1921): 419–28, 427. The "domestic 'our'" is still used in the dialects of northern England.

17. Pearsall, *Canterbury Tales,* 211.

18. See J. A. Burrow and V. J. Scattergood's comments on VII. 69 in their notes for the *Riverside Chaucer,* 911. Perhaps it should come as no surprise that the only other tale in which the "domestic 'our'" occurs with greater frequency is the *Wife of Bath's Prologue,* in which Alisoun shares with us all the intimate details of her household.

When the monk asks the merchant's wife about the conjugal labor of "oure goode man" (VII. 107), he is not simply adopting her point of view. Rather there is, as Pearsall suggests, "a conspiratorial quality about 'oure goode man', an invitation to intimacy in sharing this patronising condescension and in sharing the secrets of the marital bed."[19] Similarly, when Daun John speaks with the merchant about "oure dame" (VII. 356, 363), he conspires with the audience in a joke at this cuckolded husband's expense. While the lady of the house may be the merchant's wife, she is still the monk's "owene nece sweete" (VII. 363), with Daun John's repetition of "oure dame" broadcasting the two men's joint possession. Conspiracy, intimacy, and shared possession—these are the added valences that the "domestic 'our'" carries in the *Shipman's Tale*. And the narrator's "Oure deere cosyn" is no exception.

The intimate and conspiratorial air of this expression, along with the narrator's manipulation of it to forge kinship between himself, his audience, and his characters, becomes all the more apparent when we consider the tale's hybrid narrative voice. After first introducing the merchant of "Seint-Denys" who will star in his tale, the Shipman sets the thematic tone of his fabliau by commenting on the universal politics of marital finances:

> The sely housbonde, algate he moot paye,
> He moot us clothe, and he moot us arraye,
> Al for his owene worshipe richely,
> In which array we daunce jolily.
> And if that he noght may, par aventure,
> Or ellis list no swich dispence endure,
> But thynketh it is wasted and ylost,
> Thanne moot another payen for oure cost,
> Or lene us gold, and that is perilous.
>
> (VII. 11–19)

Abandoning the fictional distance of the third-person narrator, the Shipman adopts the familiarity of the first-person plural, identifying himself with married women. In doing so, he not only claims the authority to speak for all wives but also incorporates his audience (male and female members

---

19. Pearsall, *Canterbury Tales*, 212.

alike) into that wifely community, attempting to make us complicit in the marital manipulations he describes. This abrupt pronoun shift has long been the topic of scholarly debate. For William Lawrence and Robert Pratt, the shift is a casualty of Chaucer's incomplete revision: a tale originally intended for the Wife of Bath has not been properly fitted to its new male narrator.[20] In contrast, Murray Copland and more recently Janet Thormann have seen this shift as appropriate to the Shipman, arguing that he uses it to ventriloquize the voice of the merchant's wife.[21] Although these competing readings diverge on the intended identity of the speaker, both arguments see in these lines the emergence of a hybrid narrator who shifts back and forth between male and female points of view. Thus whether an accident of textual history or a narrative ploy, the impact of the lines is similar.

If the Wife of Bath addresses her audience here, drawing us into her company of "us wyves," as she did in her *Prologue*, then all women, and the audience along with them, are all the more complicit in the machinations described. If it is the Shipman who speaks in a woman's voice, whether that of a general woman or the wife of the tale, then that falsetto voice still circumscribes all women in its proclamations, though the audience might manage ironic distance, elbowing the Shipman in his joke. Consequently, when this narrator turns to the audience and asks: "Who was so welcome as my lord daun John, / Oure deere cosyn, ful of curteisye?" it is no ordinary rhetorical question. Addressing the audience directly, once again speaking through the first-person plural, this is a woman's voice, and her question is laden with a knowing air of conspiracy. Moreover, it is a conspiracy and an intimacy in which this hybrid narrator, through the strategic manipulation of pronouns, has entangled the audience. The monk, the speaker implies, is familiar to the audience not only as the Daun John of countless fabliaux but also as "Oure deere cosyn." While audience members might resist the narrator's incorporating maneuvers, standing outside the deceptions and

20. William W. Lawrence, "Chaucer's *Shipman's Tale*," *Speculum* 33, no. 1 (1958): 56–68; and Robert A. Pratt, "The Development of the Wife of Bath," *Studies in Medieval Literature in Honor of Albert Croll Baugh*, ed. MacEdward Leach (Philadelphia: University of Pennsylvania Press, 1961), 45–79.

21. Murray Copland, "*The Shipman's Tale*: Chaucer and Boccaccio," *Medium Ævum* 35 (1966): 11–28; and Janet Thormann, "The Circulation of Desire in the 'Shipman's Tale,'" *Literature and Psychology* 39, no. 3 (1993): 1–15. For Copland, the Shipman's ventriloquizing produces a comic effect; for Thormann, by "taking up the voice of a woman, the Shipman indicates that his tale will perform the enigma of female desire and, in so doing, will contain female desire as and in male speech" (10).

intrigues that are taking place, they are nonetheless made to confront those maneuvers. Forcing us to experience conversational manipulation, the hybrid narrator prepares us for, and makes us sensitive to, the more elaborate discursive manipulations of the merchant's wife.

Like the narrator behind her, the wife of the tale begins her conversational maneuvers with the strategic use of both possessive pronouns and terms of kinship. When she wanders "pryvely" (VII. 92) into her garden in search of Daun John, the wife makes clear that she recognizes the value of calling someone "cousin," addressing the unsuspecting monk with "O deere cosyn myn, daun John" (VII. 98). More important, she understands that a kinship verbally established must be verbally maintained. Repeatedly addressing the monk as "cosyn" throughout their conversation, she continually reminds him of the relationship that has been established between them. The wife's interest, however, is not in simply proclaiming a kinship, but in exploring the uses and boundaries of that kinship. Beginning with the qualified and possessive "deere cosyn myn," the wife seeks to establish a greater intimacy with the monk than the monk has with her husband. Although he initially responds with the unqualified, "Nece" (VII. 100), the monk's seeming neutrality quickly dissipates as he introduces his rather overfamiliar question about her marital bed with the more intimate, "deere nece" (VII. 106). Throughout their privy exchange in the garden, their shifting use of epithets reveals the relationship transformations that are taking place. By the end of their discussion, "deere cosyn myn" shifts registers of intimacy to become "My deere love" (VII. 158) and the unqualified "Nece" becomes the doubly possessive, "myn owene lady deere" (VII. 196), as "cosynage" is exchanged for "affiance" (VII. 140) at the expense of the "eterne alliaunce" of brotherhood.[22]

Yet it is not solely through the strategic employment of terms of address that the wife effects such a transformation and substitution. The kinship between the monk and the merchant may consist solely in the claim of "cosynage," but the relationship between the wife and the monk is constituted by, and through, conversation. Although the wife continues with her

22. Later in the poem, the monk proves that he has mastered the wife's techniques. When he chats with the merchant with the object of requesting a loan, he first solidifies their "cosynage," addressing the merchant with "cosyn" three times in eight lines (VII. 257, 260, 264), and then seals the bargain with "myn owene cosyn deere" (VII. 279).

possessive "cosyn myn" (VII. 114) until she receives a response in kind from the monk, it is her use of conversation, or rather, her promise of forbidden conversation, that effects a change in their relationship, with epithets serving as markers of that change. When the wife suggests the possibility of illicit communication—"but to no wight . . . / Dar I nat telle how that it stant with me" (VII. 119–20), the monk responds with the possessive "my" on cue, implying that their relationship is now intimate enough to allow such a conversation to take place:

> "Allas, my nece, God forbede
> That ye, for any sorwe or any drede,
> Fordo youreself; but telleth me youre grief.
> Paraventure I may, in youre meschief,
> Conseille or helpe; and therefore telleth me
> Al youre anoy, for it shal been secree.
> For on my portehors I make an ooth
> That nevere in my lyf, for lief ne looth,
> Ne shal I of no conseil yow biwreye."
>   (VII. 125–33)

Volunteering his discreet and priestly counsel, the monk offers the wife an officially sanctioned channel through which she can reveal her heart and "privetee." Attempting to professionalize his curiosity under the guise of the confessor, the monk expresses his desire to remedy the wife's spiritual maladies, easing her "grief" (pain), curing her "meschief" (distress), and alleviating all her "anoy" (troubles). Like a conscientious shrift-father, he reassures his patient that any information she reveals will remain secret, for their conversation is bound by the seal of confession.[23] For all that it is couched in the vocabulary of spiritual healing, however, his repeated urging "telleth me," "telleth me," cannot help but reveal his eagerness to know her (and her husband's) secrets, sounding much more like idle curiosity than pastoral urging. Desperate to elicit her marital tales, he even goes so far as to swear a further oath on his breviary that he will not "biwreye" her "conseil."

---

23. The twenty-first canon—"Omnis utriusque sexus"—of the Fourth Lateran Council, responsible for mandating annual auricular confession, prohibited priests from repeating any information heard during confession. As I discuss in Chapter 1, however, the gossip of priests and parishioners alike continually troubled the confessional seal.

A master of discursive manipulation, the wife sees his oath for what it is, a "gossip's promise"—the attempt to persuade her to "biwreye" her secrets by swearing not to betray them. Understanding the customs of gossip's exchange, she responds with an appropriate and enthusiastic reciprocal assurance:

> "The same agayn to yow," quod she, "I seye.
> By God and by this portehors I swere,
> Though men me wolde al into pieces tere,
> Ne shal I nevere, for to goon to helle,
> Biwreye a word of thyng that ye me telle,
> Nat for no cosynage ne alliance,
> But verraily for love and affiance."
>   (VII. 134–40)

Far from the traditional model of shrift in which only the male priest, monk, or friar could hear the confessions of his female parishioners, the wife's hyperbolic and extended echo of the monk's oath—her gossip's promise— imagines an alternative model that licenses her to hear his confession as well. And it is precisely this wifely co-optation of confession that restructures their conversational kinship. Rather than allowing their relationship to transform into that of shrift-father and parishioner, by reciprocating the oath, the wife not only maintains their relationship as equals but reconstitutes their kinship as one in which "ech of hem tolde oother what hem liste" (VII. 142). Not a superfluous gesture, the wife's reciprocation of the oath is essential to the conversational kinship being forged.[24] The intimacy that the wife tried to effect with "deere cosyn myn" is now realized through the gossip's promise and the confessional appropriation it licenses.

The final two lines of the wife's oath, however, are problematic. Why, if she has spent the bulk of their conversation trying to make the monk reciprocate her "cosynage," does she then discount it? And why, after discounting it, does she immediately take it up again? Paul Strohm argues that the wife is "disclaiming the shoddy motives that actually drive her conduct ('cosynage' and 'alliance'—VII. 139) and claiming motives of a more elevated

---

24. For an alternative argument, see David Abraham, who claims that the wife's oath is "completely unnecessary." "Cosyn and Cosynage," 322.

sort ('love and affiance'—VII. 140)."[25] While Strohm's claim convincingly explains the shift of registers that takes place in "My deere love" and "myn owene lady deere," it does not account for the fact that the wife again adopts the title of "cosyn" once the oaths have been sworn. The wife's disavowal here is practical rather than ideological: she is about to ask the monk to renounce his "cosynage" with her husband. In convincing the monk to substitute one "cosyn" for another, she must both debase this form of "alliance" as that which is inferior and can therefore be easily disavowed, and reaffirm that precisely this kind of alliance has been forged between the monk and herself. She must expose the feigned nature of claimed "cosynage" even as she reclaims that kinship.[26]

To seal her alliance with Daun John, the wife employs her familiar conversational tactics. She tantalizes the monk with the possibility of her illicit confession, promising him a "legende of [her] lyf" (VII. 145) in which she will reveal the intimate details of her marriage. Her discursive strategy is so successful that Daun John renounces his relationship to the merchant—"He is na moore cosyn unto me / Than is this leefe that hangeth on the tree!" (VII. 149–50)—while begging her insistently to reveal her secrets: "Telleth youre grief, lest that he come adoun; / And hasteth yow" (VII. 156–57). Yet even after the monk has forsaken his "cosynage" with the merchant, the wife continues her discursive maneuvers. Titillating him with the transgressive nature of their conversational kinship, the wife occupies over half her "legende" with a series of disclaimers about the impropriety of divulging marital "privetee":

> "But sith I am a wyf, it sit nat me
> To tellen no wight of oure privetee,

---

25. Strohm, *Social Chaucer,* 101.

26. Richard Firth Green argues that the last two lines of the wife's oath (VII. 139–40) belong, not to the wife, as editorial consensus has proclaimed, but to the narrator, claiming that this change in attribution both "makes better immediate sense" and has syntactic precedents in Chaucer's corpus. Green, "Chaucer's *Shipman's Tale,*" 97. In my discussion here, I assign the lines to the merchant's wife, including them among her repertoire of conversational maneuvers. However, even if one accepts Green's claim, my argument about the disavowal remains unchanged, for this is the same hybrid narrator who has already spoken as the voice of all wives, a narrator who both understands and has practiced the machinations that are taking place. Whoever utters these lines—the merchant's wife, the Shipman in falsetto, or the Wife of Bath—the consequence is the same: "cosyn" cannot have the same value after the disavowal as before it, and as a result, the way is paved for the substitution that follows.

> Neither abedde ne in noon oother place;
> God shilde I sholde it tellen, for his grace!
> A wyf ne shal nat seyn of hir housbonde
> But al honour, as I kan understonde;
> Save unto yow thus muche I tellen shal."
>   (VII. 163–69)

Her repeated, albeit insincere, expressions of reluctance at committing such a grave infraction, followed immediately by a teasing reminder of the monk's newly established intimacy as her conversational *confidant*, advertise the scandalous nature of the secrets that she is always on the verge of disclosing. These discursive tactics replace content, for when the wife finally tells her confessional tale she never actually reveals any intimate details. Like Geffrey in the *House of Fame*, the wife in the *Shipman's Tale* uses the promise of gossip to generate interest without ever divulging anything new. Although she does provide a brief confessional disclosure, the information she provides is not secret, but rather a well-worn antifeminist refrain about the six things that women most desire.[27] Indeed, as she freely admits, prefacing her confessional narrative with "And wel ye woot" (VII. 173), the "legende" of her life is already quite familiar to the monk.

The wife's conversational maneuvers do more than create suspense; they further transform her relationship with the monk. Emphasizing both the transgression inherent in her appropriation of confession and her willingness to commit that transgression, the wife makes clear what is at stake in her gossip's promise. It is not only Daun John who disclaims a relationship with the merchant. The gossip's promise for the wife is tantamount to disavowing the sacrament of marriage, swearing allegiance to her conversational cousin at the expense of fidelity to her husband. That her confessional narrative is formulaic and commonplace does not alter the significance of its disclosure.[28] Her willingness to "biwreye" her husband's secrets exposes her willingness to betray him. Just as the gossip's promise restructures the kinship between these self-professed cousins, so the confession licensed by

---

27. Taking a cue from the Wife of Bath, the merchant's wife proclaims that the ideal husband should be "Hardy and wise, and riche, and therto free, / And buxom unto his wyf and fressh abedde" (176–77).

28. Cf. Karma Lochrie's argument about the dynamic of disclosure operating in orthodox confession: "the objects of confessional disclosure were always less the secrets themselves than the ritualized telling and sacerdotal listening." Lochrie, *Covert Operations*, 31.

that promise once again transforms the relationship, as intimate and illicit conversation with a male gossip serves as prelude to much more intimate and serious transgressions, in which dear cousins become "deere" loves.[29] We might be tempted to dismiss the betrayal of confession that takes place at the hands of the monk and the merchant's wife as a consequence of the fabliau's generic constraints. That is, we might attribute the introduction of confessional practice into the narrative to the monk's clerical office and, in turn, read the slippage between the confessional and the sexual as a foregone conclusion. After all, one of the most consistent features of the fabliau is the clerical intruder who betrays his professional obligations by cuckolding his spiritual charges. Indeed, several fabliaux depict monks, friars, and parish priests who exploit confession as a venue for seduction and an opportunity for intimacy, rendering into fiction concerns raised by orthodox and heterodox preachers alike about the ways in which private auricular confession might be abused. Richard FitzRalph complains about the scandalous behavior of friars who conflate the hearing of "conseile" with the commission of sin: "And freres procureþ þe contrarie for to here þe priuyeste counseile of wymmen, of queenes, & of alle oþere, & leggeþ [lie] hed to hed."[30] For Lollard writers, this conflation was not merely the fault of corrupt clerics but the unavoidable consequence of the model of private confession established by the Fourth Lateran Council: "bi þis priueye shrift a frere & nunne may synne to-gidre; and close hemsilf in a chaumbre bi lok in-sted of feyned assoylynge [absolution]."[31] The confessional appropriations depicted here, however, do more than provide the occasion for sexual transgression; they detail the exploitation of confessional speaking itself. Although the monk may have introduced confession into his conversation with the merchant's wife in order to seduce her, it is the wife who remakes confessional practice, transforming it into a mutual exchange of secrets, a reciprocal catharsis through which both parties could unburden themselves of all their "meschief"—"ech of hem tolde

---

29. The slippage between the conversational and the sexual depicted here is precisely the accusation that orthodox clerics levy against idle talk. In penitential discussions of chastity, wives, widows, and virgins alike are warned that trafficking in jangles leads to more illicit exchanges. See, for example, the *Book of Vices and Virtues*, 250–51 and 256–57.

30. Richard FitzRalph, *Defensio Curatorum*, in *Dialogus inter Militem et Clericum, Richard FitzRalph's Sermon: "Defensio Curatorum" and Methodius: "Þe Bygynnyng of þe World and þe Ende of þe Worldes,"* ed. Aaron Jenkins Perry, EETS, o.s. 167 (London: Kegan Paul, Trench, Trübner, 1925), 73/13–15.

31. *English Works of Wyclif,* 330.

oother what hem liste." It is the wife who turns confessional speaking into conversational manipulation, speaking not plainly but artfully, turning her "confession" into a self-aggrandizing "legende." And it is the wife who uses confession to curry the monk's favor, telling a good tale as preface to requesting the hundred franks. What is more, the betrayal of confessional speaking enacted by the monk and the merchant's wife is taken up by the women in Dunbar's *Tretis of the Tua Mariit Wemen and the Wedo,* a text unconstrained by either the expectations of the fabliau or the inherent susceptibility of male-female intimate exchange. Indeed, the confessional appropriations of these three women are more explicit, more systematic, and more egregious than those of the monk and the merchant's wife.

Sisterly Shrift

Like the wife of the *Shipman's Tale,* Dunbar's Wedo establishes kinship through conversation, transforming her companions from "wemen ȝing" (young women) (41) into her "sisteris in schrift" (251). She too uses the gossip's promise and her co-optation of confession to create conversational intimacy. But while the wife of the *Shipman's Tale* utilizes wifely confession as a means to greater intimacy with her male *confidant,* the Wedo views the sisterly shrift of her all-female coterie as an end in itself. Dunbar's *Tretis* shifts emphasis from kinship formation to confessional practice, analyzing the Wedo's appropriation of confession through the lens of officially sanctioned shrift and its dual functions of spiritual healing and instruction. By depicting these women's idle talk as a co-optation of confession, Dunbar does not simply imagine a carnivalesque inversion of orthodox practice. Rather he explores the utility of this discursive appropriation both for the women who engage in it and for his own poetic practice.

Although the *Tretis* begins as if it belonged to the literature of *amour courtois,* with the narrator describing his three female characters in a manner befitting any romance heroine,[32] the poem quickly shifts from the courtly to the confessional, as the Wedo's *demande d'amour* acts as a call to shrift:

---

32. James Kinsley calls attention to Dunbar's "jocular" echoing of the courtly love tradition, briefly analyzing the relationship of the *Tretis* to alliterative romance. *Poems of William Dunbar,* 259–61, 259.

Bewrie, said the wedo, ȝe woddit wemen ȝing,
Quhat mirth ȝe fand in maryage sen ȝe war menis wyffis;
Reveill gif ȝe rewit that rakles conditioun,
Or gif that ever ȝe luffit leyd upone lyf mair
Nor thame that ȝe ȝour fayth hes festinit for ever,
Or gif ȝe think, had ȝe chois, that ȝe wald cheis better.
Think ȝe it nocht ane blist band that bindis so fast
That none undo it a deill may bot the deith ane?

(41–48)

[Reveal, said the Wedo, you young wedded women,
What mirth you find in marriage since you became men's wives,
Reveal if you rue that reckless condition,
Or if you ever loved a man more in your life
Than them to whom you have fastened your faith forever
Or if you think, if you had the choice, that you would choose better.
Do you not think it is a blessed band that binds so fast
That nothing can sever it except death alone?]

Asking the wives to "bewrie" and "reveill" their marital experiences, the Wedo invites them to make a wifely confession—an intention she underlines when she encourages the second wife to "confesse us the treuth" (153). Her terminology not only highlights the confessional aspect of the conversations that will take place but hints at the ways in which her appropriation of confession will deviate from the traditional model. While "confess" and "reveal" comprise the vocabulary of self-revelation that belongs to confession generally, "bewrie" appears in penitential manuals only as an example of behavior inappropriate to confession.[33] Explaining the importance of self-accusation, *Handlyng Synne* instructs,

Þy shryfte shal be al of þy selue,
Of þyn owne propre dede,

---

33. Klaus Bitterling identifies these words as "marking what is to follow as confession in a pseudoreligious sense," briefly analyzing the scene in terms of the women's parodic and hypocritical use of religious discourse. "*The Tretis of the Twa Mariit Wemen and the Wedo: Some Comments on Words, Imagery, and Genre,*" *Scottish Studies* 4 (1984): 337–58, 344. He does not distinguish "bewrie" from the other words of self-revelation.

And bewreye noon ouþre, y þe forbede.
Þyn owne folye þou shalt seye,
And none ouþer body bewreye.
(11620–24)³⁴

[Your confession should be solely about yourself, about your own deeds. I forbid you to reveal anyone else's (deeds). You shall speak of your own folly and not betray any other person.]

"Bewrie" denotes the divulging of others' sins, rather than the revealing of one's own transgressions—an act expressly forbidden by ecclesiastical authority.³⁵ By beginning her call to confession with an incitement to this inappropriate activity, then, the Wedo announces the deviation inherent in her confessional appropriations. She encourages the women to "bewrie," that is, both to reveal and betray, not themselves but their husbands. Whereas the wife of the *Shipman's Tale* continually negotiates between the illicit and the proper, flirting with conversational impropriety, the Wedo both embraces and inspires transgressive speech.

By proposing the *demande,* the Wedo positions herself as shrift-mother to the two younger wives. Accepting the Wedo's proposition as they perform their confessions, these two women reveal both the uses and the conditions of sisterly shrift. For the first wife, the verbal transgression enjoined by the Wedo's call to "bewrie" constitutes the sole function of wifely confession. Contrite speech is replaced by a devastating catalogue of her aged husband's faults:

I have ane wallidrag, ane worme, an auld wobat carle,
A waistit wolroun na worth bot wourdis to clatter,

---

34. Mannyng repeats this prohibition several times during his discussion of confession: "Þogh þe prest aske, bewreye þou no deyl; / Bewreye weyl þyn owne dede, / But noun ouþer, y þe forbede" (11648–50). Although "bewreye" here refers to self-revelation, it is used only for the purpose of drawing a contrast with backbiting. In the majority of other instances, both in this text and in other penitential manuals, the act of confessing is described by the words, "tell," "say," and "show," rather than "bewrie."

35. As I discuss in Chapter 1, self-accusation was a universal condition of orthodox shrift. Penitential manuals frequently admonish parishioners not to gossip about their neighbors. See, for example, the prohibition declared by preacher of *Jacob's Well:* "breke noȝt / þi schryfte in accusyng oþers synnes, as þe husbonde tellyth þe wyves defawtes, & "þe wyif þe husbondys defawȝtes. telle þin / owne synnes, & noȝt þi neyȝbouris synnes" (182/15–17).

Ane bumbart, ane dron bee, ane bag full of flewme,
Ane scabbit skarth, ane scorpioun, ane scutarde behind.

(89–92)

[I have a worthless fellow, a worm, an old caterpillar man,
A used up wild boar worth nothing but clattering words,
A lazy fellow, a drone bee, a bag full of phlegm,
A scabbed monster, a scorpion, a skitterer behind.]

Shifting from long lines to quick clauses as she moves from polemics to practicalities, the wife's speech escalates to a flyting frenzy, hurling a seemingly endless list of abuse at her absent spouse. As her words "clatter" loudly about the audience's ears, she condemns her husband for being worth nothing but chatter, embodying antifeminist proverbs about women's speech even as she attempts to reinscribe them on her aging husband. Hers is a far cry from traditional confession in both content and condition. Not only does she reveal her husband's shortcomings instead of her own, but also she speaks in a manner wholly inappropriate for shrift, reveling in invective rather than humbly admitting her flaws.[36] That is, the Wedo's appropriation of orthodox confessional practice licenses both the first wife's disgust and her vehement expression of it in a language quite shocking for one so "swanquhit of hewis" (swan-white in hue) (243).[37]

Although transgressive speech is an essential element of the second wife's confession, her performance outlines a more complicated model of sisterly shrift than that of her companion, one that intersects with, as well as deviates from, the traditional ecclesiastical model. Even before this second wife begins, the Wedo stresses the confessional rather than merely transgressive nature of their conversation. She solicits this wife's confession not simply with an invitation to "bewrie," but with an assurance of reciprocity: "And syne my self ʒe exeme one the samyn wise, / An I sall say furth the south dissymyland no word" (and then you shall examine me in the same way,

36. As countless Middle English penitential manuals remind parishioners, humility is an essential condition of confessional practice. See *Jacob's Well*, 182/23–32; *Book of Vices and Virtues*, 180/23–181/20; and *Handlyng Synne*, lines 11456–90.

37. See Edwina Burness's detailed analysis of the women's use of "unfeminine" language and rhetorical devices in "Female Language in *The Tretis of the Twa Mariit Wemen and the Wedo*," *Scottish Studies* 4 (1984): 359–68, 366.

and I shall speak the truth without dissimulating a word) (156–57). The Wedo's pledge resonates with the language of confessional practice. By introducing the role of examination ("exeme")—the process by which a confessor probes the conscience of his parishioners—the Wedo highlights her role as shrift-mother.[38] By emphasizing the importance of truth, one of the necessary conditions of traditional shrift, the Wedo makes clear that she is aware of that traditional model. Moreover, her reassurance resembles officially sanctioned methods of encouragement suggested to parish priests in pastoral manuals. As John Mirk explains, the priest, when faced with a reluctant female parishioner, should hint at his own transgressions, saying, "Parauentur I haue done þe same, / And fulhelt [quite probably] myche more, / ȝef þow knew all my sore."[39] The important difference, of course, is the word, "if" (ȝef). While Mirk's model priest proposes an impossible condition, implying that he has sinned but never intending to reveal those secret transgressions, the Wedo promises to divulge all her "privetee." Although she serves as shrift-mother for the two younger women, the Wedo makes clear that her appropriation of confession, like that of the *Shipman's Tale,* is reciprocal.

For the second wife, this reciprocity is a necessary but not sufficient condition to induce shrift. Before she will "bewrie" her "conseil," she requires a gossip's promise: "I protest, the treuth gif I schaw, / That of ȝour toungis ȝe be traist" (I protest, that if I show the truth, that you two will be trusty of your tongues) (158–59). The wife's protestation illustrates the function of that promise for the confessee: in order for her to "schaw" her "treuth," that is, reveal her "privetee," she must be assured that her confession will remain secret. Here, as in the *Shipman's Tale,* the women's gossip requires its own confessional seal, one that appears to be more reassuring than its orthodox rival. The reciprocation of the gossip's promise has a transformative effect on the second wife: "With that sprang up hir spreit be a span hechar. / To speik, quod scho, I sall nought spar; there is no spy neir" (with that her spirit sprang up a span higher, to speak, she said, I will not spare, there is no spy near) (160–61). The women's conversational community, sealed by an oath of secrecy, creates a space in which the second wife can speak as she has previously been unable, for fear that her speech might be

---

38. For a discussion of the role of interrogation during confession, see Tentler, *Sin and Confession,* 82–94. Mirk's *Instructions for Parish Priests* provides a contemporary depiction of this practice, lines 805–1398.

39. *Instructions for Parish Priests,* lines 794–96.

reported.[40] Like the first wife, the second speaker does not intend to give a humble confession. Quite the opposite, her once-abject spirit has risen much higher at the prospect of speaking and sparing nothing. Hers is not, however, simply a carnivalesque or a parodic model of confession in which all things are precisely as they should not be, in which transgressive speech is an end in itself.[41] Rather what Dunbar depicts, through the speech of this second wife, is the function of these women's confessional practice, illustrating its "spiritual" and medicinal value.[42]

Much like its orthodox counterpart, wifely shrift cures the afflictions of the soul.[43] Describing the process of confession, the second wife speaks in graphic physiological detail of venting spleen and purging disease:

> I sall a ragment reveil fra rute of my hert,
> A roust that is sa rankild quhill risis my stomok;
> Now sall the byle all out brist that beild has so lang.
> For it to beir one my breist wes berdin our hevy;
> I sall the venome devoid with a vent large
> And me assuage of the swalme that suellit was gret
> (162–67)

> [I shall reveal a long discourse from the root of my heart
> A rancor that is thus festered while my stomach turns in disgust;
> Now shall all the bile burst out that so long has suppurated;
> For to bear it on my breast was an over heavy burden;
> I shall discharge the venom with a large gust
> And alleviate the swelling that swelled so great.]

40. Her assertion that "there is no spy neir" reminds us both that the spying narrator has outwitted these three women and that we in the audience are positioned alongside that narrator as spies, eavesdropping and passing judgment on the women's conversation. See Domna C. Stanton's compelling discussion of male narrators who spy on women at a lying-in: "Recuperating Women and the Man Behind the Screen," *Sexuality and Gender in Early Modern Europe, Institutions, Texts, Images*, ed. James Grantham Turner (Cambridge: Cambridge University Press, 1993), 247–65, esp. 252–53.

41. For arguments of this type, see Bitterling, *"The Tretis"*; and Deanna Delmar Evans, "Dunbar's *Tretis:* The Seven Deadly Sins in Carnivalesque Disguise," *Neophilologus* 73, no. 1 (1989): 130–41, esp. 134–35.

42. I am not of course arguing that Dunbar is sympathetic to the complaints of these women, but rather that in his construction of the second wife's response, he shows precisely how wifely confession might serve its participants.

43. As Bitterling argues, "The medicinal aspect of confession was insisted upon by all authors discussing the necessity of shrift." *"The Tretis,"* 346.

Although her rhetorical excess might appear to tend toward transgressive flyting, the second wife's talk of her swollen boils and suppurating wounds resonates with the language of penitential manuals, which depict sin as a wound desperately in need of confession's healing balm. As the preacher of *Jacob's Well* explains to his parishioners, the "conscyens nedyth to be pourgyd, wyth a drawyng salue of clene schryfte" lest the "wounde of dedly synne rotyth & festryth" in the soul.[44] In the *Tretis*, confession purges the festering wounds of the second wife's spirit. However, there is no threefold model of contrition, confession, and penance in this wifely appropriation of shrift. The cure for a diseased soul is quite simply to speak. Revealing the "ragment [long discourse]" of her marital grievances, the second wife releases her "venome," "byle," and spleen through equally venomous language. As David Parkinson claims, "Abusive language now has recreative, even medicinal virtues."[45] Just as the gossip's promise lifts the prohibition on unrestrained speech, so it releases the "our hevy" burden under which the second wife has suffered. The weight of sin described in penitential manuals becomes, in this wifely appropriation, the "berdin" of conversational censorship, from which this wife is released through the process of shrift. The transgressive speech incited by the Wedo and practiced by the first wife is here brought to fruition, as the second wife demonstrates the recuperative value of this unorthodox confessional practice.

While the second wife illustrates the curative function that wifely shrift performs for the confessee, the Wedo, playing her role as shrift-mother, explores its pastoral use. She recognizes that confession constitutes one of the Church's most important sites of instruction and social control and intends to exploit fully its educative potential, framing her shrift as a sermon:[46]

> God my spreit now inspir and my speche quykkin
> And send me sentence to say substantious and noble,
> Sa that my preching may pers ʒour perverst hertis
> And mak yow mekar to men in maneris and conditiounis
>
> (247–50)

44. *Jacob's Well*, 179/2 and 179/4.

45. David Parkinson, "Prescriptions for Laughter in Some Middle Scots Poems," *Selected Essays on Scottish Language and Literature*, ed. Steven R. McKenna (Lewiston, N.Y.: Edwin Mellen Press, 1992), 27–39, 30.

46. "Second only in importance to the pulpit as a place of instruction was the confessional." Patterson, "'Parson's Tale,'" 336. Tentler outlines the power of private auricular confession to exert social control in *Sin and Confession*, esp. 51–53.

[God inspire now my spirit and quicken my speech
And send me wisdom to speak substantively and nobly,
So that my preaching may pierce your perverse hearts
And make you meeker to men in manners and conditions.]

Beginning with an invocation and claiming the ability to pierce the perverse hearts of her congregation, the Wedo's "preaching" sounds alarmingly like an official sermon.[47] It is as if, despite the riotous laughter shared by these three women and their assurances of mutual self-revelation, the Wedo has used her co-optation of confession as a trap, tricking the two wives into revealing their "perverst hertis" so that she may correct them according to proper doctrine. That is, the Wedo's tactics at first appear to be modeled on those of orthodox priests, like Jean Gerson, who employ a variety of interrogational stratagems to coax confessions out of reluctant speakers.[48] But the Wedo's is to be a wifely sermon, confessional in its mode, in which she will "show" her sisters in shrift both how she has been a "schrew" (251) and, more importantly, how she has been able to get away with it.[49] Deviating from the traditional pastoral syllabus of Pater Noster, Ave, and Creed, the subject of the Wedo's "lesson" (257) is doubleness:

Be constant in ȝour governance and counterfeit gud manneris
Thought ȝe be kene, inconstant and cruell of mynd;
Thought ȝe as tygris be terne, be tretable in luf
And be as turtoris in your talk thought ȝe haif talis brukill;
Be dragonis baith and dowis ay in double forme
(259–63)

47. Bitterling argues that "invocations of God and prayers to the Holy Ghost" are "especially common in sermons, Saint's legends, and instructions for confession." "*The Tretis,*" 344.

48. See Tentler's discussion of interrogational practice, including his detailed account of some of Gerson's more egregious strategies. *Sin and Confession,* 82–95, esp. 91–92. Such confessional machinations have led scholars to interpret confessional practice as a kind of game in which the sinner's subterfuge is pitted against the priest's resourcefulness. See Lochrie, *Covert Operations,* 33–38.

49. The Wife of Bath's lessons about marital manipulation echo in the Wedo's sermon, as does the parodic preaching depicted in *Gilote et Johane,* an early fourteenth-century Anglo-Norman interlude recently edited by Carter Revard, "The Wife of Bath's Grandmother: Or How Gilote Showed Her Friend Johane That the Wages of Sin Is Worldly Pleasure, and How Both Then Preached This Gospel Throughout England and Ireland," *Chaucer Review* 39, no. 2 (2004): 117–36. See also my discussion of the gossips' unorthodox pastoral practices in Chapter 4, below.

[Be constant in your behavior and counterfeit good manners
Though you be savage, inconstant, and cruel of mind;
Though you be fierce as tigers, be maleable in love
And be as turtledoves in your talk though you have brittle tails;
Be both dragons and doves always in double form.]

Teaching her companions how to counterfeit "gud manneris," masking a cruel and inconstant heart with sweet words, the Wedo draws the text of her confession-sermon from antifeminist discourse. Although there is nothing surprising about the fact that the Wedo preaches and embodies antifeminist commonplaces about women's inconstancy, her "lesson" on doubleness acquires a new and problematic resonance in this confessional context. As the Wedo told her companions earlier in their conversation, speaking the truth, "dissymyland no word" (157), is a necessary condition of shrift—both wifely and patristic. Proper confession should "be symple & noʒt double in thynkyng oon, and tellyng an-oþer."[50] Moreover, as late medieval penitential manuals make clear, one of the goals of shrift is to make heart and tongue "acorde in one."[51] Enjoining a division between "mynd" and "talk," the Wedo's lesson is absolutely antithetical to confessional practice. She teaches the wives how to sin with their tongues through the very institutional practice designed to control and contain verbal transgression.[52]

The theme of doubleness runs throughout the Wedo's sermon-confession as she instructs the young wives in the arts of marital manipulation, showing them how she has avoided the "ruffill of [her] renoune and rumour of pepill" (destruction of her reputation and the rumor of the people) (332). Among lessons on cuckolding husbands without consequence, withholding the conjugal debt until one receives satisfactory remuneration, and appropriating the heir's inheritance for oneself, the Wedo teaches her charges the value of trustworthy female companions. Describing how she made her second husband do women's work, she reveals that she enlisted her close female friends as witnesses to her marital mastery, further humiliating her henpecked spouse: "Than said I to my cummaris in counsall about: / Se how I cabeld ʒone cout with kene brydill" (then I said to my council of

---

50. *Jacob's Well,* 181/9–10.
51. Ibid., 181/14.
52. The Sins of the Tongue were a popular topic for penitential manuals and constituted a common subject for examination and instruction during confession. See also Craun, *Lies, Slander, and Obscenity,* 113–56.

gossips, see how I secured that colt with a sharp bridle) (353–54). Her "cummaris in counsall" are invited to "se" how she has tamed her husband; and it is only at their witnessing that her triumph is complete. Her gossips are privy to the intimate details of her marriage and only they have that privilege—if anyone outside this "counsall" were to witness her shrewish antics, she would be labeled, and perhaps even punished, as a scold.[53] That is, while enjoining doubleness everywhere else, the Wedo declares that in confessional gossip with one's "cummaris," heart and tongue can accord together.

Recognizing the conventions of the confessional, the Wedo pretends to maintain her "professional" distance by addressing the two wives as her spiritual children. She presents the learning of her lessons as a kind of rite of passage though which her charges will make the transition from young girls to wise women—"Ladyis, leir thir lessonis and be no lassis fundin" (Ladies, learn these lessons so that you are not taken for young girls) (503). Indeed, by insuring that her congregation shares a common set of knowledge, the Wedo's confessional instruction ushers these wives into a community of the faithful, not the orthodox community forged by officially sanctioned shrift but the community of "cummaris." It is not coincidental that at the conclusion of the Wedo's sermon, when the women pass around the wine as they have done after each confession, the narrator claims that they "carpit full cummerlik" (chattered like gossips) (510). Revealing their "hertis," sharing the privy details of their marriages, and witnessing the Wedo's manipulative triumphs, these women have become "cummaris in counsall" through their confessional gossip.[54]

While the wife of the *Shipman's Tale* employs her adaptation of confession as means to attain conversational intimacy, the Wedo appropriates confession *as confession,* claiming for her wifely co-optation all the powers and functions of authorized shrift. The *Shipman's Tale* focuses on language and

---

53. For a discussion of the punishments to which scolds were condemned, see Bardsley, "Sin, Speech, and Scolding"; and Lynda E. Boose, "Scolding Brides and Bridling Scolds: Taming the Woman's Unruly Member," *Shakespeare Quarterly* 42, no. 2 (1991): 179–213. For a detailed discussion of one specific punishment, the "cucking-stool," see John W. Spargo, *Juridical Folklore in England Illustrated by the Cucking-Stool* (Durham: Duke University Press, 1944).

54. Just as the dual significations of "biwreye" point to the connections between the women's secret sharing and their betrayals, so the multiple significations of "conseil" indicate the various activities in which these "cummaris" engage. "Counseil" delineates the secrets they share, the discussions they have, the advice they give, and the meetings they convene. *Middle English Dictionary,* s.v. "counseil," 1, 2, 5, 8.

its power to construct relationships, using confessional gossip to reveal the affinity between the exchange of secrets and more intimate exchange. Dunbar's *Tretis*, however, as it ruminates over the transgressive speech of the three women, points to a more worrying affinity between the gossips' confessional conversations and officially sanctioned shrift. Through the Wedo's appropriations, the "sacred seal" of confession begins to resemble the gossip's promise, and shrift's spiritual medicine looks a lot like gossip's "healing talk."[55] Knowing the "herte and privetee" of her companions better than the "parisshe preest," the Wedo, by co-opting confessional practice, not only usurps the office of the parish priest but threatens to undermine the institutional power of confession itself.

The Wedo's exploitation of confession licenses her appropriation of other pastoral practices. In addition to sermon, she co-opts the saint's life, identifying the narrative of her marital exploits as a "legeand of [her] lif" (504). Dunbar, here, makes explicit what was only suggested in the *Shipman's Tale*, transforming the brief narrative of the merchant's wife into the Wedo's 230-line sermon-confession. While the Wedo's proclamation, like that of her predecessor, is certainly a case of what Strohm terms "flagrant self-dramatization," it is also something more.[56] In this text so preoccupied with the dynamics of confession in which the Wedo seizes the powers of pulpit, the term "legeand" cannot help but resonate more problematically than mere self-dramatization might suggest. Indeed, the Wedo indicates what is at stake in her appropriation of "legeand," announcing her contestation with Latin textual culture: "This is the legeand of my lif, thought Latyne it be nane" (504). That is, the Wedo is not just exaggerating the woes of her marriage, she is proclaiming (albeit comically) her right to remake pastoral and textual practice, to rewrite the idea of legend as she has remade confession.

Just as the Wedo uses her co-opted shrift to conflate a number of pastoral practices, so Dunbar exploits confessional gossip to combine a range of literary traditions. Scholars have long struggled to solve the puzzle of the *Tretis*'s literary provenance. Suggesting Dunbar's possible sources, critics have seen in the *Tretis* the influence of the *Wife of Bath's Prologue*, Lydgate's *Pain and*

---

55. Patricia Spacks's suggestive description acquires a penitential resonance in the late medieval period. Spacks, *Gossip*, 57.

56. Paul Strohm, "*Passioun, Lyf, Miracle, Legende*: Some Generic Terms in Middle English Hagiographical Narrative, Part II," *Chaucer Review* 10, no. 2 (1975): 154–71, 163.

Sorrow of Evil Marriage, and the *Parlement of Thre Ages.*[57] The text's genre has proven to be as elusive as its source. The *Tretis* draws on an array of literary traditions: antifeminist writings, the literature of courtly love, alliterative poetry, the *chanson d'aventure,* the "gossips' songs" or "alewife poems," and the *chanson de mal mariée.*[58] Seeking an explanation for the poem's at times conflicting attributes, scholars have attempted to identify a single genre that would account for its multiple features. Roy Pearcy offers the most convincing of these readings. Refuting earlier claims that the *Tretis* is a *chanson de mal mariée,* he argues that Dunbar models his text on a previously unidentified medieval subgenre, the *jugement.*[59] But even Pearcy's suggestive category cannot fully account for the all the features that coalesce in this poem. The *Tretis* is a generic amalgam, a deliberate mixture of diverse literary conventions. It is a "gossips' song" and a *jugement,* a *chanson de mal mariée,* and an alliterative debate. It combines antifeminist polemic and courtly *blazon,* pastoral practice and vulgar flyting. And this conflation, I would argue, is precisely the point.

By using confessional gossip to structure his poem, Dunbar provides his characters with a framework that will allow for the greatest rhetorical freedom, not in order to provide a realistic picture of what women talk about when they are alone, but so that he can experiment with forms of speaking. Gossip's transforming talk in this confessional context allows both the characters and their poet to combine and reinvent discursive conventions. The conversational catharsis licensed by the women's confessional appropriations has less to do with the content of the women's talk than with its form,

57. The influence of the Wife of Bath has been well attested. See James Kinsley, "*The Tretis of the Tua Mariit Wemen and the Wedo,*" *Medium Ævum* 23, no. 1 (1954): 31–35; Derek Pearsall, *Old and Middle English Poetry* (London: Routledge and Kegan Paul, 1977), 278; and Francis Lee Utley, *The Crooked Rib: An Analytical Index to the Argument about Women in English and Scots Literature to the End of the Year 1568* (Columbus: Ohio State University Press, 1944), 282–83. For Dunbar's indebtedness to Lydgate, see Kinsley, *The Poems of William Dunbar,* 264–65. Thorlac Turville-Petre has argued that the *Parlement* provides the structural precedent for the *Tretis.* Turville-Petre, *The Alliterative Revival* (Cambridge: D. S. Brewer, 1977), 118–21. For a history of the debate over Dunbar's sources, see Bitterling, "*The Tretis,*" esp. 337–40.

58. Kinsley, *Poems of William Dunbar,* 260–61; Bitterling, "*The Tretis,*" esp. 337–40; Utley, *Crooked Rib,* 282–83; Turville-Petre, *Alliterative Revival,* 118–21.

59. Roy J. Pearcy, "The Genre of William Dunbar's *Tretis of the Tua Mariit Wemen and the Wedo,*" *Speculum* 55, no. 1 (1980): 58–74. After demonstrating how little the poem has in common with the *chanson,* Pearcy's thorough and suggestive essay details the features that the *Tretis* shares with other *jugements:* three female protagonists, belonging to the upper bourgeoisie or lower aristocracy, who in a courtly setting participate in a narrative "game" in which all three women offer their own contribution to be judged by a third party (61–62).

for the secrets shared by these women, like the "privetee" disclosed by the wife of the *Shipman's Tale,* are the overly familiar refrains of antifeminist discourse. The surprise of the poem inheres not in the fact that the women are unsatisfied with their husbands' sexual prowess or that they scheme to get marital sovereignty, but rather in that fact that their speech defies expectations. My point is not that the *Tretis* is a narrative enactment of the Wedo's lesson on doubleness, in which courtly beauties tell sordid tales.[60] Rather, I want to suggest that Dunbar's poem is an exploration of the rhetorical possibilities created when generic conventions collide: when the pastoral meets the venomous and the alehouse comes into the courtly garden. Drawing on idle talk's powers of transformation, Dunbar uses confessional gossip to experiment with generic conventions about female speech. Like Dunbar's *Tretis,* the texts I discuss in the next chapter defy expectations about women's speech. But where Dunbar frames the speech of his characters in unconventional ways, these "gossips' songs" highlight the unorthodox content of gossips' idle talk, as they "carpit full cummerlik with cop going round" (510).

---

60. For arguments of this type, see Bitterling, "*The Tretis,*" and Evans, "Dunbar's *Tretis.*"

THE GOSPEL ACCORDING TO GOSSIPS, OR

HOW GOSSIP GOT ITS NAME

In the middle of the Chester play of the *Deluge,* Noah's industrious wife is suddenly transformed into a "good gossip."[1] Disobeying her husband's commands, Mrs. Noah refuses to board the ark because she is unwilling to leave her drinking companions behind: "But I have my gossips everyechone, / one foote further I will not gone" (201–2). Demonstrating a surprisingly sympathetic commitment to her female community, she justifies her insubordination by asserting the mutual support that gossips owe one another: because her gossips have loved her well, she will not allow them to drown while she has the means to save them. This female alliance supersedes her matrimonial bonds, for as she explains to Noah, unless he lets her friends aboard he can row off and get himself a new wife. In fact, her responsibilities as a gossip trump all others. As her son invokes her obligations to both family and faith, Mrs. Noah chooses instead to perform her duties as a gossip, sharing strong wine and singing a "good gossippes songe." So compelling are ties of friendship that she will not sever them voluntarily: only when she is dragged onto the ark by one of her sons does she abandon her drinking companions.[2]

1. R. M. Lumiansky and David Mills, eds., *The Chester Mystery Cycle,* EETS s.s. 3 (London: Oxford University Press, 1974), 42–56, line 228.
2. The surprising nature of Mrs. Noah's defiance here is all the more remarkable when we compare this scene to its companion in the Towneley cycle. There, *uxor* Noah is motivated by an

Privileging female community over secular and religious authority, the Chester Mrs. Noah has become for critics the standard bearer of medieval gossips.[3] Indeed, she stands as a literary homage to tippling female characters, such as the infamous Elinor Rumming, for her transformation is not part of the original medieval play-text but rather is a sixteenth-century interpolation[4]—a set piece echoing the tropes of a popular late medieval subgenre, the "gossips' song" or "alewife poem."[5] Mrs. Noah and her gossips resonate with the idle and drunken women of these texts, but do so in a way that suggests both the appealing strength of these female communities and the threat such communities might pose to patriarchal authority. Consequently, scholars have used the "good gossips" of the Chester play to recu-

---

obstinate disposition: she refuses to board the ark because she wants to persist in her spinning. Her family's tactics of persuasion are pragmatic rather than ideological. Instead of invoking familial obligation, her daughters-in-law appeal to her instinct for self-preservation. More striking still, Towneley's *uxor* Noah boards the ark willingly as soon as the waters reach an uncomfortable level. David Bevington, ed., *Medieval Drama* (Boston: Houghton Mifflin, 1975), 290–307.

3. Linda Woodbridge suggests that Mrs. Noah initiates the "drunken gossips tradition" that figures so prominently in antifeminist satires of the early seventeenth century. *Women and the English Renaissance: Literature and the Nature of Womankind, 1540–1620* (Urbana: University of Illinois Press, 1984), 224–43, 234. See also Gail McMurray Gibson, "Scene and Obscene: Seeing and Performing Late Medieval Childbirth," *Journal of Medieval and Early Modern Studies* 29, no. 1 (1999): 7–24, esp. 14–15; Mary Wack, "Women, Work, and Plays in an English Medieval Town," in *Maids and Mistresses, Cousins and Queens: Women's Alliances in Early Modern England*, ed. Susan Frye and Karen Robertson (Oxford: Oxford University Press, 1999), 33–51; and Patricia Anne Anderson, "Gossips, Ale-wives, Midwives, and Witches," Ph.D. diss., SUNY Buffalo, 1992, esp. 78–80.

4. Oscar L. Brownstein, "Revision in the 'Deluge' of the Chester Cycle," *Speech Monographs* 36, no. 1 (1969): 55–65; and Lawrence M. Clopper, "The History and Development of the Chester Cycle," *Modern Philology* 75, no. 3 (1978): 219–46. Clopper has demonstrated that the Chester cycle underwent two major revisions over the course of the sixteenth century: the first during the period 1505–32, when the Old Testament and Nativity sequences were both expanded and revised; the second in the decade leading up to the final performance in 1575. It is likely that the revisions to the Noah play occurred during the first period of revision.

5. Quite popular at the time of the Chester revisions, the "alewife group" or "gossips' songs" include several late fifteenth-century poems, "John Crophill's Ale-pots," *A Talk of Ten Wives on the Husbands' Ware*, and the English carol known as the *Good Gossips*, as well as a number of early sixteenth-century texts: the *Ballad of Kynd Kittok* (c. 1508), Skelton's the *Tunning of Elinor Rumming* (c. 1521), *Cryste crosse me spede* (c. 1534), Dunbar's *Tway Cummeris* (c. 1503–7), and the *Tretis of the Twa Mariit Wemen and the Wedo* (c. 1508). For a survey of the genre, see Francis Lee Utley, *The Crooked Rib*, entries 79, 107, 172, 193, 195, 251, 277, 336; Rossell Hope Robbins, "Poems Dealing with Contemporary Conditions," in *A Manual of the Writings in Middle English*, ed. A. E. Hartung and J. B. Severs (New Haven: Yale University Press, 1975), 5:1463–65; and Anderson, "Gossips, Ale-wives, Midwives, and Witches," 72–112. On the genre's Chester associations, see Greene, ed., *Early English Carols*, 466–68; and Wack, "Women, Work, and Plays," 38.

perate from antifeminist stereotype both the gossips' songs and the historical women on whom they reflect.

Given that vivid depictions of drinking women are a universal feature of the gossips' song, it is hardly surprising that critics have considered the medieval tavern the key to explicating these poems. Much recent historical and literary scholarship has focused on the women who frequented and ran the English alehouses.[6] As Judith Bennett has argued, brewing was the most common occupation for late medieval women. But while brewing provided supplemental income, it also inspired public scorn: civic and religious authorities alike condemned English alewives for inciting as well as engaging in disreputable behavior. Looking through this socioeconomic lens, scholars have interpreted the good gossips as both a source and a symptom of the alewives' disrepute.[7] Although this rich work has recovered much about the lives of historical women and has offered a useful context through which to consider the gossips, it has also produced a one-dimensional picture of them. In a sense, this approach has taken the good gossips of the English carol at their word, "Whatsoever any man thynk, / We com for nowght but for good drynk," for even though critics have explored the gossips' camaraderie and conversation, their analysis has been circumscribed by tavern conviviality.[8]

By focusing solely on alewives, scholars have overlooked the gossip in the gossips' songs. That is, they have largely ignored both the gossip's legitimate role in late medieval society and her connection to the idle talk that eventually takes her name. As we have seen, the term "gossip" originally signifies a state of spiritual kinship, denoting either the relationship between godparent and godchild or the coparental bond forged between parent and godparent.

6. Judith M. Bennett, "Misogyny, Popular Culture, and Women's Work," *History Workshop Journal* 31 (1991): 166–88, "The Village Ale-Wife: Women and Brewing in Fourteenth-Century England," in *Women and Work in Pre-Industrial England*, ed. Barbara Hannawalt (Bloomington: Indiana University Press, 1986), 20–38, and *Ale, Beer, and Brewsters in England: Women's Work in a Changing World, 1300–1600* (New York: Oxford University Press, 1996); Wack, "Women, Work and Plays"; and Anderson, "Gossips, Ale-wives, Midwives, and Witches."

7. Bennett, "Misogyny, Popular Culture, and Women's Work" and *Ale, Beer, and Brewsters*, esp. 122–44; Wack, "Women, Work, and Plays," esp. 38; and Anderson, "Gossips, Ale-wives, Midwives, and Witches." For a critique of this methodology, see Ralph Hanna III, "Brewing Trouble: On Literature and History—and Alewives," in *Bodies and Disciplines: Intersections of Literature and History in Fifteenth-century England*, ed. Barbara A. Hanawalt and David Wallace (Minneapolis: University of Minnesota Press, 1996), 1–18.

8. The *Good Gossips* in *Early English Carols*, ed. Greene, 251, no. 419 Aa, stanza 21. A notable exception is Gibson, who compares Mrs. Noah's drowned and therefore silenced gossips to the empowering space of the lying-in. "Scene and Obscene," 14–15.

While critics have acknowledged this connection, in their analysis they rarely go beyond paying etymological lip service. Yet as I will argue throughout this chapter, the literary phenomenon of the gossips can only be fully understood through the lens of baptismal sponsorship. Gossips, both historical and literary, exist at the intersection between the social and the pastoral, a space of teaching and conversation, feasting and alliance, drinking and support. The "good gossips" reveal anxieties about the consequences of this orthodox practice—the power of the alliances that are forged; the danger of the pastoral instruction that is required. At the same time, literary representations of the gossips provide a remedy, a mechanism for controlling both these networks and their conversations, for it is through these texts that idle talk becomes not only women's work but also "gossip."

In order to explore what is at stake in the figure of the gossip, I examine two texts published by Wynkyn de Worde at the height of the good gossips' popularity: the *Fyftene Joyes of Maryage* (1507, 1509) and the *Gospelles of Dystaues* (c. 1510).[9] These two understudied texts are not themselves part of the "alewife group."[10] Rather, like the Chester play of the *Deluge*, they interpolate the English gossips into their narratives. As such, they provide rare and valuable evidence of the reception, interpretation, and use of the gossips as a literary and historical phenomenon. Both the *Gospelles* and the *Fyftene Joyes* are Middle English translations of anonymous French antifeminist narratives: *Les Evangiles des quenouilles* (c. 1466–74) and *Les Quinze Joyes de Mariage* (c. 1400).[11] Neither French text is primarily concerned with the gossips, as either drinking companions or spiritual kin: the *Evangiles* offers a humorous compendium of old wives' tales compiled by a women's spinning circle over a series of winter evenings; the *Quinze Joyes* is a collection

9. Neither text has been the subject of a modern edition; however, Diane Bornstein's *Distaves and Dames: Renaissance Treatises for and about Women* (New York: Scholars' Facsimiles and Reprints, 1978) reproduces de Worde's edition of the *Gospelles* in facsimile. The *Fyfteen Joyes* (STC 15257.5 and 15258) survives in three copies: the Bodleian has a fragment of the 1507 edition (fols. C4–C5); the Folger has an incomplete copy of the 1509 edition, which is lacking the final two joys; and the Pierpont Morgan has a complete copy. The *Gospelles* (STC 12091) survives in a complete copy in the Huntington Library (shelfmark 13067) as well as in two fragments: British Library, Harley 5919/35 (fol. D3), and Bodleian, Douce fragment, e.15 (fols. A3–A5).

10. Despite the fact that both Utley and Robbins assign the *Gospelles* to the alewife group, the text shares very few features with other texts from the genre: it is not written in verse, and with the exception of a short scene that I discuss in detail below, the women do not feast or drink nor are they referred to as gossips.

11. On the dating of the *Evangiles*, see the *Evangiles des quenouilles*, ed. Madeleine Jeay (Montreal: University of Montreal Press, 1985), 35; on the dating of the *Quinze Joyes*, see *Les Quinze Joyes de Mariage*, ed. Joan Crow (Oxford: Blackwell, 1969), xvi–xix.

of comical vignettes depicting the female arts of marital manipulation and sexual transgression. Although these French narratives do depict female characters who convene to share wine and conversation, de Worde's translators transform these women into English gossips in all their social, pastoral, and discursive complexity. What is more, these translators emphasize the word "gossip" as much as the women: one introduces the verb, "to gossip," some eighty years before the *Oxford English Dictionary*'s earliest recorded use; the other abandons his conservative translation practices to hurl a new English insult, defaming a character as a "ryght gode gossip."

Although there is very little evidence attesting to the reception history of the *Gospelles* and the *Fyftene Joyes*, their appearance under de Worde's imprint at precisely this moment helps to contextualize them within the early sixteenth-century literary marketplace.[12] Both the popularity and the subject matter of the *Evangiles* and the *Quinze Joyes* made them a perfect fit for de Worde's printshop. Their combined total of ten French imprints between 1480 and 1507 would no doubt have made them incredibly attractive as potentially profitable ventures; more important, their antifeminism complemented other texts in de Worde's catalogue, thereby appealing to his

---

12. Unlike some of de Worde's other editions, we have no indication of who may have commissioned these texts: the *Fyftene Joyes* offers no hint of patronage; the prologue to the *Gospelles* declares only that the text was translated "at the request of some my welbeloued" (y2r). Moreover, the extant copies of the two texts provide little evidence of late medieval ownership or reception. The Folger Library's copy of the *Fyftene Joyes* does, however, offer some suggestive hints about early readership. On the title page, Mr. Radulphus Kinge declares his ownership of the text, "Radulphus Kinge me comparavit," in an early to mid-sixteenth-century hand that suggests Kinge was among the book's earliest owners. Unfortunately, we know nothing further about Mr. Kinge beyond his name and what look to be his marginal comments later in the text. This early reader seems to have been particularly interested in the gossips; his only comment— "commendare solent quod consuetudo" (they are accustomed to commending whatever is the custom)—appears in the margin when the first of the gossips is introduced into the narrative as the wife's informant and her partner in crime (B4r). I am deeply indebted to Betsy Walsh and Laetita Yeandle at the Folger Library for their help in identifying and dating Mr. Kinge's hand. Rather more is known about the provenance and reception of the two French sources. The Burgundian court has been identified as the site for the composition and original audience of the *Evangiles*. See *Evangiles*, ed. Jeay, 32–38, and "Le Travail du récit à la cour de Bourgogne: Les *Evangiles des quenouilles*, *Les Cent nouvelles nouvelles* et *Saintré*," In "A l'heure encore de mon escrire": *Aspects de la littérature de Bourgogne sous Philippe le Bon et Charles le Téméraire*, ed. Claude Thiry *Les Lettres Romanes* (1997, hors série), 71–86. On the later popularity of the *Evangiles*, see Jeay, "La popularité des 'Evangiles des quenouilles': un paradoxe révélateur," *Renaissance et Réforme* 18 (1982): 166–82; and Anne Paupert, *Les Fileuses et le clerc: une étude des Evangiles des quenouilles* (Paris: Champion-Slatkine, 1990), esp. 249–51. For a summary of the critical debate surrounding the early circulation of the *Quinze Joyes*, see *Quinze Joyes de Mariage*, ed. Crow, esp. ix–xx.

established clientele. As Julia Boffey has demonstrated, de Worde "actively sought" and promoted antifeminist texts as a particular specialty of his "list."[13] Like the decision to publish translations of these French narratives, the interpolation of the English gossips into them was both economically and culturally savvy. In addition to collecting antifeminist works more generally, de Worde had effectively cornered the market on the gossips' song: all known English editions of works from the alewife group appeared under his imprint.[14] De Worde's publication of the *Gospelles* and the *Fyftene Joyes* thus capitalized upon the latest literary trend, paying homage to the gossips' songs he so aggressively pursued. The interpolation of the gossips into these texts, however, does more than simply attest to their popularity. By introducing these English characters and their practices into their French exemplars, de Worde's translators demonstrate how the figure of the gossip both resonated and was deployed in late medieval England.

My discussion begins with an investigation of the practice of baptismal sponsorship in late medieval England. As I argue throughout this first section, the legitimate features and obligations of this orthodox practice become a source of critique both for historical godparents and for the literary gossips who take their name. From the baptismal font and the gossips' feast, I turn to the *Fyftene Joyes of Maryage*, the poem that gives the fullest depiction of a late medieval gossip in all her drinking, feasting, sponsoring, and chattering splendor. Emphasizing the pastoral and social obligations of a gossip, this text explores the relationship between spiritual kinship, pastoral instruction, and idle talk. Although the text suggests the subversive potential of the gossips' meeting, it ultimately undermines this possibility, as the women's words are silenced by the passing of the gossips' cup. The chapter concludes with the *Gospelles of Dystaues* and its community of neighbors who gather together to write the gospel according to women. Like the *Fyftene Joyes*, the *Gospelles* is structured by an antifeminist joke, as the narrator

---

13. Julia Boffey, "Wynkyn de Worde and Misogyny in Print," in *Chaucer in Perspective: Middle English Essays in Honor of Norman Blake*, ed. Geoffrey Lester (Sheffield: Sheffield Academic Press, 1999), 236–51, 244.

14. Although most of the gossips' songs circulated only in manuscript, de Worde printed at least two: a *lyteel propre iest. Called cryste crosse me spede a.b.c How ye good gosyps made a royall feest* (STC 14546.5) and the *Tunning of Elinor Rumming* (STC 22611.5). Joseph Ames reproduces the surviving text of *Criste cross me spede* in *Typographical Antiquities*, vol. 2 (London: William Miller, 1812), 367–69. The location of the 1508 imprint of Dunbar's *Tretis* (STC 7350) is unknown; both Scotland and Rouen have been suggested as possibilities. See *Poems of William Dunbar*, xiii–xiv.

invites readers to see the great disparity between the Gospels and these old wives' tales. Yet as the text progresses, the joke falters, and the women's supposedly idle talk becomes no laughing matter. In fact, it is not until the women are safely transformed into gossips that the narrator is able to laugh at his own joke.

Gossips and Their Feasts

In late medieval England, women who accepted the role of "gossip" were bound by spiritual kinship to both the mother and her newborn child, undertaking a range of social and religious obligations.[15] As godmothers, they participated in the public ceremony of baptism, carrying the newborn to the church, receiving her from the baptismal font, and providing her name.[16] As the mother's spiritual kin, they supported her through labor, remained with her during the lying-in, and accompanied her to church for her purification, or churching—the ceremony through which the mother was cleansed of the impurities of childbirth and reintegrated into the community of the faith-

15. Although rather less is known about the practice of spiritual kinship in late medieval England than in other areas typically discussed by anthropologists, historians have demonstrated from the surviving evidence that baptismal sponsorship played a significant role in early English society. For the most thorough survey of the development of baptismal sponsorship as well as a review of the scholarship, see Joseph H. Lynch, *Godparents and Kinship in Early Medieval Europe* (Princeton: Princeton University Press, 1986), esp. 13–80. See also Lynch, "*Spiritale Vinculum*: The Vocabulary of Spiritual Kinship in Early Medieval Europe," in *Religion, Culture, and Society in the Early Middle Ages*, ed. Thomas F. X. Nobel and John J. Contreni (Kalamazoo: Medieval Institute Publications, 1987), 181–204; John Bossy, "Blood and Baptism: Kinship, Community and Christianity in Western Europe from the Fourteenth to the Seventeenth Centuries," *Sanctity and Secularity: The Church and the World*, ed. Derek Baker (Oxford: Clarendon, 1973), 129–43, and "The Counter-Reformation and the People of Catholic Europe," *Past and Present* 47 (1970): 51–70; and Louis Haas, "Social Connections Between Parents and Godparents in Late Medieval Yorkshire," *Medieval Prosopography* 10 (1989): 1–21, and "Baptism and Spiritual Kinship in the North of England, 1250–1450," master's thesis, Ohio State University, 1982.

16. Although midwives sometimes carried the child to church, this duty often fell to the gossip. Barbara Hanawalt, *Growing up in Medieval London: The Experience of Childhood in History* (New York: Oxford University Press, 1993), 45. In England, it was common practice for one of the godparents to give his or her name to the child, and godparents were often selected because of their names. So expected was this tradition that neighbors and family members became irate when their name was not used. Philip Niles, "Baptism and the Naming of Children in Late Medieval England," *Medieval Prosopography* 3 (1982): 95–107; Michael Bennett, "Spiritual Kinship and the Baptismal Name in Traditional Society," in *Principalities, Powers, and Estates: Studies in Medieval and Early Modern Government and Society*, ed. L. O. Frappell (Adelaide: Adelaide University Union Press, 1979), 1–13; and Haas, "Social Connections" and "Baptism and Spiritual Kinship."

ful.[17] The gossips' duties, however, were not limited to the ceremonies of childbirth. As Wit proclaims in *Piers Plowman*, "moore bilongeth to the litel barn er he the lawe knowe / Than nempnyge of a name" (more is owed to the little child before he knows the law than providing his name) (IX. 78–79). Gossips accepted responsibility for the child's spiritual and physical well-being, protecting her from "myseise and . . . myschief [illness and distress]," from "fyer and water and other perels."[18] At the same time, they forged a mutually beneficial alliance with the child's mother, establishing a "formal state of friendship" that had financial, social, and political benefits.[19] These multiple duties were not just licensed but often were required by both secular and religious authorities, yet they became the source of the gossips' ill repute.

For ecclesiastical authorities, the gossip's primary responsibility was pastoral: teaching her godchild the basic tenets of the faith.[20] Penitential manuals and instructions for priests repeatedly urge baptismal sponsors to fulfill their obligations: "God faders and godmodyrs of thys chylde whe charge you . . . that ye lerne or se yt be lerned the *Pater noster. Aue maria.* and *Credo.* after the lawe of all holy churche."[21] Asserting the significance of this duty, John Mirk places the failure to fulfill it at the top of the list of slothful

17. In recent years, building on the work of Adrian Wilson, scholars have recovered a great deal of evidence about both the ceremonies of childbirth and the ways in which they were understood in late medieval and early modern England. Adrian Wilson, "The Ceremony of Childbirth and Its Interpretation," in *Women as Mothers in Pre-industrial England,* ed. Valerie Fildes (London: Routledge, 1990), 68–107, and "Participant or Patient? Seventeenth-Century Childbirth from the Mother's Point of View," in *Patients and Practitioners: Lay Perceptions of Medicine in Pre-industrial Society,* ed. Roy Porter (Cambridge: Cambridge University Press, 1985), 129–44; Gibson, "Scene and Obscene" and "Blessing from Sun and Moon: Churching as Women's Theater," in *Bodies and Disciplines,* 139–54; Becky R. Lee, "Men's Recollections of a Women's Rite: Medieval English Men's Recollections Regarding the Rite of the Purification of Women after Childbirth," *Gender and History* 14, no. 2 (2002): 224–41, and "The Purification of Women after Childbirth: A Window onto Medieval Perceptions of Women," *Florilegium* 14 (1995–96): 43–55; and Linda A. Pollock, "Childbearing and Female Bonding in Early Modern England," *Social History* 22, no. 3 (1997): 286–306.

18. *Piers Plowman,* IX. 76; *Manuale ad usum percelebris ecclesie Sarisburiensis,* ed. A. Jefferies Collins (London: Henry Bradshaw Society, 1960), 32. The godparent's responsibility for the child's safety lasts until she reaches seven years of age.

19. Bossy, "Blood and Baptism," 133–34.

20. On the subject of godparents and pastoral instruction, see Eamon Duffy, *The Stripping of the Altars: Traditional Religion in England 1400–1580* (New Haven: Yale University Press, 1992); Nicholas Orme, "Children and the Church in Medieval England," *Journal of Ecclesiastical History* 45 (1994): 563–86; and Shulamith Shahar, *Childhood in the Middle Ages* (London: Routledge, 1990), 117–18.

21. *Manuale ad usum percelebris ecclesie Sarisburiensis,* 32.

acts—it is the first of his questions about *acedia:* "Hast þou be slowe 7 take non hede / To teche þy godchyldre pater noster 7 crede?"[22] Knowledge of these basic tenets was a prerequisite for serving as a baptismal sponsor, and godparents were tested on their knowledge at the beginning of the ceremony.[23] As the *York Manual* explains, "godparents must instruct their spiritual children in the faith; which they would be unable to do unless they themselves were first instructed in the faith."[24] This emphasis on knowledge and teaching is one of the many features that literary gossips share with their historical counterparts; the subjects of their instruction, however, are rarely the tenets of the orthodox faith. Dunbar's Wedo, for example, teaches from a pastoral syllabus of her own devising, while the women in the *Good Gossips* counsel each other about how to avoid domestic violence.[25] That spiritual kinship licenses the good gossips to disseminate their unorthodox erudition is, as we will see, one of the central anxieties of these texts.

As much as ecclesiastical authorities worried about the pastoral deficiencies of the godparents, of far greater concern was their proliferation. Spiritual kinship carried with it all the force of the incest taboo: marriage was prohibited not only between all those present at the baptismal font, but also between their kin.[26] In order to prevent an ever-widening circle of marital prohibitions, authorities sought to restrict the number of godparents to three: two godparents of the same sex as the child, one of the opposite sex.[27] However, judging from the fact that this regulation had to be repeated throughout the statutes of the period, parents often ignored this rule.[28] Medieval children were known to have "swarms of godparents"—Joan of

---

22. *Instructions for Parish Priests,* lines 1049–50.

23. *Manuale ad usum percelebris ecclesie Sarisburiensis,* 31.

24. "Patrini debent instruere filios suos spirituales in fide, quod non possent facere; nisi ipsimet in fide prius instruerentur." *Manuale et processionale ad usum insignis ecclesiae Eboracensis,* ed. W. G. Henderson, Surtees Society, vol. 63 (Durham, Eng.: Andrews, 1875), 22.

25. *The Tretis of the Twa Marrit Wemen and the Wedo, The Poems of William Dunbar,* lines 245–504; the *Good Gossips,* 250, no. 419 Aa, stanza 14. I discuss the Wedo's pastoral practice in Chapter 3, above.

26. Included under the prohibition were the priest; the priest's children; the newborn; the newborn's mother, father, and siblings; the godparents; the godparents' spouses; and the godparents' children. Mirk, *Instructions,* lines 173–78; and Atchley, "Wose," 315–16. For the statutes prohibiting such marriages, see Powicke and Cheney, *Councils and Synods II,* 1:88, 190, 234, and 636.

27. Shahar, *Childhood,* 118; Powicke and Cheney, *Councils and Synods II,* 1:31.

28. Powicke and Cheney, *Councils and Synods II,* 1:69, 183, 233, 369, 453, 590, and 635; and Bossy, "Blood and Baptism," 133.

Arc, for example, had eleven, seven godmothers and four godfathers.[29] Consequently, the proliferation of gossips in attendance at a baptism quickly became a problem for secular as well as religious authorities, as the newborn's entourage, like the unruly women of late medieval literature, threatened to disrupt public order.[30]

The gossips' reputation for disorder and excess came not just from their numbers but from their appetites. The feasting so central to the gossips' songs—the "gose or pigge or capons wynge" of the *Good Gossips* and the stinking tripe, "podynges and lynkes" of Elinor Rumming's companions—was also a ubiquitous feature of late medieval spiritual kinship.[31] Indeed, by the fifteenth century, gossips had become synonymous with feasts in popular and penitential literature, as the translator of *An Alphabet of Tales* reveals. Recounting a narrative about sacrilegious feasting, he identifies the main characters not simply as male friends, but as "gossops," insisting repeatedly on the connection between inordinate appetite and spiritual kinship.[32] What produces this reputation for gluttony is the custom of the gossips' feasts—the celebrations hosted by parents after the child's baptism and the mother's purification.[33] That these were occasions for excess is evidenced by the fact that civil and ecclesiastical authorities alike attempted to curtail them, restricting both attendance and expenditure.[34]

Yet behind the notoriety of the gossips' feast lies a legitimate practice that served a number of social and legal functions. These events enabled parents to give thanks for the child's safe delivery, to repay the godparents for their

29. Haas, "Social Connections," 5 n. 9; and Edward Lucie-Smith, *Joan of Arc* (New York: Allen Lane, 1976), 8.

30. Bossy, "Counter-Reformation," 57.

31. The *Good Gossips*, 250, no. 419Aa, stanza 6; and the *Tunning of Elinor Rumming*, in *John Skelton: The Complete Poems*, ed. John Scattergood (New Haven: Yale University Press, 1983), lines 443–44.

32. Departing from his source, the English translator identifies the gluttonous men as "gossops" three times in the space of seventeen lines. *Alphabet of Tales*, no. 117. Dunbar makes a similar connection between gossips and sacrilegious feastings in *Tway Cummeris, Poems of William Dunbar*, 197–98.

33. The term, "gossips' feast," refers to both the christening and the purification feasts. See Hanawalt, *The Ties That Bound: Peasant Families in Medieval England* (New York: Oxford University Press, 1986), 173; Lee, "Men's Recollections," 230–32; and Haas, "Baptism and Spiritual Kinship," 87–88.

34. Bossy, "Counter-Reformation," 57; and Lynch, *Godparents and Kinship*, 24–27. In 1540, Chester mayor Henry Gee attempted to limit the extravagance of the purification feast by decreeing that only the midwife and the new mother's mother, sisters, and sisters-in-law were allowed to enter the house after the purification. Rupert Morris, *Chester in the Plantagenet and Tudor Reigns* (Printed for the author, 1893), 336.

service and their gifts, and, most important, to imprint the date in the minds of those attending. Because there was no systematic recording of births in medieval England, in order to establish that an heir had attained legal age, proof-of-age juries were empanelled to hear the testimony of witnesses.[35] As documents of these proceedings reveal, feasts played a central evidentiary role. Neighbors recall attending these events or bumping into friends who were on their way to them; they reminisce about the food and wine that was served; and they vividly remember even twenty-one years later the snub of not being invited.[36] The feasts served as elaborate advertisements for the date of a child's birth, and parents threw lavish banquets in order to ensure lasting memories: one fourteenth-century feast was so extensive that "the kitchen of the manor was nearly burnt down."[37] For the gossips, these occasions provided the opportunity to reaffirm the alliances formed at the baptismal font—to assert their intimate connection to both the parents and the newborn. And it is clear from the testimony at proof-of-age inquests that neighbors recognized the gossips' privileged status. One Yorkshire witness not only remembered the godparents' names but expressed his amazement at the extravagant dishes served in their honor: the earl of Athol, it seems, had ordered that all the fish in his pond be prepared as a "repast" for his daughter's godmothers.[38] Despite its infamy, the gossips' feast in all its excess was indispensable to the social practice of spiritual kinship in late medieval England.

If the gossips' feast is a legitimate social custom suffering from an ignominious reputation, then the lying-in is a social imperative suffused with scandal. Civil and ecclesiastical authorities certainly recognized the necessity of the lying-in: not only did the mother need to recuperate from her physical travails but also she was required to withdraw from the religious and

---

35. It was not until 1538 that parish registers recorded such information at the order of Thomas Cromwell. Men came of age at twenty-one; married women at sixteen; and unmarried women at fourteen. On the function of proof-of-age documents, see Lee, "Men's Recollections," 225–27; Haas, "Social Connections," 6–7; Sue Sheridan Walker, "Proof of Age of Feudal Heirs in Medieval England," *Mediaeval Studies* 35 (1973): 306–23; and John Bedell, "Memory and Proof of Age in England, 1272–1327," *Past and Present* 162 (1999): 6–12. Despite the formulaic, and at times fabricated, nature of some of these documents, their details suggest the kinds of testimony—the kinds of memories—that were expected. See Niles, "Baptism and the Naming," 96–97.

36. Lee, "Men's Recollections," 230–32; and Haas, "Baptism and Spiritual Kinship," 87–88.

37. *Calendar of Inquisitions Post Mortem and Other Analogous Documents Preserved in the Public Record Office*, 20 vols. (London, 1904–95), 14:304.

38. *Calendar of Inquisitions*, 14:346. See also Haas, "Baptism and Spiritual Kinship," 88.

social community until she had been purified.[39] Authorities even acknowledged that this event necessitated special food and drink: to sustain her
during her labor and to aid her recuperation, the mother was traditionally
served a "caudle," a fortifying drink "consisting of ale or wine, warmed with
sugar and spices."[40] Despite these allowances, however, the lyings-in became
the subject of scathing critique and constrictive legislation. Denouncing the
fancy dishes and expensive drinks that were served at lyings-in, Chester
mayor Henry Gee attempted to curb the "gret excesse and superfluose costes
and charges" by decreeing that from henceforth "no such dishes metes and
wynes" were to be brought to any women in childbed. His citizens, it seems,
were bankrupting themselves on these events; they were no longer able to
"sustayne and maynteyne ther nessecary charge."[41] Women were spending
beyond their (and indeed the husbands') means in order to outdo both their
neighbors and their superiors, and the phrase "lying in like a countess"
became something of a popular joke about women's aspirations.[42] But for
the lying-in as for the gossips' feast, this reputation for excess obscures the
practice's numerous social functions.

A "collective female ritual," the lying-in, like the meetings in the gossips'
songs, provided the occasion for conversation and alliance as well as feasting.[43] Women recognized the lying-in as a social obligation, a declaration of
solidarity with one's neighbors.[44] These events were the female domestic
equivalent of the more public gossips' feasts, and women resented not being
invited to them just as deeply: in one extreme example, a villager was so
irate at being excluded that she burst in during her neighbor's labor to curse
her with "all the plagues of hell."[45] Lasting up to forty days, the lying-in
began with the mother's labor; encompassed the celebratory "sitting up,"

39. Wilson, "Participant or Patient?" 138.

40. Wilson, "Ceremony of Childbirth," 73–74.

41. Morris, *Chester*, 336. Because Gee treats purification feasts in the same decree and refrains from mentioning christening feasts, it seems that he has an interest in curtailing specifically
female events. For Gee's campaign to assert control over the women of Chester, see Wack,
"Women, Work and Plays," 39–41.

42. Janelle Day Jenstad, "Lying-in Like a Countess: The *Lisle Letters*, the Cecil Family, and
A Chaste Maid in Cheapside," *Journal of Medieval and Early Modern Studies* 34, no. 2 (2004):
373–403. Christine de Pisan makes a similar complaint about merchant-class women who attempt
to better their social superiors through lavish displays. See Charity Cannon Willard, "Women
and Marriage Around 1400: Three Views," *Fifteenth-Century Studies* 17 (1990): 475–84, esp. 480.

43. Wilson, "Participant or Patient?" 135.

44. Pollock, "Childbearing and Female Bonding."

45. Michael MacDonald, *Mystical Bedlam: Madness, Anxiety, and Healing in Seventeenth-
Century England* (Cambridge: Cambridge University Press, 1981), 108–9.

when the new mother was first able to move about the chamber; and culmi-nated in her purification ceremony, or churching.[46] It was punctuated by two moments when historical gossips, like their fictional counterparts, were seen moving through town: the first, when they converged on the mother's house to attend the birth, and the second, when they processed to church for the purification. By the end of the sixteenth century, these processions became almost indistinguishable from the gadding about of the good gos-sips, as women, much to the consternation of civil and ecclesiastical authori-ties, came to celebrate churching less as a religious ritual than as an occasion both for being seen and for feasting with their female companions.[47] As if taking a cue from the gossips' songs, one new mother en route to her churching stopped off at the tavern to feast for several hours; although she later went to church, it was "rather to be seene, then upon any devotion," for she quickly returned to the tavern without being purified.[48] Despite their notoriety, however, the purification processions, as Gail McMurray Gibson has argued, constituted a "women's theater of considerable social and politi-cal importance."[49] Indeed, they were the mechanism through which women displayed publicly their newly forged kinship. As such they could be elabo-rate spectacles: Elizabeth Woodville, for example, was accompanied by no fewer than sixty female attendants.[50] Behind these public processions were the private conversations that took place during the lying-in, where women could speak freely with "noman hem a-monge."[51] These female communi-ties, Becky Lee demonstrates, were structured by a "complex web of ties and allegiances, grounded in friendship, duty, and socio-economic status."[52] Both affirming and taking advantage of these ties, the women's talk was

46. For a detailed discussion of the various stages of the lying-in and their duration, see Wilson, "Ceremony of Childbirth," 70–83. As Wilson explains, the duration of the lying-in was determined by the mother's financial means. On the complex meanings of the purification ritual, see Wilson, "Ceremony of Childbirth," 78–83; Lee, "Male Recollections," esp. 227–29; and David Cressy, "Purification, Thanksgiving and the Churching of Women in Post-Reformation En-gland," *Past and Present* 141 (1993): 106–46.

47. Wilson, "Ceremony of Childbirth," 88–93.

48. The woman, Jane Minors, was not alone in her sentiment, for, as the authorities com-plained, such abuses were "publique & notoriouse." W. H. Hale, *A Series of Precedents and Proceedings in Criminal Causes, Extending from the Year 1475 to 1640, Extracted from Act-books of Ecclesiastical Courts in the Diocese of London* (London: F. and J. Rivington, 1847), 216.

49. Gibson, "Blessing from Sun and Moon," 147.

50. Ibid.

51. *A Talk of Ten Wives on Their Husbands' Ware, Jyl of Breyntford's Testament*, ed. F. J. Furnivall (London, 1871), 29–33.

52. Lee, "Male Recollections," 235.

anything but idle. While the gossips' songs attempt to trivialize this conversation, late medieval men were perfectly capable of recognizing its power: John Paston II sent his mother, Margaret, to attend the duchess of Norfolk's lying-in so that she could act as his representative in negotiations that would otherwise be interrupted by this period of female seclusion.[53] That is, the talk of these wives was not just about their "husbands' wares"—it was integral to their socioeconomic life.

Announced at the baptismal font and reaffirmed during the purification procession, the alliances forged during the lying-in extend far beyond the ceremonies of childbirth. The coparental bond established through baptismal sponsorship created "a formal state of friendship," akin to that of "blood-brotherhood or of fraternity in general."[54] Bound by spiritual kinship, gossips were obliged to cooperate, to protect one another, and to honor each other's requests.[55] In choosing their allies, parents adopted a number of strategies. Occasionally they used baptismal sponsorship to intensify existing kinship networks, binding family members more closely to one another, but the most common practice was to select gossips who could extend these networks, allying themselves with members of the community outside their family.[56] Parents made godparent connections both vertically and horizontally, choosing gossips who were above them in social standing in order to seek advancement and choosing those who were below them to strengthen loyalties.[57] Although evidence concerning the nature and impact of these coparental alliances is scarce, the information we do have suggests that this practice played a significant role in late medieval England.[58] Gossips raised one's profile at court: Elizabeth Verdon enjoyed a long-standing and intimate alliance with Queen Isabella, her daughter's godmother.[59] They

53. *Paston Letters and Papers of the Fifteenth Century,* ed. Norman Davis, pt. 1 (Oxford: Clarendon Press, 1971), no. 271. See also Frances and Joseph Gies, *A Medieval Family: The Pastons of Fifteenth-century England* (New York: Harper Collins, 1998), 271.

54. Bossy, "Blood and Baptism," 133–34.

55. Lynch, *Godparents and Kinship,* 196–98; Bossy, "Blood and Baptism," 133–34.

56. Haas, "Social Connections," 9–10; Niles, "Baptism and Naming," 101. A small percentage of cases show that baptismal sponsorship was occasionally used to bind children of the same generation more tightly together or to oblige older wealthy relatives to look after the financial well-being of both the child and its parents. See, for example, the case of Ralph Shirley III and his nephew, discussed by Christine Carpenter, *Locality and Polity: A Study of Warwickshire Landed Society, 1401–1499* (Cambridge: Cambridge University Press, 1992), 217.

57. Haas, "Social Connections," 8–16.

58. Bossy, "Blood and Baptism," 133–34; Niles, "Baptism and the Naming," 102–3; and Haas, "Baptism and Spiritual Kinship." For a more cautious view, see Hanawalt, *Ties That Bound,* 259.

59. Niles, "Baptism and the Naming," 102.

performed favors: William Caxton printed Chaucer's *Boece* at the request of his "gossib."[60] They enabled professional advancement: Richard Quatermayns appears to have helped his gossip, Tom Fowler, to achieve political office.[61] Above all, gossips enjoyed unfettered access to and increased influence over each other, a fact John Paston II knew all too well. Ever the schemer, he attempted to capitalize upon the bishop of Winchester's intimacy with his "godsip," the duke of Norfolk. Not only did he ask the bishop to intercede with the duke on his behalf, but also he encouraged him to broach the subject at the gossips' feast. John II recognized the social and legal significance of the gossip relationship, for he calls attention to it not only in his letters to his brother but also in his petition to Edward IV: John attests that he lobbied the duke "by þe means of his godsip þe Bisshop."[62]

That such alliances were seen as both powerful and problematic is evidenced by the fact that ecclesiastical authorities sought to prevent certain groups from entering into them. From the earliest days of the practice, nuns and monks were forbidden from acting as baptismal sponsors for fear that they would be united to the child's parents "by an improper or shameful bond of closeness."[63] Late medieval authorities continued to assert this prohibition, expanding it to cover other clergymen.[64] For Richard FitzRalph, friars were to avoid becoming "gossippes" to men or women, "leste sclaundre arise by occasioun þerof among freres."[65] The responsibilities incurred by spiritual kinship thus extended beyond instructing the child in the tenets of the faith, for these secular alliances were seen not only to conflict with devotional obligations, but also to bring disrepute to the clerical orders.[66] Anxieties about the gossips' alliances, however, were not restricted to the clergy. Indeed, the literary phenomenon of the gossips reveals a deep con-

60. William Caxton, epilogue to *Boecius de consolacione philosophie* (London, 1478), fol. M5v. STC 3199.

61. Christine Carpenter, ed., *Kingsford's Stonor Letters and Papers, 1290–1483* (Cambridge: Cambridge University Press, 1996), headnote to letter no. 150.

62. *Paston Letters,* nos. 358 and 294. For a detailed account of the negotiations of John II, see Frances and Joseph Gies, *Medieval Family,* 270–72.

63. Lynch, *Godparents and Kinship,* 154.

64. See, for example, the reiteration of the prohibition in the *Manuale et processionale ad usum insignis ecclesiae Eboracensis,* 21. As Haas has argued, the "ban was honored in the breach." "Social Connections," 13.

65. FitzRalph, *Defensio Curatorum,* 73/12–13.

66. Bossy, "Blood and Baptism," 134.

cern about the social consequences of women's spiritual kinship—both the networks they forge and the pastoral care they provide.

The Joys of Gossiping

The gossips' excessive feasting, controversial pastoral care, and problematic alliances play a recurring role in the *Fyftene Joyes of Maryage*. First printed by de Worde in 1507 and then reprinted in 1509, the *Fyftene Joyes* is a Middle English verse translation of the anonymous early fifteenth-century prose satire, the *Quinze Joyes de Mariage*. Composed by an anonymous translator, de Worde's edition is based on the earliest printing of this text, published in Lyon (1480–90).[67] Its title is an irreverent parody of such devotional works as the *Quinze Joyes de Notre Dame*, the *Fifteen Oes*, and the *Fyfftene Ioyes of Oure Lady*.[68] However, rather than asking readers to meditate on the wounds of Christ or the joys of Mary, the text dwells on the pitfalls of marriage and the wiles of women, standing as an homage to and expansion of the body of misogamic and antifeminist literature so popular in the later Middle Ages.[69] Each of its fifteen chapters details some manifestation of female sinfulness and marital woe: adultery, wanderlust, profligacy, and intractability, to name a few. It is into this context that the gossips are interpolated; that is, the *Fyftene Joyes* is not a narrative exclusively concerned with

67. Quite popular in France, the *Quinze Joyes* went through at least seven printings in the years between 1480 and 1520. *Quinze Joyes de Mariage,* ed. Crow, xii; Joan Crow, "The 'Quinze Joyes de Mariage' in France and England," *Modern Language Review* 59 (1964): 571–77; and Maria Lobzowksa, "Two English Translations of the XVth Century French Satire 'Les Quinze Joyes de Mariage,'" *Kwartalnik Neofilologiczny* 10 (1963): 17–32. As Crow explains, the Lyon imprint preserves a shorter text than that of any of the manuscripts, considerably truncating Joys 8–15. De Worde's translator follows the Lyon text quite closely and does not appear to have had access to any more complete version of the narrative. Although Robert Copland has often been identified as the translator of the *Fyftene Joyes,* Mary Erler has dismissed this attribution on the basis of autobiographical evidence in the poem's prologue. Robert Copland, *Poems,* ed. Mary Carpenter Erler (Toronto: University of Toronto Press, 1993), 110.

68. On the history and devotional use of these poems, see Rebecca Krug, "*The Fifteen Oes,*" in *Cultures of Piety: Medieval Devotional Literature in Translation,* ed. Anne Clark Bartlett and Thomas H. Bestul (Ithaca: Cornell University Press, 1999), 107–17, 212–16. The Middle English poems the *Fyfftene Ioyes of Oure Lady* and the *Fifteeen Joys and Sorows of Mary* have been attributed to John Lydgate. *The Minor Poems of John Lydgate,* ed. Henry Noble MacCracken, EETS, o.s. 192 (London: Oxford University Press, 1934), 260–79.

69. A. E. B. Coldiron, "Paratextual Chaucerianism: Naturalizing French Texts in Early Printed Verse," *Chaucer Review* 38, no. 1 (2003): 1–15. On the popularity of such literature, particularly in de Worde's printshop, see Boffey, "Wynkyn de Worde."

a gossips' meeting, but rather one in which these women play a supporting yet significant role. And while the *commeres* certainly appear in the original French source, de Worde's translator elaborates upon them, emphasizing not merely their scheming and debauchery, but their spiritual kinship and all the duties it entails. If, as A. E. B. Coldiron suggests, de Worde's translator attempts to "domesticate and tame" for an English audience a potentially disruptive French narrative, then a significant part of his project was devoted to reinterpreting the gossips.[70]

Indeed, English readers seem to have been particularly interested in the gossips who appear in this text, for each new translation to enter the English marketplace both highlights and reinvents these women. The *Quinze Joyes* enjoyed considerable popularity in England, and its publication history suggests the multiple ways in which this text and its gossips were interpreted. After de Worde's second edition, the *Quinze Joyes* next appeared in the English marketplace when it was singled out by Archbishop Whitgift in his 1599 proclamation banning satires. Adam Islip, who had four months earlier been fined for printing this "booke disorderly," was required to submit all copies to the bishop of London "to be burnte."[71] According to late sixteenth-century authorities, the text, as well as Islip's printing of it, was unruly, threatening moral order. Four years later, the text reappears as the *Batchelars Banquet* (STC 6476.2), an updated prose edition that translates medieval French fashions—clothing, pastimes, and turns-of-phrase—into seventeenth-century English ones.[72] Under its new less sacrilegious title, the text not only avoided the censors but also became quite successful, appearing in at least four subsequent editions. The late seventeenth century saw

70. Coldiron argues that de Worde's edition of the *Fyftene Joyes* engages in "paratextual Chaucerianism," using an "indirect evocation of what would have been loosely recognizable as Chaucerian" (13n2) to accommodate to the English marketplace the potentially subversive misogyny of the *Quinze Joyes*. For Coldiron, the translator's rhymed iambic pentameter lines and "post-Chaucerian" prologue both serve to make the text appear more familiar to an English audience. Coldiron, "Paratextual Chaucerianism." The translation's Chaucerian undertones have been discussed by Lobzowksa, "Two English Translations," 19–26.

71. Edward Arber, *A Transcript of the Registers of the Company of Stationers of London, 1554–1640*, 5 vols. (London, 1875–94), 4:316r–v and 397. There is no indication of whether this "XV ioyes of marriage," also identified as the "25 Joies of Mariage," is based on the 1509 verse translation or a later version of the text. See Crow, "'Quinze Joyes de Mariage' in France and England," 575–76.

72. *The Bachelor's Banquet*, ed. Faith Gildenhuys (Ottawa: Dovehouse Editions, 1993), 22–30; Lobzowska, "Two English Translations"; Crow, "'Quinze Joyes de Mariage' in France and England," 575–76. Henceforth, I will refer to the *Batchelars Banquet* by its modernized title, *Bachelor's Banquet*; all quotations from this text come from Gildenhuys's edition.

yet another reinvention of the *Quinze Joyes,* this time as the *XV Comforts of Rash and Inconsiderate Marriage* (Wing F885). Appearing in six editions between 1682 and 1703, this new prose translation removed all traces of the French original and added three new chapters particularly pertinent to late seventeenth-century England.[73]

Each of these translators updates his French exemplar to suit his English audience; and each of them makes considerable changes to scenes in which the gossips appear. Indeed, these three translations sketch a brief history of the gossips' reputation and their increasing association with idle talk. The translator of the *Bachelor's Banquet* reserves his most creative and elaborate additions for the gossips' conversations, providing a detailed and lively rendition of these women's words. With cup going round and innuendo running rampant, the gossips gossip about their neighbors, bemoaning the fact that their companion's husband "keeps queans even under her nose" and joking that "F . . . loves Mistress G" while "G. himself loves . . . his maid N."[74] By contrast, the translator of the *XV Comforts* truncates both the gossips' conversation and their involvement in the text, dismissing them as "Gossiping Baggages," whose tongues "oyld with Liquor" are "interlarded with smutty discourse."[75] By the late seventeenth century, the gossips have become idle women engaged in trifling and unseemly conversation. The transformations enacted by the translator of the *Fyftene Joyes,* however, suggest that the gossips had a much more complicated reputation in late medieval England, for he emphasizes not simply their idle talk but their duties to one another—their pastoral care, their political alliances, and their mutual support.

The spiritual kinship de Worde's translator depicts in the *Fyftene Joyes* is steeped in late medieval English customs. His exploration of the gossips therefore begins in the space where such female alliances are forged—the lying-in. When the wife's labor pains begin in the "Third Joy," the husband rushes about town gathering together the "gossyppes," who "must her kepe of chylde whyle she lyeth in," keeping her company and aiding in her recuperation. Once they have arrived, the husband must cater to their needs:

---

73. Crow, "'Quinze Joyes de Mariage' in France and England," 576–77. The additional three joys are first included in the 1683 edition. In one, the husband ends his days in Barbados; in another, having spent all his money, the husband turns to a life of crime, ending up on the gallows.

74. *Bachelor's Banquet,* ed. Gildenhuys, 63.

75. *The XV Comforts of Rash and Inconsiderate Marriage* (London, 1683), 20 and 59.

> The gossyppes come and this good man must gete
> Suche vytayles as they may well drynke and ete
> So that they may in suche a wyse be eased
> As they shall holde them well content & pleased
> This done the wyfe and gossyppes talke togyder
> (C6v)

Barely implied in the French source, where the husband simply makes sure that the women are comfortable, this gossips' feast is the invention of the English translator.[76] Reflecting English practice, he describes the feast as recompense for the gossips' service, referring to it as "theyr paye" (C7r). Food and drink are indispensable here, not only sating the women's appetites but also ensuring that they consider themselves suitably compensated. While the French *commeres* are pleased because someone is waiting on them hand and foot, the gossips are not content until they feel their services have been appropriately valued.[77] Only after the feast is provided can these kinswomen talk together.

In the hands of the medieval translator, the gossips' conversation does not devolve into either "smutty discourse" about their neighbors' sexual exploits or disparaging remarks about their husbands' sexual inadequacies; rather it serves as the occasion for pastoral care. That is, unlike their successors in the *Bachelor's Banquet* and the *XV Comforts*, the women in the *Fyftene Joyes* use their idle talk to teach. Their pastoral obligations, however, are to the new mother, not the newborn child, who is mentioned only once in the entire scene. Having already sponsored the child's entrance into the community of the faithful, these women now welcome the new mother into the community of gossips. Just as the object of their pastoral care has shifted, so does the subject of their lessons. Rather than tenets of the orthodox faith, the new mother gets an education in gossip's lore.

The first lesson on the women's pastoral syllabus is how to interpret as a

---

76. Leaving out any specific mention of a feast, the Lyon text declares, "Or conuient il que le bon homme quiere et que il face tant quil soient bien aises." *Les Quinze Joyes de Mariage, Texte de l'Édition Princeps du XVe Siècle,* ed. Ferdinand Heuckenkamp (Halle: Max Niemeyer, 1901), 20. Henceforth, this text will be referred to as the Lyon edition. The translator of the *Bachelor's Banquet* goes a step further than his English predecessor, detailing the dishes that are served: "sugar, biscuits, comfits and caraways, marmalade and marchpane [marzipan], with all kind of sweet suckets and superfluous banqueting stuff" (62).

77. As the narrator of the Lyon edition explains, "se tiennent bien aises quiconques ayt peine de le querir" (20).

gossip. When the women discover that they are not as comfortable as they might be, that their "paye" is insufficient, they immediately seek to teach the new mother how to recognize her husband's deficiencies. Speaking for the entire community, one gossip announces her shock at the dire circumstances in which their charge finds herself:

> Gossyp, I mervayle moche and so doth all
> This felawshyp that it so is befall
> And we have wonder what it may amount
> That your husbande doth make so lytell count
> Of you or of your yonge chylde here in trouthe
> A gentyll herte wolde pyte haue and routhe
>
> (C7r)

A gossip, the new mother learns, must assess every situation through her companions' eyes. Her predicament is unacceptable because all the "felawshyp" consider it to be so, and to be part of that fellowship, she must embrace its interpretation. Here again, the English translator expands upon his source, so that the women do not just complain about the husband's lack of attentiveness but rather offer their interpretation of it. The husband, they explain, pales in comparison to other men, because a "gentyll herte" would take better care of his wife. More important, he would take better care of her gossips. Proof of the husband's spousal neglect lies in his lack of consideration for her companions: "It doth appere he leuoth [sic] you but lyte / Whereof bothe ye and we may haue dyspyte" (C7r). Because the husband undervalues the gossips, he must not love his wife.[78] A quick study, the young mother immediately embraces the gossips' hermeneutics, parsing her husband as an "euyll man" (C7v).

Interpretation serves as prelude to action, for the central unit in the gossips' curriculum is how to "tame" a husband. Echoing the words of countless fictional wives, the gossips proclaim that the key to success in marriage is always having the last word. While this lesson on marital sovereignty is not in itself surprising, within its details lies an account of the duties that gossips owe one another beyond the space of the lying-in. Like the Wife of Bath's sermon, this lesson is drawn from experience: one of the gossips re-

---

78. The French *commeres* in the Lyon edition simply declare that he does not love her, rather than identifying the consequence-turned-cause of that neglect (20).

counts the story of how she successfully domesticated her own recalcitrant husband. The teacher introduces her autobiographical narrative by marking the new mother's status as fledgling member of the fellowship: she is the only one present who is unfamiliar with the tale that all the "gossyppes that be here they know well" (C7v), for gossips are privy to the intimate details of each other's marital tribulations. Opening with a statement of its authenticity—"I shall tell you truely by my fayth"—and culminating in the miraculous transformation of a notoriously domineering husband into a docile servant, her story functions as an exemplum teaching the new mother both how to tame a husband and how to use one's gossips to do so. Gossips, the speaker explains, serve as witnesses to the wife's marital dominance. Not only are they called upon in this exclusively female court to testify to the wife's successes, but also they are sought by the husband himself to hear his complaint—his testimonial to his wife's sovereignty: "And he hath tolde my gossyp sykerly / That he in me coude put no remedy" (C7v). Now that the new mother is a member of this fellowship, these duties are owed to her as well. As women, the gossips could not testify at proof-of-age inquiries, but here, as the new mother's spiritual kin, keepers and interpreters of her matrimonial secrets, they can act as witnesses, not to her child's age but to her marital mastery.

While both the women's conversation and the duties it implies are steeped in antifeminist commonplaces, they also move beyond this humor. The gossips here do not simply teach the wife how to play a part in the stereotypical battle for the breeches. Rather de Worde's translator depicts them fulfilling their pastoral duties. Unlike their English successors, these medieval gossips use the lying-in as an opportunity to educate their young charge, and they take their obligation seriously, promising to return the next morning "to se / The manner all how she shall gouerned be" (C8r). That is, they intend to return in order to assess how well their student has learned her lessons, both how she will be governed by the gossips' lore and how she will use that lore to govern her husband. The other English versions of this narrative provide no hint of such an obligation, no sense that there would be a compelling reason to return beyond the promise of another feast and an opportunity to antagonize the husband further. In the *Bachelor's Banquet,* the women's counsel is at best a kind of public service announcement for wives—"the wrong that he doth you doth likewise touch us and all other good women that are in your case"—and at worst a means to torment the husband (64). The women's conversation in the *XV Comforts* is even further from any kind of pastoral intent; the narrator curses these "Baggages," who "by their advice set the Husband and Wife at variance" (20). By contrast, the gossips in the *Fyftene Joyes*, for all that they embody antifeminist stereotypes, reveal that there is much more at stake in the activities of their female fellowship than gluttony and marital sovereignty.

For the translator of the *Fyftene Joyes*, the scene of the lying-in provides an opportunity to ruminate on the role of the English gossips. So interested is he in the possibilities this practice allows that he reprises the scene in the "Eighth Joy." While this second lying-in does indeed appear in all versions of the narrative, the late medieval English translator chooses to expand upon it, lingering at the mother's bedside before turning to the subject of pilgrimage that occupies the majority of the chapter. In both his French source and the translations of his successors, this repetition serves as the briefest reminder of the gossips' hedonism, which in turn foreshadows the excesses of the upcoming pilgrimage. These other texts provide little more than a declaration that the women amuse themselves both with celebrations that bankrupt the husband and with conversation that partakes of all manner of mischief.[79] The translator of the *Fyftene Joyes*, however, uses this scene to distill the gossips and their lying-in to their essential components, both orthodox and subversive.

In fact the repetition of this scene allows the translator to define what it means to be a gossip serving at a lying-in or, to use his words, to define what it means to "gossyp" (I3r). Each of the events and lessons of the previous gathering are rehearsed, but here they assume the atmosphere of habit. The gossips arrive "as is the guyse." Their feast is invoked metonymically in the cup that "besely gooth rounde." In accordance with English custom, there is a celebratory "sy[tt]yng vp" and the events culminate when the now veteran mother is "puryfyed with solempnyte."[80] Most importantly, the lesson on marital governance has already been learned: several of the moth-

79. One of the manuscripts, MS Phillipps 8338, reminds the reader that such a scene has already been described in the third chapter: "Les commeres viennent, comme dit est par cy devant ou chappitre de la tierche joye de mariage." *Quinze Joyes de Mariage*, ed. Crow, 54/24–26.

80. This mention of the purification, like the vast majority of details in this scene, is lacking in the Lyon edition, which simply states, "Elle couche longuement et les commeres viennent Et feront les leuailles grans et belles Si aduient quelle a deux ou trois de ses comeres qui sont auecques elle en la maison pour galer et sera aladuanture sil ni a quelque fatras dont ie me tais" (The wife has a long lying-in and the gossips arrive. And they make a great and merry sitting up. It happens that she has two or three of her gossips who are staying with her in her house in order to amuse themselves. It will be a surprise if they don't engage in some foolery that I will not mention.) (59).

er's favorite gossips stay in the house "to rule merely / With her."[81] And because their pastoral duty has already been fulfilled, now when the women speak, they "talke of tryffles." Summarizing their activities, the translator declares that these women visit the mother to "gossyp in her company." His phrasing here is remarkable, not the least because he uses the verb, "to gossip," some eighty years before it seems to have been current in English usage.[82] Given recent critiques of dictionary methodology, I do not wish to argue that our late medieval translator coined this verb, though this is of course a possibility. Rather I want to suggest that his use of this word reveals his preoccupation with defining what it means to be a gossip.

This translator's impulse toward definition is not shared by either his source or his successors; there is no trace of the verb "to gossip" in either of the later English texts, and the Lyon imprint offers no hint of what inspired its use.[83] Indeed, throughout this short scene, the translator has been transforming his source to highlight those features of the gossips in which he has been particularly invested. Where the Lyon text uses *galler,* an Old French verb meaning to amuse oneself or to have a good time, the English text asserts that women "*rule* merely."[84] While merriment is certainly implied by *galler,* the notion of domestic governance, of women's rule, is wholly unconnected to it. In fact, elsewhere in the narrative, this word has sexual overtones, referring to various amusements that men and women enjoy together.[85] Similarly, when the Lyon text proclaims the gossips will no doubt involve themselves in some tomfoolery—"sera aladuanture sil ni a quelque fatras" (59)—our English translator declares that the women might chance

81. This scene comically illustrates Natalie Zemon Davis's claim that the lying-in provided women with the opportunity to invert domestic power dynamics. "Women on Top," in *Society and Culture in Early Modern France* (Stanford: Stanford University Press, 1975), 145. See also Wilson, "Ceremony of Childbirth," 85–88.

82. The first instance provided by the *Oxford English Dictionary* (s.v. "gossip") comes from the *Comedy of Errors* in 1590. Similarly, the *Middle English Dictionary* offers no evidence that this verb form existed in the late Middle Ages, restricting its entries to the noun, "godsib."

83. Declaring only that the women come "pour galler," the Lyon text omits the phrase, "et parler de leurs choses," which is present in the manuscript tradition as well as in another incunable imprint of the text, the 1499 Treperel edition. Although there is no evidence to suggest that de Worde's translator had access to any other edition, it is possible that his exemplar contained this phrase. Even if this is the case, that idea that the translator would define the act of gossiping as gossips talking about their things supports rather than contradicts my argument here.

84. Emphasis mine. Marcel Cressot, *Vocabulaire des Quinze Joies de Mariage* (Geneva: Slatkine Reprints, 1974), 47.

85. *Quinze Joyes de Mariage,* ed. Crow, 69. See also Jean Rychner, ed., *Le XV Joies de Mariage* (Paris: Librairie Minard, 1963), 11:111–12, 13:59, and 15:5.

to *talk* of trifles, emphasizing their conversation over their tendency toward mischief.[86] The cumulative effect of these seemingly minor changes is considerable. In just thirteen lines, this translator identifies gossips as spiritual kin who feast, rule the domestic realm, accompany one other to religious ceremonies, and delight in idle talk.

While de Worde's translator uses the lying-in to define the English gossips, in order to reveal the consequences of their spiritual kinship, he explores the duties that these women owe one other beyond the ceremonies of childbirth. Like the historical gossips on whom they reflect, the women of the *Fyftene Joyes* enter into a lifelong relationship with one another. The alliances forged at the lyings-in, the network of witnesses and advisors introduced there, are called upon throughout the wife's marital career. Gossips act as informants and intercessors, negotiating with the husband on the wife's behalf. When the wife wants to go on pilgrimage in the "Second Joy," it is her gossip who persuades the husband to allow her departure, bombarding him with justifications until he capitulates to the verbal siege. Similarly, when the wife desires a new dress in the "First Joy," it is her "euer trewe" gossip who provides her with the information necessary to hoodwink her husband (B4r). But nowhere are the gossips' duties more evident than in the poem's final chapter. Here, in the "Fifteenth Joy," the full ramifications of the gossips' alliance are revealed. Here, too, the medieval English translator finally silences these women's conversation, even as he reveals its subversive potential. Moreover, this final scene appears to have been particularly prone to reinterpretation. Not only does our translator adapt the text, but the two major incunable French editions along with both early modern English translations also offer different renditions of this scene.[87] That is, the gossips' alliance appears to have caused trouble both inside and outside the text.

At the core of the gossips' alliance is an obligation to come to one another's aid and it is this duty upon which the "Fifteenth Joy" reflects. The chapter opens with the husband catching his wife and her lover in flagrante delicto. While he chases after the young gallant, the wife escapes to her

86. Brent Pitts translates *fatras* variously as "hullabaloo" (128), "shenanigans" (129), and "tomfoolery" (78). Brent A. Pitts, trans., *The Fifteen Joys of Marriage* (New York: Peter Lang, 1985).

87. Although the variant scenes in the two incunable French editions no doubt result from incomplete exemplars, because the two editions employ quite different tactics for dealing with the lacuna, these adaptations rise to the level of interpretation.

mother's house, where after some subterfuge she finally admits what has happened. Recognizing that they must find a "remedye / To cesse the noyse of people and the crye" (M4v), the mother turns to her most trusted allies, telling the chambermaid to summon her war counsel:

> Go to my gossyppes suche and suche and say
> I recommaunde me to them all and pray
> They wyll come and dysporte them here with me
> Loke that thou fynde them out where so they be
> Say that I haue to do with them a thynge
> Whiche truely I wyll shewe at theyr comynge
>
> (M4v)

In hands of de Worde's translator, the mother's speech becomes more than just the invitation that appears in other versions of the narrative.[88] Through its humorous mixing of etiquette and innuendo, it recapitulates the gossips' defining features. By having the mother demand that her companions be sought out no matter their location, the translator both establishes the gossips as invaluable advisors and reminds readers that these gadabout women are not where they are supposed to be. To establish that these women are bound by obligations that extend beyond friendship, he gives the mother's invitation the air of a formal request: she recommends herself to her gossips in a gesture typically employed in formal correspondence rather than informal conversation.[89] Similarly, the mother's tactics of persuasion recall the gossips' earlier activities. First she offers entertainment, suggesting that they come and "dysporte" with her as they have done before; then she entices them with the promise of some yet undisclosed story, which she will reveal once they arrive. So persuasive is this summons that "all the gossyppes comen on a rewe." With the female collective thus reconvened, the gossips can proceed with the business at hand.

88. The invitation in the Lyon edition is far less detailed: "Va dire a mes commeres telle et telle que ie leur prie quelles se viengnent esbatre auec moy et que iay vn pou afaire delles" (Go and tell my gossips such and such that I invite them to come and amuse themselves with me and that I have a small matter to discuss with them.) (80). Even more succinct are the narrator's remarks in the *Bachelor's Banquet*, "She sends for her especial gossips and companions whose counsels in like cases she doth use" (130). The invitation has been omitted from the *XV Comforts*, which completely excises the gossips' meeting from the chapter.

89. As many of the examples provided under the *Middle English Dictionary* entry for *recommaunden* reveal, such recommendations usually appear as a gesture of respect for or supplication to a social superior.

Here, as in the "Third Joy," the women's conversation cannot begin without a feast. Just as the husband attempted to compensate his wife's gossips for their services at the lying-in, so this mother offers her companions "a poor repast" to thank them for their "werkes" (M5r). While other versions of the narrative reduce this connection to a joke about the women's notorious tippling, proclaiming that the first thing the gossips do when they arrive is drink the best wine in the house, de Worde's translator expands the joke to ruminate not simply on the women's feasting but on the duties the feast both enables and supplants:

> No Pater nester aue ne no crede
> Wyll they reherce nor oryson in dede
> Unto the tyme the dronken haue and fedde
>
> (M4v)

By invoking the Pater Noster, Ave Maria, and Creed—the pastoral syllabus for baptismal sponsorship—he reminds readers that these women are not just drinking companions but spiritual kin.[90] They are the mother's gossips, who attended her lying-in and who sponsored the troubled young wife who now sits before them. Clearly part of the joke here is that these women privilege feasting over their orthodox pastoral duties: their charge's circumstances betray their neglected spiritual obligations. But even as the translator asks readers to laugh at the gossips' dereliction of their official duties, he emphasizes the unconventional pastoral care these women are here to provide. For if feasting has usurped their religious obligations, then it has strengthened their social alliances. The gossips' may be unconcerned with their charge's moral failings, but when they notice that she is unable to partake of the festivities—that "she hathe lytell lust to play" (M5r)—they immediately offer their services.

The support the gossips provide is their conversation, as they analyze the significance of the wife's predicament in order to protect both her physical safety and her public reputation. And it is this conversation that particularly interests de Worde's translator, for he dilates their exchange to almost twice

90. Although the Lyon edition also contains a reference to the Pater Noster and Ave Maria, the allusion seems to be less about the pastoral syllabus and more about the speed with which the women guzzled the wine: "les premieres choses quilz font sans dire pater ne aue maria elle boiuent du meilleur en actendant" (The first thing they do without so much as saying the Pater Noster or Ave Maria is to drink the best wine in the house.) (80).

its original length.[91] Elaborating upon a joke in his source, he transforms the women into legal scholars, experts in the intricacies of matrimonial law.[92] As a result, their idle talk develops into a full-blown debate. They argue from experience that adultery has legal precedent; indeed, it is a "custome of the countre and the lawe / Whiche can not hurte the value of a strawe" (M5r). Not only have they been caught in similar circumstances, escaping unscathed, but also they have frequently witnessed many similar cases which were resolved "Withoute restraynt or revocacyon." The women do not simply converse, they engage in learned disputation—"grete dyspycyon," an activity usually reserved for theologians, lawyers, and royal advisors.[93] Every gossip recognizes her duty to participate in the discussion, so that all of the women "speke and answer on a rowe." In order to arrive at a sound conclusion, they debate all sides of the issue: "One dooth allegge an other dothe replye / The thyrde sayth thenne all is not worthe a fly." This desire for thoroughness compels them to ask for additional evidence, inquiring how this slander came into being, not only so that they can fully assess the situation but also, the translator implies, so that they can discover the illicit details of this adulterous narrative. In short, these gossips take their obligations seriously, devising how they might best come to their companion's aid.

Yet despite their lively debate, the gossips' conversation appears decidedly ineffectual, for the translator's joke is not simply the humorous incongruity between women's words and scholarly discourse but the fact that, for all their effort, the gossips' idle talk accomplishes little. Their arguing "vp and doune," the translator proclaims, comes "all to late." What is more, their disputation gives way to unproductive chatter, as the women "crye and clappe" (M5r). Echoing the condemnations of proverbs and penitential manuals, the translator makes these gossips emblems of female garrulity;

---

91. Moreover, the scene in the Lyon edition is already a significant expansion of the brief conversation in the manuscript tradition.

92. The joke in the Lyon edition concerns the women's suitability as legal witnesses: "dieu scet selles seroyent bien propres a faire vng grant tourbe et commes ilz alegueroient les stilles et coustumes de pais" (God knows they would make a fitting troop of witnesses, as they would argue the legal proceedings and customs of the country.) (81). Randall Cotgrave's *A Dictionarie of the French and English Tongues* (London, 1611), explains that a *turbe* is "a troope (consisting at the least) of tenne witnesses; two such troopes being required to the approuement of an vnwritten custome or for the exposition of a written one" (fol. Kkkk1v).

93. The examples provided in both the *Middle English Dictionary* (s.v. "desputeision") and the *Oxford English Dictionary* (s.v. "dispicion") all suggest the scholarly rather than colloquial connotations of this word.

indeed, they become personifications of the idle talk that "clappeth as a mille"—of jangling in all its pastoral infamy.[94] Whereas earlier de Worde's translator had been interested in exploring the possibilities of this talk, in this final scene he forecloses those possibilities. Even though the women have reached a verdict "agaynst this wedded man," they have not yet found a remedy. They gather provisions to "make the good man and his frendes blynde," but the translator makes clear that these provisions are to furnish future feasts: the women will convene often to "drynke and ete" and speak of this matter "with wordes softe" (M5v). While the women plan to "pro-cede" against the poor husband, waging a verbal campaign against him and his friends, the details of their verbal siege remain unspoken. That is, even as he suggests that the gossips' words have subversive potential—the power not only to convince but to blind men—de Worde's translator diffuses their conversation, supplanting their verbal warfare with unproductive speech. At the close of the chapter, and indeed the poem, readers are left with a familiar image of the women as they "drynke and ete and make them wele at ease" (M5v) as threatening conversation is replaced by a gossips' feast.

The translator's silencing of the women's conversation stands in marked contrast to other versions of the narrative. While his English successors are far less interested in the debate of the gossips' war counsel, they revel in the women's verbal campaign. The *Bachelor's Banquet* depicts in vivid detail the garrulous guerilla warfare in which the women in engage.[95] First, under the pretext of seeing how the poor husband is faring, two of the "chief" gossips pay a visit, chastising him for believing the slanderous rumors about their gossip and assuring him that they have known her all their life and she has always been virtuous (132). Next the chambermaid, who has acted as the gossips' herald, arrives "with her five eggs" to defend her mistress's honor (132). When the husband objects that he has seen it with his own eyes, the gossips explain that he must have misinterpreted the scene: "God forbid that every man and woman which is alone together should do evil" (133). Throughout the afternoon, one by one, each of the gossips arrives to give

---

94. *Parson's Tale,* X. 406. The idea that jangling is like the clapper of a mill that is never still is a commonplace in medieval penitential literature. See *Jacob's Well,* 148/24–25; and Bartlett Jere Whiting, *Proverbs, Sentences, and Proverbial Phrases from English Writings Mainly Before 1500* (Cambridge: Belknap Press, 1968), C276 and M556.

95. Interestingly, the translator of the *XV Comforts,* after omitting the gossips' meeting, refuses to give the gossips credit for the verbal siege. While a "Female Gang of her Friends and Relations attaque the Husband," he is adamant about not identifying them as "gossips" (100).

"her verdict." One feigns loyalty to the husband, assuring him that she would tell him if she thought anything were amiss. Another declares that this suspicion is the "devil's work," while her companion expresses concern that the wife's grief is life threatening. As a finishing touch, the mother-in-law arrives in a state of high distraction, railing against the husband for bringing such slander upon her daughter. On cue, the women console her and renew their attack on the husband, coming "upon him thick and three-fold" (133). Overwhelmed by the verbal bombardment, the husband capitulates, entreating the gossips to broker a reconciliation with his wife. With this final image of the gossips magnificent in their triumph, the translator of the *Bachelor's Banquet* concludes his text.

Part of the disparity between these two English versions no doubt results from the fact that they are working from different exemplars. The Lyon edition on which de Worde's text is based does not preserve the scene of the gossips' siege, while the Rosset edition, which serves as the source for the *Bachelor's Banquet*, does.[96] However, to view the silencing of the gossips in the *Fyftene Joyes* as an accident of textual history is to miss the tactics in which de Worde's translator has been engaged. Throughout the scene, he has been working to foreclose the possibilities of the gossips' speech, making it seem ineffectual and unproductive. His exclusion of the chapter's final scene is the culmination of this strategy. Other editors faced with an incomplete text here take pains to showcase the potency of the gossips' speech. Jean Treperel, who published an edition of the *Quinze Joyes* in Paris (1499), compensated for his faulty exemplar by composing his own version of the final chapter; central to his reconstruction is a scene in which one of the wife's gossips employs a variety of conversational tactics to hoodwink the husband.[97] More important, de Worde's translator has demonstrated his willingness to amend his exemplar where he finds it deficient. In the "Thirteenth Joy," when the husband returns from war to discover that his wife has remarried, de Worde's translator allows him to both challenge the usurper to a duel and debate the situation with his wife, rather than simply

96. Crow has argued that *Bachelor's Banquet* is based on one of two imprints by François Rosset: the 1595 Paris edition or the 1596 Rouen edition. Crow, "'Quinze Joyes de Mariage' in France and England," 576.

97. The Treperel edition drastically rewrites "le quinziesme ioye." As Crow argues, it "looks as if the editor, having lost his original text, has had to make it up from memory." Crow, "'Quinze Joyes de Mariage' in France and England," 571. The text of this edition has been reproduced in *Der Treperel-Druck der Quinze Joyes de Mariage*, ed. Arthur Fleig (Griefswald: Julius Abel, 1903). The "Fifteenth Joy" appears on 44–45.

accept it. Though the husband is of course unsuccessful, the addition nonetheless brings the chapter to a more satisfying resolution.[98] Moreover, this
translator has already included a scene in which a gossip lays verbal siege to
the husband: in the "Second Joy," he provides a detailed account of a gossip's deft conversational maneuvers. That is, de Worde's translator has not
only the disposition but also the means to expand the final scene of the
"Fifteenth Joy" to include the gossips' conversational triumph. He chooses
instead to close his text with an image of the gossips' feast.

The translator of the *Fyftene Joyes* highlights the subversive potential of
the gossips' spiritual kinship—their unorthodox pastoral care and problematic alliances—only to foreclose these possibilities by reducing the women's
words to the conviviality of the gossips' feast. The antifeminist humor that
he has both embraced and resisted ultimately has the last laugh, for the feast
that had been so central to his exploration of the English gossips becomes
the method for containing them. In this concluding gesture, de Worde's
translator both pays tribute to the gossips' songs and demonstrates the principal on which they operate: women's troubling conversations are silenced
by the passing of the cup, as the literary gossips' drunken gatherings are
used to trivialize the conversational communities of the historical women
who stand behind them.

Gossips and the *Gospelles*

Like the *Fyftene Joyes,* the *Gospelles of Dystaues* uses the gossips' feast to
diffuse the potency of women's speech. Here, however, the conversation
belongs not to a community of spiritual kinswomen who share the arts of
marital manipulation, but rather to a gathering of neighbors, who convene
to compose the gospel according to women. That is, in the *Gospelles,* the
gossips' feast is used not to illuminate the goings-on at a lying-in, but to
contain the problematic teachings of a female textual community. While the
Fyftene Joyes explores English gossips in all their complexity, the *Gospelles of
Dystaues* deploys them as a stereotype to denigrate female erudition. This
tactic belongs not just to de Worde's translator, Henry Watson, who interpolates the gossips into his French source, but to de Worde himself, who
includes a series of woodcuts that reveal the larger implications both of the

98. Crow, "'Quinze Joyes de Mariage' in France and England," 575.

gossips' feast and of the narrative more generally.[99] In de Worde's edition, text and image work in tandem to turn female erudition into idle talk.

At the center of these interpolative strategies lies a single image—a woodcut that de Worde incorporates to frame the gossips' feast. Playing on the stock figure of the schoolmaster, the woodcut depicts a woman sitting at a pulpit, reading from an open book to three male children (figure 2). De Worde had used the image before. As part of the series he commissioned to accompany Stephen Hawes' *Example of Virtue* (1509), the image first represented "dame sapyence," sometime schoolmistress to the poem's male dreamer.[100] Dame Sapience reappears several times in de Worde's publications. At times she depicts allegorical figures, such as Lady "Gramer," Lady "Logyke," and Lady "Rethoryke"; at times she represents historical women, like the duchess of Bologne.[101] But despite her changing identity, in all cases, the woman in this woodcut is a figure of female erudition who lectures to male audiences on topics essential to their success. In the *Gospelles of Dystaues,* however, this woodcut functions quite differently. Presiding over the gossips' feast, this woman who not only reads but teaches from her book, resonates with and is implicated in this celebratory gathering of loquacious women. Indeed, the image, along with its textual companion, the gossips' feast, is deployed in de Worde's edition to condemn female "scholars" and the unauthorized "textual communities" gathered around them—both within the fictional confines of the *Gospelles* itself and in the historical communities beyond it.[102]

99. Henry Watson has been identified as the "H.W.," who appears in the prologue to the *Gospelles*: "at the request of some my welbeloued I. H. W. haue translated this treatyse þat conteyneth the texte of the gospelles of dystaues" (fol. y2r). All abbreviations have been silently emended.

100. *Example of Virtue,* fol. Bb2v. The woodcut is no. 1258 in Edward Hodnett, *English Woodcuts 1480–1535* (Oxford: Oxford University Press, 1973). A facsimile reproduction of Hawes's poetry is available in Frank J. Sprang, *The Works of Stephen Hawes* (Delmar: Scholars' Facsimiles and Reprints, 1975).

101. The three allegorical figures appear in Hawes's *Pastime of Pleasure* (1509), fols. C1r, C3v, and C5r; "Ydain duchesse of Boulyon" appears in the *Knyght of the Swanne* (1512), fol. M1v.

102. Brian Stock first used the term "textual community" to describe the ways that religious/ heretical groups in the eleventh and twelfth centuries organized themselves around and through the shared interpretation of a core group of texts. *The Implications of Literacy: Written Language and Models of Interpretation in the Eleventh and Twelfth Centuries* (Princeton: Princeton University Press, 1983), esp. 88–92. More recently, scholars have employed the term to refer to various late medieval reading communities. See, for example, Felicity Riddy's discussion of women's textual communities in "'Women Talking About the Things of God': A Late Medieval Sub-Culture," in *Women and Literature in Britain, 1150–1500,* ed. Carol M. Meale, 2nd ed. (Cambridge: Cambridge University Press, 1996), 104–27. For an alternative account of women's textual com-

These additional features of de Worde's edition might at first appear superfluous in light of the text's relentless parodying of female learning. Composed by Henry Watson, de Worde's apprentice and one of his most prolific translators, the *Gospelles* follows its source, the anonymous French satire *Les Evangiles des quenouilles* (c. 1466–74) quite closely.[103] Unlike his colleague, the anonymous translator of the *Fyftene Joyes,* Watson does not endeavor to resist the antifeminist humor of his French exemplar but rather revels in its every detail. Depicting a community of women who use their spinning circle to produce a compendium of female "science," the *Gospelles* repeatedly invites its audience to laugh at these women who pretend to be scholars. So relentless is the parody that it is tempting to see this narrative as a sustained and successful antifeminist joke, in which laughter functions to nullify—to "adnychyll," to use Watson's Middle English word—the real possibility of women's knowledge.[104] Indeed, as Gretchen Angelo has argued, the author of the *Evangiles* uses this device in order to establish his own authority as a writer, valorizing male textual production over female orality by representing these women's work as a "deformed imitation of male scholarly discourse."[105] However, despite the fact that the narrative is structured by this

---

munities, see Rebecca Krug, *Reading Families: Women's Literate Practice in Late Medieval England* (Ithaca: Cornell University Press, 2002), esp. 12–16.

103. Watson was, along with Robert Copland and Andrew Chertsey, one of de Worde's three main translators. Like Copland, Watson also served as one of de Worde's apprentices, though we have no evidence to suggest that he embarked on a printing career of his own. Between 1502 and 1518, Watson translated six texts for de Worde, the *shyppe of fooles* (STC 3547), the *chirche of the euyll men and women* (STC 1966), *Valentine and Orson* (STC 24571.3), the *hystorye of Olyuer of castylle* (STC 18808), the "noble history of King Ponthus" (STC 20107), and the *Gospelles*. N. F. Blake, "Wynkyn de Worde: The Later Years," *Gutenberg Jahrbuch* (1972): 128–38, esp. 129–30; H. S. Bennett, *English Books and Readers, 1475 to 1557*, 2nd ed. (Cambridge: Cambridge University Press, 1969), 159–63; and Boffey, "Wynkyn de Worde," 244.

104. In one of his few departures from the French text, Watson claims that men, through their derisive attitude toward both the *Gospelles* and women more generally, "adnychyll," rather than simply ignore ("ygnorent"), the great nobility of women (A2r). All quotations from the *Evangiles* are taken from *Les Evangiles des quenouilles,* ed. Jeay.

105. Gretchen V. Angelo, "Author and Authority in the *Evangiles des quenouilles,*" *Fifteenth-Century Studies* 26 (2000): 21–41, 29. Although the *Gospelles* has been all but ignored by critics, the last decade has seen a renewed interest in the *Evangiles.* The conversation has focused on the contestation between male and female methods of textual production, a subject scholars have identified as a particular preoccupation of the Burgundian court. Along with Angelo, see Laura Doyle Gates, "Distaff and Pen: Producing the *Evangiles des quenouilles,*" *Neophilologus* 81, no. 1 (1997): 13–20; Catharine Randall, "Gossiping Gospels: The Secret Strength of Female Speech in *Ancien Régime* France," *Women in French Studies* 8 (2000): 97–115; and Kathleen Loysen, *Conversation and Storytelling in Fifteenth- and Sixteenth-Century French Nouvelles* (New York: Peter Lang, 2004), 18–57.

Figure 2. Woodcut illustration of a woman at a pulpit reading, c. 1510. The *Gospelles of Dystaues*, D2r. Huntington Library 13067. Reproduced by permission of the Huntington Library, San Marino, Calif.

antifeminist joke, there remains something more complicated and troubling about the female erudition it represents, a subversive potential that the text's humor alone cannot fully dismiss. This is not to say that the *Gospelles* ultimately celebrates female erudition, but rather to suggest that as the text progresses, the women's teachings threaten to escape the humor that licensed them.[106] And it is to contain this potential, to reassert the narrative's structuring joke, that Dame Sapience and her gossips' feast are deployed.

The specter of female erudition is conjured early in the text of the *Gospelles*. As the narrator introduces his subject, he explicitly draws a parallel between the project of the *Gospelles of Dystaues* and the project of the Gospels themselves. Just as the words of Christ were recorded by the four evangelists so that they should not be forgotten but rather forever illuminate the world, so too the "wordes and auctorytees of the auncyent women" must be recited by female evangelists—"syxe matrones wyse & prudent"—to ensure that they remain forever in women's memories (A2v). There must be six "doctresses" rather than four, the narrator explains, because "in euery wytnesse of vyce there must be .iii. women for two men" (A2v), that is, in a court of law it takes three women to equal the testimony of two men.[107] By mentioning the witnessing of vice, the narrator suggests just how far the *Gospelles* are from Holy Writ. In fact, he is at constant pains to reassure his audience that the activity of these six wise matrons is not biblical translation—that their text is not the Gospels rendered in the vernacular by female biblical scholars who spin for their day jobs. Establishing the parameters of his joke, the narrator reassures his audience that the women's lessons are not the serious work of Scripture but inconsequential female knowledge.

The narrator is in a position to vouch for the trivial nature of the women's "wordes and auctorytees" both because he has been a student of their text since his youth (A2r) and, more important, because he is a member of their conversational community: "it is trouth that vpon a nyght after souper for to take my disporte & passe the tyme Ioyously in the longe wynter nyghtes bytwene Crystmas and Candelmas last past I transported me into the hous of a well aeged damoysell my neyghbour nere where as I was accustomed for to resorte & deuyse with her for dyuers of her neyghbours came theder for to spynne and deuyse of dyuers small and Ioyous purposes wherat

106. Adopting a more sympathetic view of the text, Randall argues that the *Evangiles* testifies to the "secret strength" of female speech, suggesting that it was "probably" by a female author. "Gossiping Gospels," 97–115, 97.

107. *Evangiles*, ed. Jeay, 152.

I toke grete pleasure and solace" (A3r–v). The narrator is not just a scribe but a *confidant*, privy to the diverting conversations of his female companions. It is no accident that their conversations take place between Christmas and Candlemas. Not only is this the time of the year when the nights are at their longest—a period, as Madeleine Jeay explains, of carnivalesque rejoicing particularly auspicious for old women[108]—but also it marks the time between Mary's childbirth and her purification. That is, the narrator joins the women's community during the period of the holy lying-in. In the *Gospelles*, however, the male narrator's attendance at this all-female gathering is not represented as inappropriate or illicit. Indeed, the verbal alliance forged between the women and their new male "gossip" appears to defy both social and literary conventions. This scribe-narrator is not the hypervirile monk achieving bodily intimacy through conversational familiarity that Chaucer gives us in the *Shipman's Tale;* rather he is an "aeged" cleric, long since past the days of doing "Venus werke."[109] At the same time, he is not a conversational outsider, eavesdropping on the women's conversations in order to record secretly every venomous word.[110] Rather, he is "accustomed" to attending such gatherings and has been invited by the company of women for the express purpose of writing down what they say. What is more, he takes pleasure in hearing and *participating* in the conversations of these women, "devising" with them "of small and Ioyous purposes." His position as the *Gospelles*'s textual disseminator is predicated on his congenial relationship with this community.[111] In turn, his congenial relationship with the community is dependent on the nature of their "devising." So long as their "devising" consists of chatter and discussion, rather than interpretations and proclamations, he will participate.[112] So long as the purposes of which they devise remain "small," that is trivial and idle, he is content.

Far from idle, however, these women have much more serious "werke"

108. Ibid., 154.

109. Even when the women offer him a young damsel as payment for his services, he refuses, claiming, albeit with a hint of irony, that he awaits "nothynge but the messanger of god for to call [him] vnto the Ioye eternell" (E5v).

110. Cf. Dunbar's narrator in the *Tretis of the Twa Mariit Wemen and the Wedo.* See also Stanton's compelling discussion of male narrators who spy on women at a lying-in: "Recuperating Women," esp. 252–53.

111. Fully aware of their companion's literary reputation, the women determine that he should be their scribe, because they asssume that he "shold do theyr werke well seynge that other tymes [he] had wryten of ladyes vn-to theyr laude & praysynge" (A3v).

112. See *Middle English Dictionary*, "devisen," 7a, 7b, and 8a. Throughout the text, the narrator plays upon both the trivial and nontrivial denotations of the word "devise."

in mind.[113] They seek an authoritative and authorizing text, which sets out the learning of ancient women, in order to counter the multitude of texts—defamatory ballads and contagious books (A3v)—that slander their sex. They understand that in order to legitimate their knowledge, they need a textual monument to that knowledge. They need to produce the gospel according to women. While the content of the *Gospelles* departs radically from Scripture, it does not take as its subject the topics that other antifeminist texts might lead us to expect. Unlike the talk of their predecessors in the *Fyftene Joyes,* the conversation of the doctresses is not a discourse on the means of attaining sovereignty, property, and sexual license in marriage. Nor is it an excuse for wives to wax lyrical about their husbands' waning sexual prowess. Rather, it is an anthology of women's lore—a compendium of "old wives' tales," cataloguing superstitions, prognostications, and herbal remedies.[114] The doctresses teach other wives how to predict the sex of a child (A7r), how to prepare a proper diet for a pregnant woman (fish heads produce overly large mouths [B1r]), how to get rid of warts (B8v), and how to make a husband love one child more than another (they must each eat a piece of the same dog's ear [D7v]). The lessons are relatively tame, even socially conservative perhaps, suggesting the consequences for women who are not diligent in their household duties.[115]

Although these "old wives tales" keep female erudition in the realm of the trivial, their method does not. The doctresses understand that an authoritative text must have a particular appearance and genealogy. That is, they recognize the role that Scholasticism plays in legitimizing texts. The *Gospelles* thus comes complete with glosses, "þat some wyse and dyscrete matrones haue added and yet shal in multeplyenge þe texte" (A4v). Their "auctoritee," however, is not drawn solely from the scholarly apparatus, from the fact that *Gospelles* looks like an authoritative text, but instead derives in part from the erudition of the doctresses themselves. These wise matrons boast impeccable credentials, having "sene and herde recorded by

---

113. The women make explicit the fact that they consider their project not "disport" but "werke," decreeing that the six days of their dictation will correspond to the six workdays of the week (A4v).

114. Madeleine Jeay traces in the text some 250 authentic Picard and Flemish folk beliefs. *Savoir faire: une analyse des croyances de* Evangiles des quenouilles, *Moyen Français* 10 (Montréal: Ceres, 1983).

115. Some of the chapters, for example, read as lessons in home economics, as the doctresses explain the consequences for a wife who leaves her yarn unspun (B7v–8r) or who does not change her sheets regularly enough (C4r).

[their] predecessours dyuers thinges of the olde testament & the newe & other thynges true & of good auctoryte" (A4v). The doctresses' expertise in reciting the *Gospelles of Dystaues* emanates from their knowledge of the true Gospels, among other worthy texts, and is described as a textual tradition handed down orally from their mothers before them. Most importantly, textual authority is drawn from the authorizing community that assembles to hear it.[116] The more women—wives, widows, and maids—who come to hear the readings, the greater the "auctoryte" of the text.[117] As Laura Doyle Gates has argued, this brand of scholarship, with its multiple authorities and its multiplying text, is a far cry from medieval Scholasticism.[118] This is what happens, the narrator seems to chuckle, when women pretend to be scholars. Yet for all its humorous multiplicity, the women's conversational community and its organization around a central text resembles quite closely Brian Stock's description of religious/heretical textual communities in the High Middle Ages. These women share knowledge of a core text, they meet to discuss the interpretation of that text, and they are guided in their instruction by charismatic leaders—the doctresses—who boast interpretative mastery over this shared text.[119]

It is in the figure of this community's most charismatic leader that the least trivial and most troublesome moments in the *Gospelles of Dystaues* occur—those moments that connect this fictional community with unauthorized historical communities in late medieval England. On the fourth day of the

116. This is not unlike the community the author facetiously invokes at the opening of his text: "Assemble than for to verefye & put forth the wordes and auctorytees of the auncyent women" (A2r).

117. Unanimously approving Dame Isengryne's plan for the *Gospelles*, the women "sayd that withouten faute they wolde be there & prayed some of theyr neyghbours as well yonge as olde þat they wolde be there to auctoryse better theyr chapytres" (A5r).

118. Gates enumerates the ways in which the "scholasticism" of the doctresses falls short of the orthodox practice it emulates: the lack of a complete authorizing text, the lack of a "closed community" of scholars, and the lack of a "rigid hierarchy" between text and gloss. "Distaff and Pen," 16. See also Karma Lochrie's discussion of the "multiplying" of sources enacted by the Wife of Bath. *Covert Operations,* 58.

119. Stock, *Implications of Literacy,* 88–92. What is more, although the doctresses and their assistants share little socially or spiritually with the nuns and devout laywomen, who for Felicity Riddy constitute a late medieval English subculture, these "textual communities" resonate with one another nonetheless. Both meet to share and discuss a text that they know well, both perpetuate a textual tradition that is bequeathed from women to their female "heirs," and both share a textuality that is at once spoken and written, participating in a textual community that is also a speech community. Riddy, "Women Talking About the Things of God," esp. 106–13.

proceedings, the narrator announces the arrival of Dame Sebylle of the Mar-reys, a worthy wife whose reputation precedes her: "And in what place or assemble that she was in she had alwaye the last worde for to make conclu-syon and so she toke alwaye auauntage for the whiche cause there came dyuers wyues whiche had not ben there before" (C6r). The quintessential female "auctorytee," Sebylle is revered by "assistants" everywhere because she has the last word in all matters interpretative. Heretofore, while the chapters may have bored the male narrator with their "folysshe reasons," there has been little in the gospels to make him uncomfortable.[120] A true "archewyf," Sebylle is sure to make him ill at ease. Although she, like her colleagues, does speak of matters concerning the household economy, the subject on which she has the last word is sex. At first, she speaks only in the abstract, with gospels outlining the consequences for forbidden relation-ships. But we can only imagine the narrator's discomfort when she moves from the abstract to the practical. Detailing the cure for an impotent rooster, Sebylle explains how garlic can make a "cocke feble and nyce" able "to kepe the better his ryghtes towarde the hennes" (C8v). Eager to add her authoritative gloss, one of the "wyse and dyscrete matrones" (A4v) cannot help but capitalize on Sebylle's innuendo, responding that she wishes there were such an herb for "nyce husbandes" (C8v). It is difficult to imagine the narrator taking solace in this particular type of devising.

Throughout the course of Sebylle's lecture, the narrator becomes increas-ingly ostracized from the community of women who previously were his conversational familiars. While he has marked his difference from that com-munity throughout the text, critiquing the value of both their project and their conversation—he refers to their lore as "babyll" (C1v) and their meet-ings as a marketplace selling only words (A5v)—it is only when Sebylle speaks of impotence, that he seeks solace in a community of men: "It dys-pleased me moche that I myght not haue the company of ony man for to laughe & passe the tyme for certaynly the countenaunce and manere of them was ryght sauage and straunge and to my thynkynge it semed them that all the worlde sholde be gouerned by theyr constytycyons and wordes" (D1r). Whereas at the beginning of the text, the narrator passed the time devising with his female neighbors, now he requires men's company in order to

---

120. One possible exception might be Isengryne's quasi-sexual cure for the "sekenes in her pappes," which one of the matrons takes up as a joke. But the digression is brief and contained (B1v).

laugh at his own joke. His nervous laughter here reveals the fact that humor is no longer capable of containing these women's words. We might be tempted, influenced by the binary oppositions that structure so much of late medieval antifeminist discourse, to read the narrator's remarks as being provoked by the mention of impotence—the sterile clerk being offended by hypervirile women. But there is a more compelling reason for the narrator's rant. Sebylle's contentious chapters are not just about sex, but about punishment for illicit sex. In fact, what Sebylle and her assistants "devise" over the course of several chapters comes dangerously close to an alternative manual of penance. Sebylle, it appears, is not just an "archewyf" but a heretic.

That Sebylle's gospels move from the trivial to the heretical seems plausible in light of her lineage. As the narrator explains, "her estate and conuersacyon" (C6r) are inextricably linked. On her grandmother's side, Sebylle comes from Savoy, "where out came fyrste the vaudoys of whiche scyence she hadde reteyned a grete parte" (C6r). Established in the late twelfth century by Valdes, the Vaudois (or Waldenses) were a religious sect dedicated to the ideal of evangelical poverty whose preaching earned them condemnation as heretics by the Council of Verona in 1184. As Jeay explains, Savoy was one of the strongholds of the movement, which recruited its members from subaltern, laboring classes and attracted "les femmes déclassées"—a social class to which Sebylle and her conversational community clearly belong.[121] Though the movement continued throughout the later Middle Ages and into the early modern period (in fact it still exists in a modified form), by the fifteenth century, the inquisitors had diffused the sect's heretical power, rendering the name synonymous with sorcery, a science in which many of the doctresses in the *Gospelles* are trained.[122] Sebylle's "penitential" gospels, however, tend toward the heretical rather than the magical.[123] She deals not in charms and curses, but in penance and restitution.

Like the writers of orthodox penitential manuals, Sebylle is concerned

---

121. *Evangiles*, ed. Jeay, 168. For the most recent scholarship on the Waldenses, see Euan Cameron, *The Reformation of Heretics: The Waldenses of the Alps, 1480-1580* (Oxford: Clarendon Press, 1984), and *Waldenses: Rejections of Holy Church in Medieval Europe* (Oxford: Blackwell, 2000); Peter Biller, *The Waldenses, 1170-1530: Between a Religious Order and a Church* (Aldershot: Variorum, 2001); and Gabriel Audisio, *The Waldensian Dissent: Persecution and Survival, c. 1170-1570*, trans. Claire Davison (Cambridge: Cambridge University Press, 1999).

122. *Evangiles*, ed. Jeay, 168.

123. While Jeay notes the connection between Sebylle's heretical background and her discourse on sexual taboo, she does not discuss the "pentitential" dimension of the scene: "Le jeudi, Sébile des Mares qui passe pour Vaudoise, reprend sans ordre les thèmes déjà traités . . . plus

with the dividing and subdividing of sin: what manner of person committed the sin and with whom, were they of the clergy, were they married, was it habitual or a singular occurrence, were they kin, and so on.[124] These subdivisions are immediately evident in Sebylle's "penitential" chapters, as each one outlines a different consequence and cure for the various manners of transgression. Chapter 3 covers questions of kinship, detailing the punishment due to a man who knows his gossip carnally,[125] while chapter 4 discusses sexual transgression involving the clergy: a man who has sex with a nun, a religious or a secular priest who has sex with a woman.[126] The fifth chapter treats the other partner in the illicit couplings in chapter 4, the priest's "companion,"[127] with chapter 6 complicating the question by discussing what happens when the priest's companion is a married woman.[128] Finally, chapter 7 tackles the problem of adultery when both parties are married.[129]

But the interest in categorization—form rather than content—is all that

directement reliés à sa biographie, une série de tabous sexuels touchant les personnes consacrées et l'inceste par affinité spirituelle." *Evangiles*, 16.

124. These are exactly the kinds of questions that priests are encouraged to ask their parishioners during confession. See, for example, Mirk's *Instructions for Parish Priests*, ed. Edward Peacock, EETS, o.s. 31 (London: Kegan Paul, Trench, Trübner, 1902), esp. 38–40; and *Speculum Sacerdotale*, ed. Edward H. Weatherly, EETS, o.s. 200 (London: Oxford University Press, 1936), esp. 63–89.

125. "He that knoweth carnally his gossep at his request may never entre in to paradyse yf his godsone doo not with his good wyll the penaunce / fyrste for his godfather / and after for his moder. Glose. Crystyne the sauage sayth that who that weddeth his gossep neuerthelesse that they be Ioyned togyder carnally yet it thondreth / or maketh some orage/eyther by londe or by water" (C4v). "Gossep" here refers the mother of his godchild, denoting the coparental bond between parent and godparent of a child. In the Huntington Library's copy of the *Gospelles*, the forms for C4v and C6v have been interchanged, so that chapters three through six of Sebylle's lecture (C4v) appear before she is introduced (C5v). Because the Huntington's copy is the only complete version of the text, I follow its signature numbers.

126. "Who someuer knoweth a nonne carnally / or a woman vyoled / and deflored by copulacyon of a man of relygyon / or seculer preest / knowe for certayne that they shall all dye an euyll dethe / and with gretter payne and doloure than þe other folke" (C4v).

127. "A preestes hoore the whiche perseuereth alway in her synne unto the dethe / knowe for also true as the gospell þat she is the deuylles hors [*sic*] / and it behoueth not to pray for her in ony maner. Glose. One amongest them sayd the which knewe that artycle that the synne myght be forgyuen by þe [pray]ers of the preest and by the chyldren that they haue to[gyder] / notwithstandynge that comunely they make an e[uyl end]e" (C4v).

128. "Yf a seculer preest / or another man of relygyon knowe carnally a wedded woman / he shall never haue pardon of the synne / tyl that he haue impetred pardon of her husbande agaynst the whiche he dyde offende so greuously. Glose. Certaynly answered an olde matrone of fyue score yere" (C4v).

129. "Yf a man maryed enhabyte with the wyfe of his neyghboure he closeth the gate of paradyse hymselfe / and shal neuer entre knocke he neuer so harde. Glose. Margot clapete sayth

Sebylle's gospels share with orthodox penitential manuals, at least those manuals adhering to the decrees of the Fourth Lateran Council. The model of penance her chapters suggest completely excises the authority of the parish priest. It does not require confession—at least not auricular confession to an ordained member of the Church—nor does it rely on the fasting and prayer of the sinner as a means of atonement. By thus calling into question the parish priest's role in absolution, Sebylle's gospels resonate with the concerns of heterodox groups in both England and France. The Lollards argued against the practice of mandatory private confession, claiming that any layperson had the right to hear confession, for only God could offer absolution.[130] The Vaudois, at the time of the text's composition, similarly excised the role of the ordained priest, claiming that the *barbes,* the "lay pastors" of their sect, had the power to hear confession.[131]

Sebylle advocates more radical changes to confessional practice than just the removal of the parish priest, however. What she and her assistants suggest is a model that invokes a kind of communal cure for transgression. Prayers must come not from the sinner but from the one most implicated by the sin: the godchild whose mother slept with her gossip, the children of the priest and his concubine. Sin is not kept secret as it is in auricular confession but rather is made open. As chapter 7 describes, in order to attain salvation, the transgressors must seek forgiveness from those against whom they have transgressed. Sin must be made public in order to be cured. Here again, Sebylle's words echo those of historical heretics. Although private shrift was upheld by the Vaudois (albeit with the priest replaced by a *barbe*), public confession was advocated by some Lollards as an alternative to the secretive shrift ordained by the pope.[132] By espousing this form of penance, Sebylle's gospels, while departing from contemporary penitential manuals, have orthodox as well as heretical overtones. The practice of solemn public penance as sanctioned by the Church, replaced by the Fourth Lateran Council's mandate of auricular confession, still lingered in both England and France into the fourteenth century and perhaps beyond.[133] Moreover, the

---

that it shall neuer be opened to hym tyll he haue obteyned pardon of hym that he dyde the offence to" (C5r).

130. See Anne Hudson, *The Premature Reformation: Wycliffite Texts and Lollard History* (Oxford: Clarendon Press, 1988) esp. 294–301.

131. Cameron, *Reformation of Heretics,* 86–92.

132. Hudson, *Premature Reformation,* 297.

133. See Mary C. Mansfield, *The Humiliation of Sinners, Public Penance in Thirteenth-Century France* (Ithaca: Cornell University Press, 1995). In chapter 4, Mansfield discusses the varieties of public penance and describes the "standard" ritual of solemn public penance in which the peni-

adulterers and priests' concubines of Sebylle's lectures were among the sinners who, according to the older doctrine, received solemn public penance.[134]

Along with public penance, Sebylle's "penitential" gospels advocate a variation on the orthodox practice of "restitution," the act of making satisfaction not only to God but to the one sinned against.[135] Not formally a part of penance, restitution was considered by ecclesiastical authorities to be a necessary, but not sufficient, condition for absolution. Generally speaking, restitution was concerned with financial satisfaction and was therefore often applied to monetary transgressions: usurers were to repay the money they had gained falsely, merchants were to return their false profits to those they had cheated, knights were to repay the tenants they had exploited, and so on. The practice did, however, extend to other transgressions that had financial consequences: homicide, libel, and mutilation. The only sexual crimes requiring restitution involved men who had deflowered virgins and women whose adulterine children had usurped the inheritance of legitimate heirs.[136] Here again, the restitution was monetary. Yet Sebylle advocates seeking forgiveness from, rather than paying restitution to, the person offended. While ecclesiastical authorities agreed that this could be a possible form of secular satisfaction if the penitent was financially unable to make the necessary restitution, they did not recognize it as a form of satisfaction for injuries that were not financial in nature.[137] By contrast, there is documentation suggesting that at least some Lollards advocated exactly this kind of restitution as a proper form of penance.[138]

I am not suggesting that we should take Sebylle's gospels seriously as a

---

tent, his transgressions made public, was ritually expelled from the church on Ash Wednesday, left to beg during Lent, and ceremonially readmitted to the community of the faithful on Maundy Thursday.

134. According to Mansfield, priestly concubinage, violence against clerics and church property, adultery, usury, and blasphemy are among the sins punished with solemn public penance. *Humiliation of Sinners*, 99.

135. For a discussion of restitution, see Mansfield, *Humiliation of Sinners*, esp. 55–59 and 85–88; John Bossy, *Christianity in the West, 1400–1700* (Oxford: Oxford University Press, 1985), 45–56, esp. 46–49; Tentler, *Sin and Confession*, 340–43; and Lea, *History of Auricular Confession*, 2:43–72.

136. Tentler, *Sin and Confession*, 340–43. See also Lea, *History of Auricular Confession*, 2:50–52. In the case of adulterine children, if the wife was unwilling or unable admit the transgression to her husband, she was required to make monetary restitution, either through her own means, paying for the nurturing of the child herself, or through the child, who should enter a convent or depart to another land so as to relieve the family of its financial burden.

137. Mansfield, *Humiliation of Sinners*, 86.

138. Hudson, *Premature Reformation*, 299.

heterodox treatise on penance in sympathy with either the Lollards or the Vaudois.[139] Rather, I want to take note of the way in which, despite all the humor surrounding Sebylle's gospels, despite the fact that the narrator introduces her in such a way as to expose her erudition as ridiculous, the model of penance that she and her assistants advocate resonates in intriguing ways with more legitimate heterodox concerns. To interpret the narrator's response to Sebylle's lecture as the familiar antifeminist reaction of a sterile cleric to an oversexed woman is to miss the much more troubling threat that Sebylle poses. She has overstepped her bounds, leaving the trivial behind and coming dangerously close to the matters of proper religion in her "holy" gospels—the only lessons to receive such an accolade (D1r).[140] What is more, this fictional community and its authorizing text have come to resemble too closely those unauthorized textual communities actually convening in England and France. And it is this overstepping that causes the narrator to retreat to a community of more rational (and presumably orthodox) men, to make explicit his joke about how funny it would be if the words and constitutions of women governed the world.

Threatening to undo the antifeminist joke on which the *Gospelles* is structured, Sebylle's teachings do not simply raise the hackles of the text's narrator; they provoke a response from both de Worde and his translator. For it is here that Henry Watson transforms these doctresses and their assistants into gossips and it is here that the image of Dame Sapience appears. As Sebylle concludes her reading and the narrator invokes the specter of female rule, one of the assistants suggests "a lytel Joyous banquet" to celebrate the noble teaching of the doctresses, declaring that through their gospels women "shal come to haue domynacyon ouer the men" (D1v). Her proclamation has a metamorphic effect on her audience: formerly a good neighbor, Mehalte Ployarde becomes "a ryght gode gossep" (D1v), who steals food from her husband to feast with her female companions. Through Mehalte's trans-

---

139. The text actually seems to have more in common with Lollard writing on the subject than it does with ideas of the contemporary Vaudois. The Vaudois, as I argue above, supported the idea of private confession as well as the notion of continual prayer as penance. See Cameron, *Reformation of Heretics*, 90–92. This partial resonance with Lollard polemic may account for the fact that the *Gospelles* were never reprinted in England and enjoyed much less popularity there than the *Evangiles* did in France. That is, it may be that the ideas expressed in the text, however comic, came too close to heresy in an English context.

140. While the other doctresses' lessons are considered wise, good, and of great authority, only Sebylle's are declared to be "holy" by her audience.

formation, Watson announces to English readers that what these women share is not a "lytel" banquet but a gossips' feast.

Departing from his usually conservative translation practices, Watson interpolates the English gossips into this French narrative. In the *Evangiles,* Mehault is not a *commere,* but "une bonne galoise" (1065), not a baptismal sponsor but "[une] femme qui aime le plaisir"—a woman who loves pleasure.[141] The pleasure enjoyed by the "galoise" is of a sexual nature as other occurrences of the word reveal.[142] In the *Livre du Chevalier de La Tour,* the "Galoys" are men and women given over to sexual license. Similarly, in the *Quinze Joyes de Mariage,* the "galoise" of the "Seventh Joy" is a promiscuous wife who believes her husband's sexual prowess to be severely lacking. When William Caxton encounters the "galoyses" in 1484, he leaves the word in the original French, offering no Middle English equivalent.[143] De Worde's anonymous translator, facing Caxton's interpretative challenge two decades later, translates the "galoise" twice: once as "a felowe good" and the second time as a "gossyp."[144] In the *Gospelles of Dystaues,* however, Watson's "ryght gode gossep" is not characterized by the sexual license of the "galoise"—at least not at this moment in the text.[145] Rather, as the first assistant to take up the rallying cry for female domination through the doctresses' words, she is both a champion of women's speech and a woman who loves to feast with her companions at her husband's expense. In short, Mehalte Ployard is a "ryght gode gossep" not in the company of the gossyp-galoise, but in the tradition of the English gossips' songs.

Borrowing the tactics of his anonymous colleague, Watson uses the gossips' feast to trivialize the women's problematic teachings. Feasting and female erudition are inextricably linked here by the assistant's proclamation: let us feast, for it is through the teaching of the doctresses that we shall gain domination over the men. By accepting one half of the proposal, the women accept the other, and as a result, Sebylle's threatening gospels are subsumed

141. *Evangiles,* ed. Jeay, 192.

142. Randall Cotgrave makes the sexual license of the "galoise" explicit: she is "a scurvy trull, scabby queane, mangie punk, filthy whore," fol. Rr7v.

143. *The Book of the Knight of the Tower,* trans. William Caxton, ed. M. Y. Offord, EETS, s.s. 2 (London: Oxford University Press, 1971), 161–63.

144. *Fyftene Joyes,* fols. H1r and H2v.

145. Later in the text, Mehalte, much to the surprise of her younger companions, declares that she still loves to "wynche" (D2v). Further distancing Mehalte from the sexual license of the *galoise,* Watson replaces an obscene remark about her sexual endeavors—the French text announces that she "savoit assez du bas voler"—with a claim about her ability to pilfer successfully (D1v).

by the gossips' feast. Whereas before the women praised one another for their words of wisdom, now they laud each other's culinary suggestions. Both types of language, the narrator suggests, are equally valuable, that is, valueless—"soo many reasons without effecte" (D1v). Moreover, the feast continues to taint the women's conversation long after their appetites have been sated; indeed, it disrupts the next day's gospels. When the women convene the following evening, instead of immediately commencing their scholarly work as they have done on each of the preceding nights, they take "tyme for to deuyse" (D2v)—to chatter idly—about the events of the feast. Exclaiming that they haven't had that much fun in ages, they jokingly criticize one another for their gluttony: "Ihesu neyghboure how ye dronke yester nyght" (D2v). Our good gossip, Mehalte Ployarde, was, it seems, the worst offender; she drank as if "all was hers," leaving companions to wonder whether she arrived home safely without waking up her husband. A true "good gossip," Mehalte uses the invocation of her husband as an opportunity to impugn his sexual prowess. And as the women begin to complain about their husbands' wares, their previously subversive conversation degenerates into antifeminist stereotype. By associating the doctresses and their assistants with the drunken chattering of the gossips' songs, Watson makes both the women and their teachings easy to dismiss.

Standing between the feast and the women's "devising" about it, between the "ryght gode gossep" and her idle talk about her husband's ware, is the image of Dame Sapience (figure 2). The woodcut is strikingly different in both theme and composition from the program of illustration that precedes it. Until this point, the woodcuts have been explicitly connected to the text. Borrowed from de Worde's edition of the *Fyftene Joyes of Maryage,* they depict the doctresses through factotum images in which the name of each speaker appears in a banner above her head. In addition, each of the preceding images has been a composite of three smaller woodcuts.[146] The first (figure 3) acts as a frontispiece, depicting the diligent scribe-narrator flanked by two doctresses (Abunde and Isengyne);[147] the second (figure 4) heralds

---

146. The blocks de Worde uses here, which appeared for the first time in his edition of the *Fyftene Joyes,* are copied from Antoine Vérard. As Martha Driver explains, the technique of composite images, refined by Johann Grüninger and popularized by Vérard, is adopted by de Worde by 1507. Martha Wescott Driver, "Illustration in Early English Books: Methods and Problems," *Books at Brown* 33 (1986): 1–49, esp. 34–45 and figures 27, 30, and 32.

147. The image appears twice on both the title page and its verso. In both instances, the image is a composite made of five smaller pieces, the three central images and two ornamental borders.

Figure 3. Dame Isengryne, Dame Abunde, and the ever-toiling narrator, from the *Gospelles of Dystaues*, A1r and v. Reproduced by permission of the Huntington Library, San Marino, Calif.

ke vpon her to rede the fyrſt monday where as was aſſig
ned/⁊ ſayd that withouten faute they wolde be there/⁊
prayed ſome of theyr neyghbours as well yonge as olde
ƥ they wolde be there to auctoryſe better theyr chapytres
¶This charge toke ryght gladly dame Iſengryne ⁊ ſayd
that ſhe wold do her beſt/in ſaynge this ſhe torned her to
warde me and requyred me right louyngly that J wolde
be her ſecretary/⁊ in lyke wyſe dyde all the other/⁊ that
they wolde make me be rewarded by ſome of them the
whiche were the yongeſt at my cheſynge/ for the whiche
rewarde J thanked them and helde me for content.

¶The ordynaunce of the fyrſt daye/⁊ of the deſcryp-
cyon of dame Iſengryne of Glaye ⁊ what ſhe was.

Figure 4. Three Doctresses: Dames Isengryne, Abunde, and Gamberde,
from the *Gospelles of Dystaues*, A5r. Reproduced by permission of the
Huntington Library, San Marino, Calif.

Dame Isengryne's outline of their scholarly endeavor by presenting three of the doctresses (Isengryne, Abunde, and Gamberde) who will bring her plan to fruition; and the third (figure 5) portrays a changing of the guard between two doctresses who are attended by a council of "assistants."[148] In each of these images, the women stand in conversation. Their authoritative text is either wholly absent or hidden from view on the male scribe's writing table. Given this pattern, what we expect from the fourth woodcut is an image composed of three smaller blocks, one of which would depict the evening's *lectrice,* Gamberde the Faee, already familiar to us from her earlier appearance in the text (figure 4). What we see instead, however, is a full block image of Dame Sapience reading from her authoritative text. While the male scribe is still nominally present—one of the children writes on a scroll—this "doctress" preaches not to a congregation of women, but to a male audience.

Although it is clear that de Worde deviates markedly from his program of illustration by introducing an image of Dame Sapience at this point in the narrative, his reasons for doing so are not immediately obvious. Turning to the French incunable editions of the *Evangiles* offers little insight into this interpretive dilemma. Matthias Huss's program of illustration, which recurs in all four of his editions as well as Claude Nourry's 1501 printing, is designed specifically for the text.[149] There are four distinct images, two of which are repeated, so that a woodcut marks the opening of each day's lecture. In two of the images, the women's distaffs are clearly present. Three of the woodcuts illustrate the narrative's setting: the male scribe is seated with his implements of textual production readily visible while a doctress speaks from her lectern. A fourth depicts the scribe entering the room while one of the women lifts up his coat to reveal the legs beneath it. In the French program of illustration, the relationship between image and text is for the most part quite straightforward; the woodcuts depict the scenes that unfold in the narrative.

Unlike de Worde's images, the French program of illustration indicates no thematic or compositional break after Sebylle's lecture. Rather, the

148. The doctress whose banner is lacking the type that would identify her is in all likelihood Transeline, who speaks just before Abunde, the doctress on the left of the frame. The image appears just before Abunde begins her gospels.

149. For the dates and descriptions of Huss's editions, see *Evangiles,* ed. Jeay, 38–40; plates between pages 24 and 25 reproduce both the Huss and de Worde woodcuts.

Upon the wednesday at the houre accustomed
came and assembled all the wyues the whiche
were accustomed for to come theder to here þ
lecture and redynge / and there came with the
dyuers other as wel yonge as olde that hadde
not ben there before / by the Instruccyon of theyr neygh-
boures. And they thus assembled came dame Abunde of þ
ouen that for that nyght had ben establysshed for to rede
her gospel so as she dyde. But before that I procede to the
chapytres of the same I wyll wryte of her estate and maner. It is trouthe that in her yonge aege she was a chappe
woman of lecherye all by tayle / and thenne afterwarde
she helde a fayre shoppe at bruges amonge þ marchautes

Figure 5. Dame Abunde, (Dame Transeline?) and the congregation of
assistants, from the *Gospelles of Dystaues*, C2r. Reproduced by permission
of the Huntington Library, San Marino, Calif.

woodcut that appears is a repetition of an earlier image.[150] That de Worde did not reproduce the French woodcuts in his edition does not prove that he is using his own images for particular effect. It could simply be that the French copy-text on which the translation was based did not contain Huss's images and therefore de Worde had no access to them.[151] Alternatively, the cost of commissioning a new set of illustrations, even pirated ones, may have been too high for such a small text. Although these economic and practical constraints may account for de Worde's reuse of blocks from the *Fyftene Joyes,* they do not explain why de Worde changes his program of illustration at exactly this moment in the text, especially when he had a factotum image of Gamberde already to hand.[152] Similarly, we cannot attribute the break to a shortage of blocks: this textual moment would not have occurred in the same form as any of the previous composites. Moreover, judging from his use of composites in the *Fyftene Joyes,* there were plenty of these factotum women available for use. The change is not due to space constraints, as de Worde has used smaller ornamental blocks throughout the text to finish lines and complete columns. Finally, it would be a mistake to dismiss the placement and selection of the image as merely accidental, the result of a carelessly produced volume. De Worde has taken considerable care with this little text, generously (and regularly) employing decorative borders, line-filling ornaments, and grotesque initials in addition to these woodcuts.[153] The appearance of this learned woman in the middle of a gossips' feast, then, must be intentional.

150. It depicts the scribe, seated with pen and scroll in hand, and a doctress seated in a lecturer's chair, attended by an audience of spinning women. The woodcut occurred previously at the opening of Dame Isengryne's lecture on the first day. I base my discussion of the images' placement on Techener's facsimile, *Les Euangiles de connoilles faictes en lonneur et exaulcement des dames, Les Joyeusetez facéties et folastres imaginations* 1 (Paris: Techener, 1829). Although this facsimile falsely purports to be a reproduction of the 1493 printing by Jehan Mareschal, Jeay has identified this text as Matthias Huss's third imprint, c. 1485–87. See *Evangiles,* ed. Jeay, 39 n. 79.

151. This seems quite probable as the edition to which de Worde's *Gospelles* bears the closest textual relation—the Rouen imprint—did not include illustrations. *Evangiles,* ed. Jeay, 36–50.

152. Martha Driver notes de Worde's "tendency to economical reuse of blocks." "Illustration in Early English Books," 32. While taking an image from the *Example of Virtue* is hardly uneconomical, the discarding of the Gamberde images is striking nonetheless, especially as he has already quite happily reused both the Abunde block (three occurrences) and the Isengryne block (two occurrences).

153. He seems to have paid the same care and attention to decoration in the *Gospelles of Dystaues* that he paid to many of his verse romance publications. Much recent scholarship, including the work of Carol Meale, Seth Lerer, and A. S. G. Edwards has revealed de Worde's careful attention to the placement of illustrative woodcuts in his publications. Carol M. Meale, "Caxton, de Worde, and the Publication of Romance in Late Medieval England," *The Library* 14,

Framed by idle chatter, this image of female erudition invites multiple interpretations. It is possible, as Catharine Randall argues, that the woodcut represents a female discourse so authoritative that it infantilizes the male scribe, thus illustrating the triumph of "female tradition and experience" over male scholarly authority that she sees depicted in the narrative more generally.[154] But given that the image is flanked by the feasting and idle talk that discredit female discourse, such a sympathetic reading seems unlikely. More plausibly, Dame Sapience might stand as an admonition to the women chattering idly around her—her embodiment of substantive scholarship shaming their foolish endeavor. Yet neither the text nor Watson's particular translation of it has been interested in differentiating among women. Quite the contrary, the text has continually moved to conflate different kinds of speech and different kinds of women. The narrator, through his repeated use of the word "devise" has equated all manifestations of female conversa-tion, from the "scholarly" to the ridiculous. Pleasant conversations on win-ter evenings and joyous reminiscences of drunken feasts, gospels and prognostications, homeopathic remedies and alternative models of penance are ultimately synonymous, reducible to the category of "devising." Simi-larly, Watson's translation transforms all manner of women, scholars and gluttons alike, into "ryght gode" gossips. And it is precisely through this conflationary logic that de Worde's woodcut must be understood. Indeed, the image functions in service of this agenda, equating legitimate female scholarship—for there is nothing parodic about the image itself—with the jangling of the gossips' feast. Set in this context, the erudition that this fe-male scholar imparts becomes nothing more than the "reasons without ef-fecte" spouted by the gossips in the surrounding text.

That this figure of female erudition becomes implicated in and tainted by the gossips' feast has ramifications beyond the *Gospelles of Dystaues*. Taken out of her safe allegorical context and placed in the company of this suspect textual community, Dame Sapience becomes a woman rather than

no. 4 (1992): 283–98; Seth Lerer, "The Wiles of a Woodcut: Wynkyn de Worde and the Early Tudor Reader," *Huntington Library Quarterly* 59, no. 4 (1998): 380–403; and A. S. G. Edwards, "Poet and Printer in Sixteenth-Century England: Stephen Hawes and Wynkyn de Worde," *Gu-tenberg Jahrbuch* (1980): 82–88.

154. Randall, *Gossiping Gospels*, 102–3, 103. Randall argues that the *Evangiles* exalts the po-tency of female speech. Because she uses de Worde's woodcuts to offer a reading of the French text, she overlooks both the impact of the gossips' feast and the ways in which this image would resonate in its English context.

an abstract virtue, a female scholar who has the ability to disseminate texts—unauthorized, potentially heretical texts, unaccompanied by clerical interpretation. She is a woman who not only reads from a book but also teaches from it; she is her own interpretative guide. In short, she is a woman who could quite easily be mistaken for a Lollard. As Claire Cross has argued, Lollard women were "reasoners in scripture," interpreters of text who taught their neighbors and family members.[155] Although much recent scholarship by Shannon McSheffrey and Rebecca Krug, among others, has quite rightly called into question the extent of both the literacy and agency of women in Lollard conventicles, the fact remains that countless women were brought before tribunals for their connection with these unauthorized textual communities.[156] While not all Lollard women were able to read Lollard tracts from the page, they were nonetheless capable of disseminating the interpretations of those tracts and in certain instances of standing in for the tracts themselves.[157] Moreover, textual communities with female members did not have to be heretical to be problematic. As Felicity Riddy has demonstrated, even textual communities of orthodox women, both aristocratic and religious, aroused the suspicion of ecclesiastical authorities.[158] Any woman with a book who is not guided in her interpretation by a male cleric is cause for concern. Any such community can easily slip into heresy—a potential comically underscored by Sebylle's "penitential" gospels.

When de Worde printed the *Gospelles of Dystaues*, cultural anxieties about unauthorized textual communities and about the unregulated circulation and consumption of unsanctioned texts ran high. Clerics like Reginald Pecock asserted their professional right to textual composition and dissemi-

---

155. Claire Cross, " 'Great Reasoners in Scripture': The Activities of Women Lollards, 1380–1530," *Medieval Women,* ed. Derek Baker (Oxford: Blackwell, 1978), 359–80.

156. Shannon McSheffrey, "Literacy and the Gender Gap in the Late Middle Ages: Women and Reading in Lollard Communities," *Women, the Book, and the Godly,* ed. Lesley Smith and Jane H. M. Taylor (Cambridge: D. S. Brewer, 1995), 157–70, and *Gender and Heresy: Women and Men in Lollard Communities, 1420–1530* (Philadelphia: University of Pennsylvania Press, 1995); and Krug, *Writing Families,* 114–52.

157. For example, Alice Colins of Ginge, famous for her ability to recite texts, was frequently called before a Lollard conventicle to serve *as* the text. Alice "could recite much of the Scriptures, and other good books; and therefore when any conventicle of these men did meet at Burford, commonly she was sent for." John Foxe, *Acts and Monuments,* ed. George Townsend (London, 1843), 4:238. See also McSheffrey's insightful argument that this account of Alice's "performance" actually demonstrates women's lack of agency in Lollard conventicles. "Literacy and the Gender Gap," 162–63.

158. Riddy, "Women Talking About the Things of God."

nation in response to Lollard texts.[159] With Henry VIII's accession to the throne, the Church renewed its campaigns against the Lollards.[160] Lutheran texts were arriving from the Continent and being disseminated by English presses in "alarming numbers."[161] And even de Worde himself was brought before the authorities for circulating heretical texts to women. According to the records of the consistorial court of the bishop of London, in 1524, de Worde was summoned before Bishop Tunstall for printing the *Ymage of Love,* "alleged to contain heresy."[162] After confessing both to printing the text and to distributing sixty copies to the nuns of Syon Abbey, de Worde was warned and ordered to recall all copies of the text in circulation.[163]

In this vigilant early sixteenth-century climate, de Worde's woodcut of the female scholar reading from her book, situated thus on the pages of the *Gospelles of Dystaues,* stands as an emblem for problematic textual communities. What is being subverted by the gossips' feast in de Worde's edition of the *Gospelles,* then, is not just the comic threat posed by Sebylle and her "penitential" gospels, but also the very real anxieties about unauthorized female textual communities throughout England. That de Worde is concerned with diffusing this threat is evidenced by the text's final image (figure 6). In it "Dame Berthe the horned" is seated hearing the plea of a male "suitor."[164] Gone is the pulpit, gone is the atmosphere of erudition, gone are the well-dressed students. Most importantly, the open book has vanished. The troublesome text has been replaced by the distaff, symbol of domesticity rather than learning. A man stands before Berthe the Horned but dressed in tatters, he awaits redress not instruction. What remains of female

159. The opening of Pecock's the *Reule of Love,* for example, speaks to precisely this anxiety about unsanctioned "preachers" instructing audiences with inappropriate texts. Reginald Pecock, *The Reule of Crysten Religioun,* ed. William Cabell Greet, EETS, o.s. 171 (Millwood: Kraus Reprint, 1987). See Krug's insightful analysis of Pecock's professionalist agenda, *Writing Families,* 137–38.

160. Cross, "Great Reasoners in Scripture." See also John A. F. Thompson, *The Later Lollards, 1414–1520* (London: Oxford University Press, 1965).

161. Henry R. Plomer, *Wynkyn de Worde and His Contemporaries from the Death of Caxton to 1535; a Chapter in English Printing* (London: Grafton, 1925), 93. Plomer provides a summary of these records, 90–94. See also N. F. Blake's account, "Wynkyn de Worde: The Later Years," 132–33.

162. Plomer, *Wynkyn de Worde,* 94.

163. For a discussion of the rationale behind the Consistorial Court's decision to label the *Ymage of Love* heretical and the role that Syon Abbey played in that decision, see Krug, *Reading Families,* esp. 203–6.

164. Hodnett, no. 1011. As the oldest of the doctresses at eighty, it is perhaps appropriate that Berthe appears as the "wydred old wenche" who rejects the proposal of Godfrey Gobelive in the *Pastime of Pleasure* (M4r). This is the only other text in which the image occurs.

clusyon of theyr gospelles / and after whan I hadde taken
my gobettes / bothe paper / pêne / and ynke I transpozted
me to the place accustomed . And I comen theder sat me
downe in my syege accustomed . Dyuers of ꝑ scolers was
comen theder alredy that began foz to voyde theyr dystas
ues. foz they myght not spynne foz the honoure of the sa-
terdaye and of the vyrgyn Mary. I had not soiournued the
re but a whyle whan dame Berthe ꝑ hozned came accom-
panyed with dyuers of her frendes and neyghbcures / foz
to rede her gospell and contynue as to doo that whiche she

Figure 6. Dame Berthe the horned and her "suitor," from the *Gospelles
of Dystaues*, E2v. Reproduced by permission of the Huntington Library,
San Marino, Calif.

erudition, here, is an antifeminist caricature: a grotesque woman who rules lower-class men with her distaff. Safely translated into "gossips," the doctresses and their assistants—and the female textual communities that stand behind them—are returned to the realm of antifeminist stereotype. Far more than an imported antifeminist satire, the *Gospelles of Dystaues*, as de Worde prints it and Watson translates it, brings to the English literary marketplace a text that both suggests the dangerous potential of women's textual communities and demonstrates a particularly English method for controlling them—a text whose "gossip" transforms female erudition into idle chatter.

The *Gospelles of Dystaues* closes with the "conclusyon and excusynge of the auctor," a few brief remarks that present the audience with instructions on how to read this narrative. Addressing men and women alike—"you my lordes and also my ladyes"—this "auctor" attempts to avert any misconceptions regarding the teachings of the doctresses, advising readers not to seek the "apparaunce of ony trouth" in their words. The *Gospelles* is not intended to be a "good introduccyon" to this female "science," he declares, but rather is meant "to shewe and declare the fragylyte of theym that soo deuyse ryght often whan they be togyder" (E6r). That is, the purpose of this text is to reveal the moral weakness of those women who engage in such trifling and unproductive speech.

In the *Gospelles*, as in the *Fyftene Joyes*, subversive female speech is translated into idle talk. Like the revised pastoral syllabus taught at the lying-in, the doctress's unorthodox penitential theory becomes synonymous with the "devising" so integral to the gossips' feast. Both texts raise the specter of women's pastoral instruction, revealing the possibilities and consequences of female alliances. Whereas the translator of the *Fyftene Joyes* explores the English gossips in all their complexity, depicting the troubling teaching they espouse, Henry Watson uses the reputation of the English gossips to foreclose those disturbing possibilities. In both texts, by making these women "crye and clappe," by having them overindulge in food and drink, in short by transforming them into "ryght gode" gossips, de Worde's translators attempt to dispel the problematic connection between women's speech and pastoral practice.

Through their interpolations, the *Gospelles of Dystaues* and the *Fyftene Joyes of Maryage* reveal what is at stake in the figure of the gossip and, by extension, in the gossips' songs, whose tropes they not only echo but illuminate. These literary gossips are not simply drinking companions who meet at the local tavern; they are spiritual kin who engage in unorthodox pastoral instruction, teaching each other far more than either the tenets of the orthodox faith or the location of the finest wine. Despite the texts' insistent disclaimers to the contrary, the conversation of these women is not merely the "talk of tryfles" or the devising of "small and Joyous purposes"; rather it is speech of social and religious consequence. Moreover, in these women's words audiences hear echoes of the historical gossips, women bound by both pastoral obligation and a formal state of friendship, whose conversations participate in and enable negotiations integral to their socioeconomic life. The gossips' talk, both fictional and historical, is anything but idle. Indeed, the *Gospelles* and the *Fyftene Joyes,* as well as the alewife group to which they pay tribute, reveal a deep cultural anxiety about the potential dangers posed by these women's words—words that become legible only when we recognize the pastoral responsibilities and social conventions that define the "gossips" rather than the tavern conviviality that circumscribes them.

At the same time, however, the "good gossips" of late medieval literature are precisely the mechanism through which trifling talk becomes women's work. English translators and poets use these literary figures to trivialize both the women and their words, conflating one with the other and subverting both in the passing of the gossips' cup. By the early seventeenth century, as the *Bachelor's Banquet* reveals, gossips were synonymous with the idle talk that takes their name. But it was during the late medieval period, in the words exchanged at the gossips' feast and the aspersions cast in the gossips' songs, that the not-so-idle talk of these not-so-idle women became "gossip."

CONCLUSION

In the morality play *Mankind*, the three mischievous villains—Nought, New-Guise, and Nowadays—run through the audience taking up a collection. These rascals explain that unless the crowd gives up its gold coins, the main attraction will not take the stage: "Gif us rede reyallys, if ye will se his abhominabull presens."[1] First heard only as a disembodied voice telling the tale of his imminent arrival, the character they advertise is none other than Tutivillus, the recording demon made infamous by late medieval penitential literature. His appearance fits perfectly with the play's earlier lessons about the dangers of idle talk. Mercy, the play's sermonizing virtue, has sternly warned the ever-prattling vices that they will repent their "idyll language" (147). Invoking the biblical admonition so popular with late medieval preachers, he reminds both the mischief-makers and their audience that on Judgment Day all men must yield accounts "for every idyll worde" (173). In *Mankind*, however, unlike the countless other texts in which this demon appears, Tutivillus does not record idle talk, he embodies it. Trafficking in jangles, he whispers false rumors about Mercy's demise. Sharing his professional secrets, he gossips with members of the audience about his tactics and makes them complicit in his machinations by asking them to keep his counsel. Tutivillus's transformation from idle talk's scribe to gossip itself makes

---

1. *Mankind, Medieval Drama*, line 465.

him a much more dangerous foe. No longer a minor demon, Tutivillus becomes the "Devell" (884) himself, master of all vices, who tempts Mankind into a life of crime with his "fablys delusory" (881).

Tutivillus, like the idle talk he represents, is characterized by contradiction: he is both dangerous and entertaining, an "abhominabull presens" and a 'worschippfull man" (465), trifling and powerful. Of all worldly temptations, only his idle talk has the power to lead Mankind astray. What is more, he is both the preacher's nemesis and his alter ego: the actor who played the role of Mercy also doubled as Tutivillus.[2] Behind the captivating attire of the gossiping demon audiences could see the moralizing preacher. Although this doubling of roles reflects the practical necessities of a small theater troupe, it also illustrates the connection between the two characters. Just as Mannyng holds his audience's attention by framing his sermons as idle talk, so Mercy uses Tutivillus as a vehicle for conveying his pastoral lessons to Mankind. Urging his "congrygacion" (188) to be vigilant against this entertaining but dangerous foe, Mercy explains that Tutivillus casts his "nett" (303) before Mankind's eyes in order to capture his imagination and cloud his vision. Dressed as the gossiping demon, he then demonstrates how difficult it is to recognize the machinations of this crafty adversary who uses every trick in his verbal arsenal to bring Mankind "to mischeff and to schame" (606).

Like Tutivillus, gossip is both entertaining and easily overlooked. For critics, gossip is either dismissed as light and trifling talk—a distraction from and a degradation of more serious kinds of speech—or relegated to the margins as transgressive discourse. Yet these tales of idle talk are "delusory" fables. And for scholars, as for Mankind, the failure to see idle talk clearly has genuine consequences. As I have argued throughout this book, taking gossip seriously offers compelling insight into late medieval English culture as well as into idle talk itself. Preachers and their congregations, poets and their audiences recognized idle talk as a serious threat and a powerful tool. Gossip in late medieval England was not considered trifling; it shaped people's lives in deeply consequential ways. Idle talk transformed social and familial relationships both for the fictional women who appear throughout the pages of late medieval plays, carols, and narrative poems and for the historical women who stand behind them. Gossip shaped the relationship between priests and their parishioners, from the pulpit and in the confessional. And for late medieval poets, it provided a tool for altering classical

2. David Bevington, *Medieval Drama*, 901.

sources as well as popular tales. Far from trivial, gossip was language with incredible force.

Idle talk was particularly problematic for ecclesiastical authorities. Despite the many pastoral tools designed to control gossip, priests and penitential writers often found themselves having to shore up their authority against it. For a man like the preacher of *Jacob's Well*, for example, idle talk was a persistent obstacle. It threatened both to drown out his voice and to expose the failures of his preaching practice. Although he represents an extreme case of the besieged cleric, neither his situation nor his failure is unique. Gossip's threat to the pulpit, however, was institutional as well as practical, for ecclesiastical authorities used idle talk as a weapon against their jangling congregations. The preacher of *Jacob's Well* saw idle talk only as a menace, but Mannyng recognized its pastoral potential, employing it to transform his exemplary narratives into the latest news. Even as he preached against gossip, Mannyng's exemplarity trafficked in its illicit specificity, delivering spectacular stories with local settings that came dangerously close to revealing "privitee."

While preachers were both vulnerable to and complicit in idle talk, late medieval poets embraced it as a powerful tool. For Chaucer, gossip was a favorite topic—a subject he pursued throughout his poetic career, theorizing about its methods and then deploying them, using gossip as the raw material of poetry, as a narrative mode, as a method for shaping interpretation, and above all as a device for experimenting with both narratives and narrative forms. Later poets may not have embraced gossip as wholeheartedly as Chaucer, yet idle talk nonetheless had a compelling fifteenth-century legacy. Writers took up gossip as both a subject and a device, using idle talk's powers of transformation to explore the permeability between pastoral discourse and women's speech. Simultaneously condemning women's talk as trifling and revealing its dangerous potential, these late medieval authors explored the connections between unruly women and their unruly words.

My exploration of idle talk in the pastoral discourse and literary texts of late medieval England accomplishes a dual agenda. First, the focus on gossip brings into the spotlight texts, practices, and characters that have been for the most part condemned to scholarly obscurity. Second, employing idle talk as a lens calls into question our assumptions about poets, texts, and practices that we take for granted. The two goals are of course interrelated. By investigating the pastoral strategies of the all-but-ignored preacher of *Jacob's Well*, we learn not just how all-pervasive a problem gossip could be, but how exemplarity functioned in practice rather than in theory. In the ears and on the tongues of late medieval parishioners, the ecclesiastical authority embodied in exemplary narrative was anything but stable. And in the hands of a writer like Mannyng, these supposedly authorized narratives became almost indistinguishable from the congregation's idle tales. Through the lens of idle talk, confession, the pastoral practice assumed almost universally to be a tool for surveillance and social control, begins to look like a venue for the latest news, not simply because wayward parishioners and less than perfect priests used it as an occasion to gossip, but because the rules governing this pastoral practice were steeped in narrative theory, designed to produce compelling tales.

Analyzing idle talk's role in the literary texts of the period produces similarly transformative readings. Considering overlooked narratives like the *Gospelles of Dystaues* and the *Fyftene Joyes of Maryage* does not merely expand the canon of late medieval antifeminist writing or attest to the popularity of the gossips' songs; it reveals what is at stake both in the figure of the gossip and in the cultural and pastoral practices that lie behind her. Although scholars have acknowledged the etymology of the word "gossip"—the spiritual kinswoman who accompanied the new mother as she gave birth and acted as baptismal sponsor to the newborn child—they have failed to consider how central this woman and her pastoral office were to the literature and society of late medieval England. The gossips and their conversations were integral to the social and economic lives of their communities. Only by paying attention to how English translators and poets deploy "gossip," both the woman and the word, can we fully appreciate the cultural influence of these women and their supposedly idle talk. Gossip illuminates canonical writers as well as marginalized texts. Examining Chaucer's corpus from the perspective of idle talk forces us to reconsider our assumptions about the nature of his poetic practice. When we recognize gossip as a poetic device, we see that the author so often hailed as "moral Chaucer" expresses both a willingness to experiment with and a skepticism of exemplarity. He uses characters whose idle talk we typically dismiss, like Harry Bailly, as well as those whose gossip we assume we understand, like the Wife of Bath, to call pastoral practice into question by performing all manner of narrative transformation. Harry's moralizing gossip is not incidental to the *Canterbury Tales;* it is fundamental to its structure. And the

Wife of Bath's idle talk serves less as an exemplum about subversive female speech, than as a model for Chaucerian poetics.

To take gossip seriously is to treat it not as marginalized speech but as the discourse of the authoritative center. Much rich and suggestive scholarship has demonstrated the ways in which gossip serves as a mode of resistance for marginalized groups.[3] But by assuming that gossip is women's work, we in a sense accept the narrative that orthodox authority tried to tell about this transforming talk. As I hope this book has demonstrated, gossip in late medieval England was the vehicle of canonical poets and ecclesiastical authorities as well as of unruly women. Parish priests and pastoral writers used gossip as a teaching tool, a device for holding the attention of their chattering congregations. Further up the ecclesiastical hierarchy, inquisitorial agents forced priests to gossip about the transgressions of their flocks.[4] And even papal information networks relied on idle talk as a source, using it to gather information about renegade nuns as well as heretics.[5]

To take gossip seriously is also to consider authoritative practices from the margins—to think about what pastoral practice looked like from the perspective of jangling congregations. In this light, exempla become entertaining stories with flexible morals that can be manipulated to suit the narrator's purposes—whether that narrator is a humble preacher, a bawdy innkeeper, a wise doctress, or an "archwyf." Through the lens of gossiping parishioners, confession, too, looks less like an instrument of social control and more like an intimate space for conversational and narrative exchange. To the disgust of some priests and the delight of others, sinners came to confession to tell their "sleueles talys."[6] They gossiped with their priest about their neighbors' transgressions and with their neighbors about their priest's pew-side manner. Confession served social as well as pastoral functions. It developed into a mechanism for airing community grievances.[7] And as the poetry of late medieval England reveals, private auricular confession served as a powerful model for the exchange of secrets. When women gossip

3. See, among others, Lochrie, *Covert Operations*, 56–92; Turner, *I Heard It Through the Grapevine*; and Deborah Jones, "Gossip."

4. Elliott, *Proving Woman*, 21–30; and Pegg, *Corruption of Angels*, 66–68.

5. See Innocent III's *nova quaedam nuper*, *Corpus Iuris Canonici*, 886–87.

6. *Jacob's Well*, 181/16.

7. Bossy, "Social History of Confession," 25.

in late medieval texts, they frame their talk as confession—"She knew myn herte, and eek my privetee / Bet than oure parisshe preest, so moot I thee!"—and employ it to forge social and familial bonds.[8] That is, idle talk allows women as well as priests to remake pastoral practice.

To take gossip seriously is, above all, to recognize its unlimited potential as a narrative device for poets and pastoral writers alike. Gossip's tidings make for entertaining tales, and its titillating rhetoric piques the curiosity of even the most resistant audience. But late medieval writers embrace gossip as narratively productive, not simply because it offers lively subject matter or a model for "narrative exchange,"[9] but because it provides them with a mechanism for transforming their sources and experimenting with inherited forms. Dunbar appropriates idle talk's shape-shifting potential for his poetry, using the gossip of his female characters to combine fabliau, romance, gossips' song, and antifeminist treatise, as he explores what happens when generic conventions collide. Recognizing that idle talk had literary cachet in late medieval England, Wynkyn de Worde's translators use gossip to adapt French antifeminist satires to the English marketplace. And of course, Chaucer embraces idle talk as an indispensable narrative tool. Gossip is the modus operandi of *Canterbury Tales,* the catalyst for his generic alchemy, the means by which he escapes the burden of classical "auctoritees," and the defining feature of his most infamous character. For Chaucer, as for the writers who followed him, idle talk transforms narratives, whether exemplary tales, classical sources, confessional stories, family romances, or antifeminist histories. To take gossip seriously is to acknowledge that in the literature of late medieval England this transforming talk is anything but idle.

8. *Wife of Bath's Prologue,* III. 531–32.
9. Spacks, *Gossip,* 263.

BIBLIOGRAPHY

Abraham, David H. "Cosyn and Cosynage: Pun and Structure in the Shipman's Tale." *Chaucer Review* 11, no. 4 (1976): 319–27.

Abrahams, Roger D. "A Performance-Centred Approach to Gossip." *Man: The Journal of the Royal Anthropological Institute* 5, no. 2 (1970): 290–301.

Adkins, Karen C. "Poison Pens: Gossip's Viral Knowledge." Paper presented at Dirt: An Interdisciplinary Conference, Center for Literary and Cultural Study, Harvard University, Cambridge, Mass., March 1996.

———. "The Real Dirt: Gossip and Feminist Epistemology." *Social Epistemology* 16, no. 3 (2002): 215–32.

Aers, David. *Community, Gender, and Individual Identity: English Writing, 1360–1430.* London: Routledge, 1988.

Aers, David, and Lynn Staley. *The Powers of the Holy: Religion, Politics, and Gender in Late Medieval English Culture.* University Park: The Pennsylvania State University Press, 1996.

Aiken, Pauline. "Vincent of Beauvais and Chaucer's Knowledge of Alchemy." *Studies in Philology* 41 (1944): 371–89.

Alexander, Jonathan, and Paul Binski. *Age of Chivalry: Art in Plantagenet England, 1200–1400.* London: Royal Academy of Arts, 1987.

Allen, Elizabeth. *False Fables and Exemplary Truth in Later Middle English Literature.* New York: Palgrave Macmillan, 2005.

Allen, Judson Boyce, and Patrick Gallacher. "Alisoun Through the Looking Glass: Or Every Man His Own Midas." *Chaucer Review* 4 (1970): 99–105.

Allen, Mark. "Mirth and Bourgeois Masculinity in Chaucer's Host." In *Masculinities in Chaucer: Approaches to Maleness in the Canterbury Tales and Troilus and Criseyde,* ed. Peter G. Beidler, 9–21. Cambridge: D. S. Brewer, 1998.

Allport, Gordon W., and Leo Joseph Postman. *The Psychology of Rumor.* New York: H. Holt, 1947.

An Alphabet of Tales, ed. Mary Macleod Banks. Early English Text Society (hereafter EETS), o.s. 126, 127. London: Kegan Paul, Trench, Trübner, 1904.

Ames, Joseph. *Typographical Antiquities.* 4 vols. London: William Miller, 1812.

Anderson, M. D. *Drama and Imagery in English Medieval Churches.* Cambridge: Cambridge University Press, 1963.

Anderson, Patricia Anne. "Gossips, Ale-wives, Midwives, and Witches." Ph.D. diss., SUNY Buffalo, 1992.

Andreas, James R. "'Wordes Betwene': The Rhetoric of the Canterbury Links." *Chaucer Review* 29, no. 1 (1994): 45–64.

Angelo, Gretchen V. "Author and Authority in the *Evangiles des quenouilles*." *Fifteenth-Century Studies* 26 (2000): 21–41.

Arber, Edward. *A Transcript of the Registers of the Company of Stationers of London, 1554–1640.* 5 vols. London, 1875–94.

Atchley, Clinton Parham Edwin. "The 'Wose' of *Jacob's Well*: Text and Context." Ph.D. diss., University of Washington, 1998.

Audisio, Gabriel. *The Waldensian Dissent: Persecution and Survival, c. 1170-1570.* Trans. Claire Davison. Cambridge: Cambridge University Press, 1999.

Ayenbite of Inwyt; or, Remorse of Conscience. Part I. Ed. Rev. Richard Morris. EETS, o.s. 23. London: Trübner, 1866.

———. Part II. Ed. Patricia Gradon. EETS, o.s. 278. Oxford: Oxford University Press, 1979.

The Bachelor's Banquet, ed. Faith Gildenhuys. Ottawa: Dovehouse Editions, 1993.

Baldwin, Ralph. *The Unity of the Canterbury Tales.* Copenhagen: Rosenkilde and Bagger, 1955.

Bardsley, Sandy. "Sin, Speech, and Scolding in Late Medieval England." In *Fama, The Politics of Talk and Reputation in Medieval Europe,* ed. Thelma Fenster and Daniel Lord Smail, 145–64. Ithaca: Cornell University Press, 2003.

———. *Venomous Tongues: Speech and Gender in Late Medieval England.* Philadelphia: University of Pennsylvania Press, 2006.

Bedell, John. "Memory and Proof of Age in England, 1272–1327." *Past and Present* 162 (1999): 6–12.

Bennett, H. S. *English Books and Readers, 1475 to 1557.* 2nd ed. Cambridge: Cambridge University Press, 1969.

———. *The Pastons and Their England.* Cambridge: Cambridge University Press, 1922.

Bennett, J. A. W. *Chaucer's Book of Fame.* Oxford: Oxford University Press, 1986.

Bennett, Judith M. *Ale, Beer, and Brewsters in England: Women's Work in a Changing World, 1300–1600.* New York: Oxford University Press, 1996.

———. "Misogyny, Popular Culture, and Women's Work." *History Workshop Journal* 31 (1991): 166–88.

———. "The Village Ale-Wife: Women and Brewing in Fourteenth-Century England." In *Women and Work in Pre-Industrial England,* ed. Barbara Hannawalt, 20–38. Bloomington: Indiana University Press, 1986.

Bennett, Michael. "Spiritual Kinship and the Baptismal Name in Traditional Society." In *Principalities, Powers, and Estates: Studies in Medieval and Early Modern Government and Society,* ed. L. O. Frappell, 1–13. Adelaide: Adelaide University Union Press, 1979.

Benson, C. David. *Chaucer's Drama of Style: Poetic Variety and Contrast in the Canterbury Tales.* Chapel Hill: University of North Carolina Press, 1986.

Benson, Larry D. *Glossarial Concordance to the Riverside Chaucer.* New York: Garland, 1993.

———. "The 'Love-Tydynges' in Chaucer's *House of Fame*." In *Chaucer in the Eighties,* ed. Julian N. Wasserman and Robert J. Blanch, 3–22. Syracuse: Syracuse University Press, 1986.

———. "The Order of *The Canterbury Tales*." *Studies in the Ages of Chaucer* 3 (1981): 77–120.

Benson, Larry D., and Theodore M. Andersson, eds. *The Literary Context of Chaucer's Fabliuax.* Indianapolis: Bobbs-Merrill, 1971.

Biller, Peter, *The Waldenses, 1170-1530: Between a Religious Order and a Church.* Aldershot: Variorum, 2001.

Bergmann, Jörg R. *Discreet Indiscretions: The Social Organization of Gossip.* Trans. John Bednarz, Jr. New York: Aldine de Gruyter, 1993.

Bevington, David, ed. *Medieval Drama.* Boston: Houghton Mifflin, 1975.

Biblia sacra iuxta Vulgatam versionem. 3rd ed. Ed. Robert Weber. Stuttgart: Deutsche Bibelgesellschaft, 1983.

Bitterling, Klaus. "*The Tretis of the Twa Mariit Wemen and the Wedo: Some Comments on Words, Imagery, and Genre.*" *Scottish Studies* 4 (1984): 337–58.

Blake, N. F. "Wynkyn de Worde: The Later Years." *Gutenberg Jahrbuch* (1972): 128–38.

Bloomfield, Morton. *The Seven Deadly Sins.* Michigan: Michigan State College Press, 1952.

Block, Edward A. "Originality, Controlling Purpose, and Craftsmanship in Chaucer's Man of Law's Tale." *PMLA* 68, no. 3 (1953): 572–616.

Blythe, Joan Heiges. "Sins of the Tongue and Rhetorical Prudence in 'Piers Plowman.'" In *Literature and Religion in the Later Middle Ages,* ed. Richard G. Newhauser and John A. Alford, 119–42. Binghamton, N.Y.: Medieval and Renaissance Texts and Studies, 1995.

Boecius de consolacione philosophie. London: William Caxton, 1478. STC 3199.

Boffey, Julia. "Wynkyn de Worde and Misogyny in Print." In *Chaucer in Perspective: Middle English Essays in Honor of Norman Blake,* ed. Geoffrey Lester, 236–51. Sheffield: Sheffield Academic Press, 1999.

Boitani, Piero. *Chaucer and the Imaginary World of Fame.* Cambridge: D. S. Brewer, 1984.

Book for a Simple and Devout Woman. A Late Middle English Adaptation of Peraldus's Summa de Vitiis et Virtutibus and Friar Laurent's Somme le Roi, edited from British Library Mss Harley 6571 and Additional 30944, ed. F. N. M. Diekstra. Mediaevalia Groningana 24. Groningen: Egbert Forsten, 1998.

The Book of Penance. Cursor Mundi, ed. Rev. Richard Morris. EETS, o.s. 69. London: Trübner, 1877.

The Book of the Knight of the Tower, trans. William Caxton, ed. M. Y. Offord. EETS, s.s. 2. London: Oxford University Press, 1971.

The Book of Vices and Virtues, ed. W. Nelson Francis. EETS, o.s. 217. London: EETS, 1942.

———. London, British Library, MS Additional 17013.

———. London, British Library, MS Additional 22283, fols. 92r–116r.

Boose, Lynda E. "Scolding Brides and Bridling Scolds: Taming the Woman's Unruly Member." *Shakespeare Quarterly* 42, no. 2 (1991): 179–213.

Bossy, John. "Blood and Baptism: Kinship, Community and Christianity in Western Europe from the Fourteenth to the Seventeenth Centuries." In *Sanctity and Secularity: The Church and the World,* ed. Derek Baker, 129–43. Oxford: Basil Blackwell, 1973.

———. *Christianity in the West, 1400–1700.* Oxford: Oxford University Press, 1985.

———. "The Counter-Reformation and the People of Catholic Europe." *Past and Present* 47 (1970): 51–70.

———. "The Social History of Confession in the Age of the Reformation." *Transactions of the Royal Historical Society* 25 (1975): 21–38.

Bornstein, Diane. *Distaves and Dames: Renaissance Treatises for and about Women.* New York: Scholars' Facsimiles and Reprints, 1978.

Boyle, Leonard E., O.P. "The Fourth Lateran Council and Manuals of Popular Theology." In *The Popular Literature of Medieval England,* ed. Thomas J. Heffernan, 30–43. *Tennessee Studies in Literature* 28. Knoxville: University of Tennessee Press, 1985.

Braswell, Mary Flowers. *The Medieval Sinner.* London: Associated University Presses, 1983.

Brown, Carleton, ed. *Religious Lyrics of the Fifteenth Century.* Oxford: Clarendon, 1939.

———. *Religious Lyrics of the Fourteenth Century.* Oxford: Clarendon, 1924.

Brownstein, Oscar L. "Revision in the 'Deluge' of the Chester Cycle." *Speech Monographs* 36, no. 1 (1969): 55–65.

Brushfield, T. N. "On Obsolete Punishments, with Particular Reference to Those of Cheshire." *Chester Archaeological and Historic Society Journal* 2 (1855–62): 31–48 and 203–34.

Bryan, W. F., and Germaine Dempster, eds. *Sources and Analogues of Chaucer's Canterbury Tales.* London: Routledge and Kegan Paul, 1941.

Burness, Edwina. "Female Language in *The Tretis of the Twa Mariit Wemen and the Wedo.*" *Scottish Studies* 4 (1984): 359–68.

Caesarius of Heisterbach. *Diaglous Miraculorum, Textum ad quatuor codicum manuscriptorum editionisque principes fidem.* 2 vols. Ed. Josephus Strange. Cologne: J. M. Heberle, 1851.

———. *The Dialogue on Miracles.* 2 vols. Trans. H. von E. Scott and C. C. Swinton Bland. London: Routledge, 1929.

Calendar of Inquisitions Post Mortem and Other Analogous Documents Preserved in the Public Record Office. 20 vols. London, 1904–95.

Calendar of Plea and Memoranda Rolls, 1413–1437, ed. A. H. Thomas. Cambridge: Cambridge University Press, 1943.

Cameron, Euan. *The Reformation of the Heretics: The Waldenses of the Alps, 1480–1580.* Oxford: Clarendon Press, 1984.

———. *Waldenses: Rejections of Holy Church in Medieval Europe.* Oxford: Blackwell, 2000.

Carpenter, Christine, ed. *Kingsford's Stonor Letters and Papers, 1290–1483.* Cambridge: Cambridge University Press, 1996.

———. *Locality and Polity: A Study of Warwickshire Landed Society, 1401–1499.* Cambridge: Cambridge University Press, 1992.

Carpenter, Nan Cooke. "Music in the English Mystery Plays." In *Music in English Renaissance Drama,* ed. John H. Long, 1–31. Lexington: University of Kentucky Press, 1968.

Carruthers, Leo. "Allegory and Bible Interpretation: The Narrative Structure of a Middle English Sermon Cycle." *Literature and Theology* 4, no. 1 (1991): 1–14.

———. "The Liturgical Setting of *Jacob's Well.*" *English Language Notes* 24, no. 4 (1987): 11–23.

———. "Richard Lavynham and the Seven Deadly Sins in *Jacob's Well.*" *Fifteenth-Century Studies* 18 (1991): 17–32, 22–23.

———. *La Somme le Roi et ses traductions anglaises: étude comparée.* Paris: AMAES, 1986.

———. "Where Did *Jacob's Well* Come From? The Provenance and Dialect of MS Salisbury Cathedral 103." *English Studies* 4 (1990): 335–40.

Carruthers, Mary. "Clerk Jankyn at hom to bord/With my gossib." *English Language Notes* 22, no. 3 (1985): 11–22.

———. "The Wife of Bath and the Painting of Lions." *PMLA* 94, no. 2 (1979): 209–22.

Carter, Susan. "Coupling the Beastly Bride and the Hunter Hunted: What Lies Beneath Chaucer's *Wife of Bath's Tale.*" *Chaucer Review* 37, no. 4 (2004): 329–45.

Casagrande, Carla, and Silvana Vecchio. *Les Péchés de la langue.* Trans. Philippe Baillet. Paris: Les Éditions du Cerf, 1991.

Cawsey, Kathy. "Tutivillus and the 'Kyrkchaterars': Strategies of Control in the Middle Ages." *Studies in Philology* 102, no. 4 (2005): 434–51.

Chaucer, Geoffrey. *Chaucer's Dream Poetry,* ed. Helen Phillips and Nick Havely. London: Longman, 1997.

———. *The Riverside Chaucer.* 3rd ed. Ed. Larry D. Benson. Boston: Houghton Mifflin, 1987.

———. *The Works of Geoffrey Chaucer.* 2nd ed. Ed. Fred N. Robinson. Boston: Houghton Mifflin, 1957.

Clarke, Peter. *The English Alehouse, a Social History, 1200–1830.* London: Longman, 1983.

Clifton, Linda J. "Struggling with Will: Jangling, Sloth, and Thinking in *Piers Plowman* B." In *Suche Werkis to Werche, Essays on* Piers Plowman *in Honor of David C. Fowler,* ed. Míceál F. Vaughan, 29–52. East Lansing: Colleagues Press, 1993.

Clopper, Lawrence M. "The History and Development of the Chester Cycle." *Modern Philology* 75, no. 3 (1978): 219–46.

———. "Lay and Clerical Impact on Civic and Religious Drama and Ceremony." In *Contexts for Early English Drama,* ed. Marianne Briscoe and John Coldewey, 102–36. Bloomington: Indiana University Press, 1989.

Coates, Jennifer. "Gossip Revisited: Language in All-Female Groups." In *Women and Their Speech Communities: New Perspectives on Language and Sex,* ed. Jennifer Coates and Deborah Cameron, 94–122. London: Longman, 1988.

Coffman, George R. "Another Analogue for the Violation of the Maiden in the 'Wife of Bath's Tale.'" *Modern Language Notes* 59, no. 4 (1944): 271–74.

Coldiron, A. E. B. "Paratextual Chaucerianism: Naturalizing French Texts in Early Printed Verse." *Chaucer Review* 38, no. 1 (2003): 1–15.

Collins, A. Jefferies, ed. *Manuale ad usum percelebris ecclesie Sarisburiensis.* London: Henry Bradshaw Society, 1960.

Cooper, Helen. "The Shape-Shiftings of the Wife of Bath, 1395–70." In *Chaucer Traditions: Studies in Honor of Derek Brewer,* ed. Ruth Morse and Barry Windeatt, 168–84. Cambridge: Cambridge University Press, 1990.

Copland, Murray. "*The Shipman's Tale:* Chaucer and Boccaccio." *Medium Ævum* 35 (1966): 11–28.

Copland, Robert. *Poems,* ed. Mary Carpenter Erler. Toronto: University of Toronto Press, 1993.

Corpus Iuris Canonici. Lipsiae: Bernhardi Tauchnitz, 1881.

Correale, Robert M., and Mary Hamel, eds. *Sources and Analogues of the Canterbury Tales.* Vol. 1. Cambridge: D. S. Brewer, 2002.

Cotgrave, Randall. *A Dictionarie of the French and English Tongues.* London, 1611.

Cox, Catherine S. "Holy Erotica and the Virgin Word: Promiscuous Glossing in the *Wife of Bath's Prologue.*" *Exemplaria* 5, no. 1 (1993): 207–37.

———. "The Jangler's 'Bourde': Gender, Renunciation, and Chaucer's Manciple." *South Atlantic Review* 61, no. 4 (1996): 1–21.

Crane, Thomas Frederick, ed. *The Exempla or Illustrative Stories from the Sermones Vulgares of Jacques de Vitry.* London, 1890.

Craun, Edwin D. *Lies, Slander, and Obscenity in Medieval English Literature: Pastoral Rhetoric and the Deviant Speaker.* Cambridge: Cambridge University Press, 1997.

Cressot, Marcel. *Vocabulaire des Quinze Joies de Mariage.* Paris: Droz, 1939.

Cressy, David. "Purification, Thanksgiving, and the Churching of Women in Post-Reformation England." *Past and Present* 141 (1993): 106–46.

Cross, Claire. "'Great Reasoners in Scripture': The Activities of Women Lollards 1380–1530." In *Medieval Women,* ed. Derek Baker, 359–80. Oxford: Blackwell, 1978.

Crow, Joan. "The 'Quinze Joyes de Mariage' in France and England." *Modern Language Review* 59 (1964): 571–77.

David, Alfred. "The Man of Law vs. Chaucer: A Case in Poetics." *PMLA* 82, no. 2 (1967): 217–25.

———. *The Strumpet Muse: Arts and Morals in Chaucer's Poetry.* Bloomington: Indiana University Press, 1976.

Davis, Natalie Zemon. *Society and Culture in Early Modern France.* Stanford: Stanford University Press, 1975.

Davis, Norman, ed. *Paston Letters and Papers of the Fifteenth Century.* Part 1. Oxford: Clarendon Press, 1971.

Delany, Sheila. *Chaucer's "House of Fame": The Poetics of Skeptical Fideism.* Chicago: University of Chicago Press, 1972.

———. "Politics and the Paralysis of Poetic Imagination in *The Physician's Tale.*" *Studies in the Age of Chaucer* 3 (1981): 47–60.

The Desert of Religion. London, British Library, MS Additional 37049.

———. London, British Library, MS Cotton Faustina B. vi. Part II.

———. London, British Library, MS Stowe 39.

Dinshaw, Carolyn. *Chaucer's Sexual Poetics.* Madison: University of Wisconsin Press, 1989.

Disbrow, Sarah. "The Wife of Bath's Old Wives' Tales." *Studies in the Age of Chaucer* 8 (1986): 59–71.

Douglas, Mary. *Purity and Danger: An Analysis of the Concepts of Pollution and Taboo.* London: Routledge, 1966.

Driver, Martha Wescott. "Illustration in Early English Books: Methods and Problems." *Books at Brown* 33 (1986): 1–49.

Duffy, Eamon. *The Stripping of the Altars: Traditional Religion in England, 1400–1580.* New Haven: Yale University Press, 1992.

Dunbar, Robin. *Grooming, Gossip, and the Evolution of Language.* Cambridge: Harvard University Press, 1996.

Dunbar, William. *The Poems of William Dunbar,* ed. James Kinsley. Oxford: Clarendon Press, 1979.

Duncan, Edgar H. "The Literature of Alchemy and Chaucer's Canon's Yeoman's Tale: Framework, Theme, and Characters." *Speculum* 43, no. 4 (1968): 641–46.

Eckhardt, Caroline D. "Genre." In *A Companion to Chaucer*, ed. Peter Brown, 180–94. Oxford: Blackwell, 2000.

Edwards, A. S. G. "Poet and Printer in Sixteenth-Century England: Stephen Hawes and Wynkyn de Worde." *Gutenberg Jahrbuch* (1980): 82–88.

Edwards, Robert. *Dream of Chaucer*. Durham: Duke University Press, 1989.

Eisner, Sigmund. *A Tale of Wonder: A Source Study of the Wife of Bath's Tale*. Wexford, Eng.: J. English, 1957.

Elliott, Dyan. *Proving Woman: Female Spirituality and Inquisitional Culture in the Later Middle Ages*. Princeton: Princeton University Press, 2004.

Les Euangiles de connoilles faictes en lonneur et exaulcement des dames, Les Joyeusetez facéties et folastres imaginations 1. Paris: Techener, 1829.

Les Evangiles des quenouilles, ed. Madeleine Jeay. Montreal: University of Montreal Press, 1985.

Evans, Deanna Delmar. "Dunbar's *Tretis*: The Seven Deadly Sins in Carnivalesque Disguise." *Neophilologus* 73, no. 1 (1989): 130–41.

Evans, Joan, and Mary S. Serjeantson, eds. *English Mediaeval Lapidaries*. EETS, o.s. 190. London: Kegan Paul, Trench, Trübner, 1933.

Fein, Susanna Greer. "Other Thought-Worlds." In *A Companion to Chaucer*, ed. Peter Brown, 332–48. Oxford: Blackwell, 2000.

———. "A Thirteen-Line Alliterative Stanza on the Abuse of Prayer from the Audelay MS." *Medium Ævum* 63, no. 1 (1994): 61–74.

Ferster, Judith. *Fictions of Advice: The Literature and Politics of Counsel in Late Medieval England*. Philadelphia: University of Pennsylvania Press, 1996.

The XV Comforts of Rash and Inconsiderate Marriage. London, 1683.

The Fifteen Joys of Marriage, ed. Brent A. Pitts. New York: Peter Lang, 1985.

Fine, Gary Alan. *Manufacturing Tales: Sex and Money in Contemporary Legends*. Knoxville: University of Tennessee Press, 1992.

———. "Rumors and Gossiping." In *Discourse and Dialogue*, vol. 3 of *Handbook of Discourse Analysis*, ed. Teun A. van Dijk, 223–37. London: Academic Press, 1985.

Fish, Stanley. *John Skelton's Poetry*. New Haven: Yale University Press, 1965.

Fisher, Ruth M. "'Cosyn' and 'Cosynage': Complicated Punning in Chaucer's 'Shipman's Tale?'" *Notes and Queries* 210 (1965): 168–70.

FitzRalph, Richard. *Defensio Curatorum*. In *Dialogus inter Militem et Clericum, Richard FitzRalph's Sermon: "Defensio Curatorum" and Methodius: "Þe Bygynnyng of þe World and þe Ende of þe Worldes,"* ed. Aaron Jenkins Perry. EETS, o.s. 167. London: EETS, 1925.

Flemming, John V. "The Summoner's Prologue: An Iconographic Adjustment." *Chaucer Review* 2 (1967): 95–107.

Fletcher, Angus. "The Sentence of Virginia in the *Physician's Tale*." *Chaucer Review* 34, no. 3 (2000): 300–308.

Folch-Pi, Willa Babcock. "Ramon Llull's Felix and Chaucer's Canon's Yeoman's Tale." *Notes and Queries* 212 (1967): 10–11.

Foucault, Michel. *The History of Sexuality*. Vol. 1: *An Introduction*. New York: Random House, 1978.

Fowler, Elizabeth. "Mysogyny and Economic Person in Skelton, Langland, and Chaucer." *Spenser Studies* 10 (1992): 245–73.

Foxe, John. *Acts and Monuments*. 8 vols. Ed. George Townsend. London, 1843.

"Frende ne sybbe who so byholdeth hys lothely lokys and his outward countenaunce." London, British Library, MS Additional 30944, fols. 3r–154v.

Fry, Donald. "The Ending of the *House of Fame*." In *Chaucer at Albany*, ed. Rossell Hope Robbins, 27–40. New York: Burt Franklin, 1975.

The Fyftene Joyes of Maryage. London: Wynkyn de Worde, 1509. New York: Pierpont Morgan Library, 21589. STC 15258.

Fyler, John M. *Chaucer and Ovid*. New Haven: Yale University Press, 1979.

Galloway, Andrew. "Marriage Sermons, Polemical Sermons, and *The Wife of Bath's Prologue*: A Generic Excursus." *Studies in the Age of Chaucer* 14 (1991): 3–30.

Ganim, John M. *Chaucerian Theatricality*. Princeton: Princeton University Press, 1990.

Garvin, Katherine. "A Note on Noah's Wife." *Modern Language Notes* 49 (1934): 88–90.

Gates, Laura Doyle. "Distaff and Pen: Producing the *Evangiles des quenouilles*." *Neophilologus* 81, no. 1 (1997): 13–20.

Gaylord, Alan T. "*Sentence* and *Solaas* in Fragment VII of the *Canterbury Tales:* Harry Bailly as Horseback Editor." *PMLA* 82, no. 2 (1967): 226–35.

Gellrich, Jesse M. *The Idea of the Book in the Middle Ages: Language, Theory, Mythology, and Fiction*. Ithaca: Cornell University Press, 1986.

Geoffrey of Vinsauf. *Poetria Nova*, trans. Margaret F. Nims. Toronto: Pontifical Institute of Medieval Studies, 1967.

Gerson, Jean. *Jean Gerson, Early Works*, trans. Brian Patrick McGuire. New York: Paulist Press, 1998.

———. *Oeuvres Complètes*. 10 vols. Paris: Desclée, 1961–73.

Gibson, Gail McMurray. "Blessing from Sun and Moon: Churching as Women's Theater." In *Bodies and Disciplines: Intersections of Literature and History in Fifteenth-Century England*, ed. Barbara A. Hanawalt and David Wallace, 139–54. Minneapolis: University of Minnesota Press, 1996.

———. "Scene and Obscene: Seeing and Performing Late Medieval Childbirth." *Journal of Medieval and Early Modern Studies* 29, no. 1 (1999): 7–24.

Gies, Frances and Joseph. *A Medieval Family: The Pastons of Fifteenth-Century England*. New York: Harper Collins, 1998.

Gluckman, Max. "Gossip and Scandal." *Current Anthropology* 4, no. 3 (1963): 307–16.

Goodman, Peter. "Chaucer and Boccaccio's Latin Works." In *Chaucer and the Italian Trecento*, ed. Piero Boitani, 269–95. Cambridge: Cambridge University Press, 1983.

Gordon, Jan B. *Gossip and Subversion in Nineteenth-Century British Fiction: Echo's Economies*. Basingstoke, Eng.: MacMillan, 1996.

The Gospelles of Dystaues. London: Wynkyn de Worde, 1507. San Marino: Huntington Library, 13067. STC 12091.

Gower, John. *Confessio Amantis*, ed. G. C. Macaulay. EETS, e.s. 81–82. London: Kegan Paul, Trench, Trübner, 1900–1901.

Grady, Frank. "Chaucer Reading Langland: *The House of Fame*." *Studies in the Age of Chaucer* 18 (1996): 3–23.

Gregg, Joan Young. "The Exempla of 'Jacob's Well': A Study in the Transmission of Medieval Sermon Stories." *Traditio* 33 (1977): 359–80.

———. "The Narrative Exempla of *Jacob's Well:* A Source Study with an Index for *Jacob's Well* to *Index Exemplorum.*" Ph.D. Diss., New York University, 1973.

Green, Richard Firth. "Chaucer's *Shipman's Tale,* Lines 138–41." *Chaucer Review* 26, no. 1 (1991): 95–99.

Greene, Richard Leighton, ed. *The Early English Carols.* 2nd ed. Oxford: Clarendon, 1977.

Gregory I. *Saint Gregory the Great, Dialogues,* trans. Odo John Zimmerman. Washington: Catholic University Press, 1959.

Grudin, Michaela Paasche. "Discourse and the Problem of Closure in the *Canterbury Tales.*" *PMLA* 107, no. 5 (1992): 1157–67.

Haas, Louis. "Baptism and Spiritual Kinship in the North of England, 1250–1450." Master's thesis, Ohio State University, 1982.

———. "Social Connections Between Parents and Godparents in Late Medieval Yorkshire." *Medieval Prosopography* 10 (1989): 1–21.

Hahn, Thomas, and Richard W. Kaeuper. "Text and Context: Chaucer's *Friar's Tale.*" *Studies in the Age of Chaucer* 5 (1983): 67–101.

Halasz, Alexandra. *The Marketplace of Print: Pamphlets and the Public Sphere in Early Modern England.* Cambridge: Cambridge University Press, 1997.

Hale, W. H. *A Series of Precedents and Proceedings in Criminal Causes, Extending from the Year 1475 to 1640, Extracted from Act-books of Ecclesiastical Courts in the Diocese of London.* London: F. and J. Rivington, 1847.

Hanawalt, Barbara. *Growing up in Medieval London: The Experience of Childhood in History.* New York: Oxford University Press, 1993.

———. *The Ties That Bound: Peasant Families in Medieval England.* New York: Oxford University Press, 1986.

Hanna, Ralph, III. "Brewing Trouble: On Literature and History—and Alewives." In *Bodies and Disciplines: Intersections of Literature and History in Fifteenth-Century England,* ed. Barbara A. Hanawalt and David Wallace, 1–18. Minneapolis: University of Minnesota Press, 1996.

———. "*Compilatio* and the Wife of Bath: Latin Backgrounds, Ricardian Texts." In *Latin and Vernacular: Studies in Late-Medieval Texts and Manuscripts,* ed. Alastair J. Minnis, 1–11. Cambridge: D. S. Brewer, 1989.

———. "Pilate's Voice/Shirley's Case." *South Atlantic Quarterly* 91, no. 4 (1992): 793–812.

Harrington, Norman T. "Experience, Art, and the Framing of the *Canterbury Tales.*" *Chaucer Review* 10, no. 3 (1974–75): 187–200.

Hartung, Albert E. "'Pars Secunda' and the Development of the *Canon's Yeoman's Tale.*" *Chaucer Review* 12, no. 2 (1977): 111–28.

Harty, Kevin J. "Chaucer's Man of Law and the 'Muses That Men Clepe Pierides.'" *Studies in Short Fiction* 18, no. 1 (1981): 75–77.

Harwood, Britton J. "Building Class and Gender into Chaucer's Hous." In *Class and Gender in Early English Literature,* ed. Britton J. Harwood and Gillian R. Overing, 95–111. Bloomington: Indiana University Press, 1994.

———. "Chaucer on 'Speche': *House of Fame,* the *Friar's Tale,* and the *Summoner's Tale.*" *Chaucer Review* 26, no. 4 (1992): 343–49.

Haviland, John Beard. *Gossip, Reputation, and Knowledge in Zinacantan.* Chicago: University of Chicago Press, 1977.

Hawes, Stephen. *The Works of Stephen Hawes,* ed. Frank J. Sprang. Delmar, N.Y.: Scholars' Facsimiles and Reprints, 1975.

Heffernan, Thomas J. "Sermon Literature." In *Middle English Prose: A Critical Guide to Major Authors and Genres,* ed. A. S. G. Edwards, 177–207. New Brunswick, N.J.: Rutgers University Press, 1984.

Helmholz, R. H. *Select Cases in Defamation to 1600.* Seldon Society, 101. London: Seldon Society, 1985.

Henderson, W. G., ed. *Manuale et processionale ad usum insignis ecclesiae Eboracensis.* Surtees Society, vol. 63. Durham: Andrews, 1875.

Herman, Peter C. "Leaky Ladies and Droopy Dames: The Grotesque Realism of Skelton's *The Tunnynge of Elynour Rummynge.*" In *Rethinking the Henrician Era: Essays on Early Tudor Texts and Contexts,* ed. Peter C. Herman, 145–67. Chicago: University of Illinois Press, 1994.

Herz, Judith Scherer. "*The Canon's Yeoman's Prologue* and *Tale.*" *Modern Philology* 58, no. 4 (1961): 231–37.

Higgs, Elton D. "'What Man Artow?': Harry Bailly and the 'Elvyssh' Chaucer." *Mid-Hudson Language Studies* 2 (1979): 28–43.

Hodnett, Edward. *English Woodcuts, 1480–1535.* Oxford: Oxford University Press, 1973.

Hoffman, Richard L. *Ovid and the Canterbury Tales.* Philadephia: University of Pennsylvania Press, 1966.

———. "Ovid and the Wife of Bath's Tale of Midas." *Notes and Queries* 211 (1966): 48–50.

Horstmann, Carl, ed. *The Minor Poems of the Vernon Manuscript.* EETS, o.s. 98, 117. London: Kegan Paul, Trench, Trübner, 1892–91.

Howard, Donald R. *The Idea of the Canterbury Tales.* Berkeley and Los Angeles: University of California Press, 1976.

Hudson, Anne. *The Premature Reformation: Wycliffite Texts and Lollard History.* Oxford: Clarendon Press, 1988.

Hussey, S. S. "Chaucer's Host." In *Medieval English Studies Presented to George Kane,* ed. Edward Donald Kennedy, Ronald Waldron, and Joseph S. Wittig, 153–61. Wolfboro, N.H.: D. S. Brewer, 1988.

Innocent III. *De miseria condicionis humane,* ed. Robert E. Lewis. Athens: University of Georgia Press, 1978.

Irvine, Martin. "Medieval Grammatical Theory and Chaucer's *House of Fame.*" *Speculum* 60, no. 4 (1985): 850–76.

Jacob's Well. Part I. Ed. Arthur Brandeis. EETS, o.s. 115. London: Kegan Paul, Trench, Trübner, 1900.

Jeay, Madeleine. "La popularité des 'Evangiles des quenouilles': un paradoxe révélateur." *Renaissance et Réforme* 18 (1982): 166–82.

———. *Savoir faire: une analyse des croyances de* Evangiles des quenouilles. *Moyen Français* 10. Montréal: Ceres, 1983.

———. "Le Travail du récit à la cour de Bourgogne: *Les Evangiles des quenouilles, Les Cent nouvelles nouvelles* et *Saintré.*" In *"A l'heure encore de mon escrire": Aspects de la littérature des Bourgogne sous Philippe le Bon et Charles le Téméraire,* ed. Claude Thiry, 71–86. *Les Lettres Romanes* (1997, hors série).

Jennings, Margaret. "Tutivillus: The Literary Career of the Recording Demon." *Studies in Philology* 74, no. 5 (1977): 1–95.

Jensen, Emily. "'Winkers' and 'Janglers': Teller/Listener/Reader Response in the *Monk's Tale*, the Link, and the *Nun's Priest's Tale*." *Chaucer Review* 32, no. 2 (1997): 183–95.

Jenstad, Janelle Day. "Lying-in Like a Countess: The *Lisle Letters*, the Cecil Family, and *A Chaste Maid in Cheapside*." *Journal of Medieval and Early Modern Studies* 34, no. 2 (2004): 373–403.

Johnston, Mark D. "The Treatment of Speech in Medieval Ethical and Courtesy Literature." *Rhetorica* 4, no. 1 (1986): 21–46.

Jones, Deborah. "Gossip: Notes on Women's Oral Culture." *Women's Studies International Quarterly* 3, nos. 2–3 (1980): 193–98.

Jonson, Ben. *The Staple of News*, ed. Anthony Parr. Manchester, Eng.: Manchester University Press, 1988.

Joseph, Gerhard. "Chaucer's Coinage: Foreign Exchange and the Puns of the *Shipman's Tale*." *Chaucer Review* 17, no. 4 (1983): 341–57.

Kail, J. D., ed. *Twenty-six Political and Other Poems*. EETS, o.s. 124. London: Kegan Paul, Trench, Trübner, 1904.

Kaiser, George. "The Conclusion of the *Canon's Yeoman's Tale*: Readings and (Mis)-readings." *Chaucer Review* 35, no. 1 (2000): 1–21.

Kean, Patricia M. *Chaucer and the Making of English Poetry*. Vol. 2: *The Art of Narrative*. London: Routledge and Kegan Paul, 1972.

Keen, William. "'To Doon Yow Ese': a Study of the Host in the *General Prologue* of the *Canterbury Tales*." *Topic* 17 (1969): 5–18.

Kelly, R. A. "*Occupatio* as Negative Narration: A Mistake for *Occultatio/Praeteritio*." *Modern Philology* 74 (1977): 311–14.

Kemmler, Fritz. *"Exempla" in Context: A Historical and Critical Study of Robert Mannyng of Brunne's "Handlyng Synne."* Tübingen: Gunter Narr Verlag, 1984.

Kendrick, Laura. *Chaucerian Play: Comedy and Control in the* Canterbury Tales. Berkeley and Los Angeles: University of California Press, 1988.

Kennedy, Thomas C. "Rhetoric and Meaning in *The House of Fame*." *Studia Neophilologica* 68 (1996): 9–23.

Kingsford's Stonor Letters and Papers, 1290–1483, ed. Christine Carpenter. Cambridge: Cambridge University Press, 1996.

Kinsley, James. "*The Tretis of the Tua Mariit Wemen and the Wedo*." *Medium Ævum* 23, no. 1 (1954): 31–35.

Kittredge, George Lyman. *Chaucer and His Poetry*. Cambridge: Harvard University Press, 1915.

Knapp, Ethan. "Chaucer Criticism and Its Legacies." In *The Yale Companion to Chaucer*, ed. Seth Lerer, 324–56. New Haven: Yale University Press, 2006.

Knight, Stephen. *Rymyng Craftily: Meaning in Chaucer's Poetry*. Atlantic Highlands, N.J.: Humanities International Press, 1973.

Kolve, V. A. *Chaucer and the Imagery of Narrative: The First Five Canterbury Tales*. Stanford: Stanford University Press, 1984.

Koonce, B. J. *Chaucer and the Tradition of Fame: Symbolism in* The House of Fame. Princeton: Princeton University Press, 1966.

Krug, Rebecca. "*The Fifteen Oes.*" In *Cultures of Piety: Medieval Devotional Literature in Translation,* ed. Anne Clark Bartlett and Thomas H. Bestul, 107–17, 212–16. Ithaca: Cornell University Press, 1999.

———. *Reading Families: Women's Literate Practice in Late Medieval England.* Cornell: Cornell University Press, 2002.

Kruger, Steven. "Imagination and the Complex Movement of Chaucer's *House of Fame.*" *Chaucer Review* 28, no. 2 (1993): 117–34.

Kurtscheid, Bertrand. *A History of the Seal of Confession,* trans. F. A. Marks. St. Louis: B. Herder, 1927.

Ladurie, Emmanuel Le Roy. *Montaillou, The Promised Land of Error,* trans. Barbara Bray. New York: George Braziller, 1978.

Langland, William. *Piers Plowman by William Langland, an Edition of the C-text,* ed. Derek A. Pearsall. York Medieval Texts. Berkeley and Los Angeles: University of California Press, 1978

———. *The Vision of Piers Plowman, a Critical Edition of the B-text.* 2nd ed. Ed. A. V. C. Schmidt. London: J. M. Dent, 1995.

———. *Will's Vision of Piers Plowman,* trans. E. Talbot Donaldson. New York: W. W. Norton, 1990.

The Lanterne of Liȝt, ed. Lilian M. Swinburn. EETS, o.s. 151. London: Kegan Paul, Trench, Trübner, 1917.

Lavezzo, Kathy. "Beyond Rome: Mapping Gender and Justice in the *Man of Law's Tale.*" *Studies in the Age of Chaucer* 24 (2002): 139–80.

Lawrence, William W. "Chaucer's *Shipman's Tale.*" *Speculum* 33, no. 1 (1958): 56–68.

The Lay Folks Mass Book, ed. Thomas Frederick Simmons. EETS, o.s. 71. London: Kegan Paul, Trench, Trübner, 1879.

Lea, Henry Charles. *A History of Auricular Confession and Indulgences in the Latin Church.* Vol. 1. Philadelphia: Lea Brothers, 1896.

Leaper, Campbell, and Heithre Holliday. "Gossip in same-gender and cross-gender friends' conversations." *Personal Relationships* 2 (1995): 237–46.

Lee, Becky R. "Men's Recollections of a Women's Rite: Medieval English Men's Recollections Regarding the Rite of the Purification of Women after Childbirth." *Gender and History* 14, no. 2 (2002): 224–41.

———. "The Purification of Women after Childbirth: A Window onto Medieval Perceptions of Women." *Florilegium* 14 (1995–96): 43–55.

Leitch, L. M. "Sentence and Solaas: the Function of the Hosts in the *Canterbury Tales.*" *Chaucer Review* 17, no. 1 (1982): 5–20.

Lerer, Seth. "*The Canterbury Tales.*" In *The Yale Companion to Chaucer,* ed. Seth Lerer, 243–94. New Haven: Yale University Press, 2006.

———. *Chaucer and His Readers.* Princeton: Princeton University Press, 1993.

———. "The Wiles of a Woodcut: Wynkyn de Worde and the Early Tudor Reader." *Huntington Library Quarterly* 59, no. 4 (1998): 380–403.

Levin, Jack, and Arnold Arluke. "An Exploratory Analysis of Sex Differences in Gossip." *Sex Roles* 12, no. 3 (1985): 281–86.

———. *Gossip: The Inside Scoop.* New York: Plenum Press, 1987.

Lobzowska, Maria. "Two English Translations of the XVth Century French Satire 'Les Quinze Joyes de Mariage.'" *Kwartalnik Neofilologiczny* 10 (1963): 17–32.

Lochrie, Karma. *Covert Operations: The Medieval Uses of Secrecy.* Philadelphia: University of Pennsylvania Press, 1999.

Lorens d'Orléans. *Somme le Roi.* London, British Library, MS Royal 19 C.ii.

Loysen, Kathleen. *Conversation and Storytelling in Fifteenth- and Sixteenth-Century French Nouvelles.* New York: Peter Lang, 2004.

Lucie-Smith, Edward. *Joan of Arc.* New York: Allen Lane, 1976.

Lumiansky, R. M. *Of Sondry Folk: The Dramatic Principle in the Canterbury Tales.* Austin: University of Texas Press, 1955.

Lumiansky, R. M., and David Mills, eds. *The Chester Mystery Cycle.* 2 vols. EETS, s.s. 3 and 9. New York: Oxford University Press, 1974.

Lydgate, John. *The Minor Poems of John Lydgate,* ed. Henry Noble MacCracken. EETS, o.s. 192. London: Oxford University Press, 1934.

———. *A Selection from the Minor Poems of Dan John Lydgate,* ed. J. O. Halliwell. Percy Society 4. London: Percy Society, 1840.

Lynch, Joseph. *Godparents and Kinship in Early Medieval Europe.* Princeton: Princeton University Press, 1986.

———. *"Spiritale Vinculum:* The Vocabulary of Spiritual Kinship in Early Medieval Europe." In *Religion, Culture, and Society in the Early Middle Ages,* ed. Thomas F. X. Nobel and John J. Contreni, 181–204. Kalamazoo, Mich.: Medieval Institute Publications, 1987.

Lyndwood, William. *Lyndwood's Provinciale,* ed. J. V. Bullard and H. Chalmer Bell. London: Faith Press, 1929.

MacDonald, Michael. *Mystical Bedlam: Madness, Anxiety, and Healing in Seventeenth-Century England.* Cambridge: Cambridge University Press, 1981.

Malone, Kemp. "The Wife of Bath's Tale." *Modern Language Review* 57, no. 4 (1962): 481–91.

Manly, John Matthews. "Chaucer and the Rhetoricians." *Proceedings of the British Academy* 12 (1926): 95–113.

———. *Some New Light on Chaucer.* London: Bell, 1926.

Manly, John M., and Edith Rickert. *The Text of the Canterbury Tales.* 8 vols. Chicago: University of Chicago Press, 1940.

Mann, Jill. *Chaucer and Medieval Estates Satire.* Cambridge: Cambridge University Press, 1973.

———. *Geoffrey Chaucer.* Atlantic Highlands, N.J.: Humanities Press International, 1991.

Manning, Stephen. "Fabular Jangling and Poetic Vision in the *Nun's Priest's Tale.*" *South Atlantic Review* 52, no. 1 (1987): 3–16.

Mannyng, Robert. *Handlyng Synne,* ed. Idelle Sullens. Binghamton: Medieval and Renaissance Texts and Studies, 1983.

———. *Robert of Brunne's "Handlyng Synne,"* ed. Frederick J. Furnivall. EETS, o.s. 119, 123. London: Kegan Paul, Trench, Trübner, 1901.

Mansfield, Mary C. *The Humiliation of Sinners, Public Penance in Thirteenth-Century France.* Ithaca: Cornell University Press, 1995.

Manuel des Pechiez. In Robert Mannyng's *Handlyng Synne,* ed. Frederick J. Furnivall. EETS, o.s. 119, 123. London: Kegan Paul, Trench, Trübner, 1901.

Marbode of Rennes. *De Lapidibus,* ed. and trans. John M. Riddle. Wiesbaden: Franz Steiner, 1977.

Maynadier, George H. *The Wife of Bath's Tale: Its Sources and Analogues*. London: D. Nutt, 1901.

McCracken, Samuel. "Confessional Prologue and the Topography of the Canon's Yeoman." *Modern Philology* 68, no. 3 (1971): 289–91.

McNeill, John T., and Helena M. Gamer, eds. *Medieval Handbooks of Penance*. New York: Columbia University Press, 1938.

McSheffrey, Shannon. *Gender and Heresy: Women and Men in Lollard Communities, 1420–1530*. Philadelphia: University of Pennsylvania Press, 1995.

———. "Literacy and the Gender Gap in the Late Middle Ages: Women and Reading in Lollard Communities." In *Women, the Book, and the Godly*, ed. Lesley Smith and Jane H. M. Taylor, 157–70. Cambridge: D. S. Brewer, 1995.

Meale, Carol. "Caxton, de Worde, and the Publication of Romance in Late Medieval England." *Library* 14, no. 4 (1992): 283–98.

Merry, Sally Engle. "Rethinking Gossip and Scandal." In *Toward a General Theory of Social Control*, vol. 1: *The Fundamentals*, ed. Donald Black, 271–302. New York: Academic Press, 1984.

"Mi dere lord seynt Johan in þe book of reuelaciones þat is cleped þe apocalips." London, British Library, MS Royal 18 A.x, ff. 16r–55v.

Middleton, Anne. "The *Physician's Tale* and Love's Martyrs: 'Ensamples mo than ten' as a Method in the *Canterbury Tales*." *Chaucer Review* 8, no. 1 (1973): 9–32.

Mill, Anna Jean. "Noah's Wife Again." *PMLA* 56, no. 3 (1941): 613–26.

Miller, Mark. "Displaced Souls, Idle Talk, Spectacular Scenes: *Handlyng Synne* and the Perspective of Agency." *Speculum* 71, no. 3 (1996): 606–32.

Miller, Robert P. "The Wife of Bath's Tale and Mediaeval Exempla." *ELH* 32, no. 4 (1965): 442–56.

Mirk, John. *Festial*. London: William Caxton, 1491. San Marino: Huntington Library. STC 17959.

———. *Instructions for Parish Priests*, ed. Edward Peacock. EETS, o.s. 31. London: Kegan Paul, Trench, Trübner, 1902.

———. *Instructions for Parish Priests*, ed. Gillis Kristensson. *Lund Studies in English* 49. Lund: Carl Bloms, 1974.

———. *Mirk's Festial*. Part I. Ed. Theodor Erbe. EETS, e.s. 96. London: Kegan Paul, Trench, Trübner, 1905.

Morris, Rupert. *Chester in the Plantagenet and Tudor Reigns*. Printed for the author, 1893.

Morrison, Susan Signe. "Don't Ask, Don't Tell: The Wife of Bath and Vernacular Translations." *Exemplaria* 8, no. 1 (1996): 97–123.

Murphy, James J. *Rhetoric in the Middle Ages: A History of Rhetorical Theory from Saint Augustine to the Renaissance*. Tempe: Arizona Center for Medieval and Renaissance Studies, 2001.

———. *Three Medieval Rhetorical Arts*. Berkeley and Los Angeles: University of California Press, 1971.

Muscatine, Charles. "Chaucer's Religion and the Chaucer Religion." In *Chaucer Traditions: Studies in Honor of Derek Brewer*, ed. Ruth Morse and Barry Windeatt, 249–62. Cambridge: Cambridge University Press, 1990.

A Myrour to Lewede Men and Wymmen: A Prose Version of the Speculum Vitae, ed. Venetia Nelson. Middle English Texts 14. Heidelberg: Carl Winter, 1981.

The Myroure of Oure Ladye, ed. John Henry Blunt. EETS, o.s. 19. London: Trübner, 1873.

Newman, Barbara. *God and the Goddesses: Vision, Poetry, and Belief in the Middle Ages.* Philadelphia: University of Pennsylvania Press, 2003.

Nicholson, Peter. "The Analogues of Chaucer's *Friar's Tale.*" *English Language Notes* 17 (1979): 93–98.

Niles, Philip. "Baptism and the Naming of Children in Late Medieval England." *Medieval Prosopography* 3 (1982): 95–107.

Orme, Nicholas. "Children and the Church in Medieval England." *Journal of Ecclesiastical History* 45 (1994): 563–86.

Ovid. *Metamorphoses,* ed. Frank Justice Miller. 3rd ed. Cambridge: Harvard University Press, 1977–84.

Owst, G. R. *Literature and Pulpit in Medieval England.* Cambridge: Cambridge University Press, 1933.

———. *Preaching in Medieval England: An Introduction to Sermon Manuscripts of the Period, c. 1350–1450.* New York: Russell and Russell, 1965.

Page, Barbara. "Concerning the Host." *Chaucer Review* 4 (1969): 1–13.

Paine, Robert. "What Is Gossip About? An Alternative Hypothesis." *Man: The Journal of the Royal Anthropological Institute* 2, no. 2 (1967): 278–85.

Parkinson, David. "Prescriptions for Laughter in Some Middle Scots Poems." In *Selected Essays on Scottish Language and Literature,* ed. Steven R. McKenna, 27–39. Lewiston, N.Y.: Edwin Mellen Press, 1992.

Patch, Howard R. "Precious Stones in the *House of Fame.*" *Modern Language Notes* 50 (1935): 312–17.

Patterson, Lee. *Chaucer and the Subject of History.* Madison: University of Wisconsin Press, 1991.

———. "Chaucerian Confession: Penitential Literature and the Pardoner." *Medievalia et Humanistica* 7 (1976): 153–73.

———. "For the Wyves Love of Bath: Feminine Rhetoric and Poetic Resolution in the *Roman de la Rose* and the *Canterbury Tales.*" *Speculum* 58, no. 3 (1983): 656–95.

———. "The 'Parson's Tale' and the Quitting of the *Canterbury Tales,*" *Traditio* 34 (1978): 331–80.

Paupert, Anne. *Les Fileuses et le clerc: une étude des Evangiles des quenouilles.* Paris: Champion-Slatkine, 1990.

Pearcy, Roy J. "The Genre of William Dunbar's *Tretis of the Tua Mariit Wemen and the Wedo.*" *Speculum* 55, no. 1 (1980): 58–74.

———. "Punning on 'Cosyn' and 'Cosynage' in Chaucer's *Shipman's Tale.*" *American Notes and Queries* 17, no. 5 (1979): 70–71.

Pearsall, Derek A. *The Canterbury Tales.* London: Unwin Hyman, 1985.

———. *Old and Middle English Poetry.* London: Routledge and Kegan Paul, 1977.

———. "Pre-empting Closure in 'The Canterbury Tales': Old Endings, New Beginnings." In *Essays on Ricardian Literature in Honour of J. A. Burrow,* ed. A. J. Minnis, Charlotte Morse, and Thorlac Turville-Petre, 23–38. Oxford: Clarendon Press, 1997.

———. "The Troilus Frontispiece and Chaucer's Audience." *Yearbook of English Studies* 7 (1977): 68–74.

Pecock, Reginald. *The Reule of Crysten Religioun,* ed. William Cabell Greet. EETS, o.s. 171. Millwood, N.Y.: Kraus Reprint, 1987.

Pegg, Mark Gregory. *The Corruption of Angels: The Great Inquisition of 1245–46.* Princeton: Princeton University Press, 2001.

Petersen, K. O. *The Sources of the Parson's Tale.* Radcliffe College Monographs 12. Boston: Athenæum Press, 1901.

Peyraut, Guillaume. *Summa de Vitiis.* Basel: Rodt, 1474.

Phillips, Susan E. "'Janglynge in cherche': Gossip and the Exemplum." In *The Hands of the Tongue: Essays on Deviant Speech,* ed. Edwin D. Craun, 61–94. Kalamazoo, Mich.: Medieval Institute Publications, 2007.

Pichaske, David R., and Laura Sweetland. "Chaucer on the Medieval Monarchy: Harry Bailly in the *Canterbury Tales.*" *Chaucer Review* 11 (1977): 179–200.

Pitts, Brent A. "Feast and Famine in the *Quinze Joyes de Mariage.*" *Romance Notes* 26, no. 1 (1985): 69–73.

Plomer, Henry R. *Wynkyn de Worde and His Contemporaries from the Death of Caxton to 1535; a Chapter in English Printing.* London: Grafton, 1925.

Plummer, John. "'Be Fructuous and That in Litel Space': The Engendering of Harry Bailly." In *New Readings of Chaucer's Poetry,* ed. Robert G. Benson and Susan J. Ridyard, 107–18. Cambridge: D. S. Brewer, 2003.

Pollock, Linda A. "Childbearing and Female Bonding in Early Modern England." *Social History* 22, no. 3 (1997): 286–306.

Powers, Eileen. *Medieval English Nunneries, c. 1275 to 1535.* Cambridge: Cambridge University Press, 1922.

Powicke, F. M. and C. R. Cheney, eds. *Councils and Synods with Other Documents Relating to the English Church, II: 1205–1313.* 2 vols. Oxford: Clarendon, 1964.

Pratt, Robert A. "The Development of the Wife of Bath." In *Studies in Medieval Literature in Honor of Albert Croll Baugh,* ed. MacEdward Leach, 45–79. Philadelphia: University of Pennsylvania Press, 1961.

The Pricke of Conscience, ed. Richard Morris. London: Philological Society, 1863.

Puhvel, Martin. "The Wife of Bath's Tale: Mirror of Her Mind." *Neuphilologische Mitteilungen* 100, no. 3 (1999): 291–300.

Quinn, William A. "Chaucer's Janglerye." *Viator* 18 (1987): 309–20.

Les XV Joies de Mariage, ed. Jean Rychner. Paris: Librairie Minard, 1963.

Les Quinze Joies de Mariage, ed. Joan Crow. Oxford: Blackwell, 1969.

Les Quinze Joies de Mariage, Texte de l'Edition Princeps du XVe Siècle, ed. Ferdinand Heuckenkamp. Halle: Max Niemeyer, 1901.

Ramsey, Lee. "'The Sentence of It Sooth Is.'" *Chaucer Review* 6 (1972): 198–97.

Randall, Catharine. "Gossiping Gospels: The Secret Strength of Female Speech in Ancien Régime France." *Women in French Studies* 8 (2000): 97–115.

Raybin, David, and Linda Tarte Holley, eds. *Closure in* The Canterbury Tales: *The Role of The Parson's Tale.* Kalamazoo, Mich.: Medieval Institute Publications, 2000.

Raymo, Robert R. "Jacob's Well." In *A Manual of the Writings in Middle English, 1050–1500.* 11 vols. Ed. Albert E. Hartung, 7:2262. New Haven: Connecticut Academy of Arts and Sciences, 1967.

Raymond, Joad. *The Invention of the Newspaper: English Newsbooks, 1641–1649.* Oxford: Clarendon, 1996.

Raymond of Peñaforte, *Summa de poenitentia, et matrimonio*. Rome: Ioannis Tallini, 1603.

Le Registre d'inquisition de Jacques Fournier, évêque de Pamiers (1318–1324). 3 vols. Ed. Jean Duvernoy. Toulouse: Edouard Privat, 1965.

Revard, Carter. "*The Wife of Bath's Grandmother:* Or How Gilote Showed Her Friend Johane That the Wages of Sin Is Worldly Pleasure, and How Both Then Preached This Gospel Throughout England and Ireland." *Chaucer Review* 39, no. 2 (2004): 117–36.

Reyes, Jesus L. Serrano. *Didactismo y moralismo en Geoffrey Chaucer y Don Juan Manuel*. Córdoba: Universidad de Córdoba, 1996.

Rhetorica ad Herennium, ed. and trans. Harry Caplan. Cambridge: Harvard University Press, 1954.

Richardson, Cynthia C. "The Function of the Host in *The Canterbury Tales*." *Texas Studies in Literature and Language* 12 (1970–71): 325–44.

Richardson, Janette. *Blameth Nat Me: A Study of Imagery in Chaucer's Fabliaux*. The Hague: Mouton, 1970.

Richardson, Thomas C. "Harry Bailly: Chaucer's Innkeeper." In *Chaucer's Pilgrims: An Historical Guide to the Pilgrims in* The Canterbury Tales, ed. Laura C. Lambdin and Robert T. Lambdin, 324–39. Westport, Conn.: Greenwood Press, 1996.

Riddy, Felicity. "'Women Talking About the Things of God': A Late Medieval Subculture." In *Women and Literature in Britain 1150–1500*, ed. Carol M. Meale, 2nd ed., 104–27. Cambridge: Cambridge University Press, 1996.

Robbins, Rossell Hope. "Good Gossips Reunited." *British Museum Quarterly* 27 (1963): 12–15.

———. "John Crophill's Ale-Pots." *Review of English Studies* 20 (1969): 182–89.

———. "Poems Dealing with Contemporary Conditions." In *A Manual of the Writings in Middle English*. 11 vols. Ed. A. E. Hartung and J. B. Severs, 5:1385–1536. New Haven: Yale University Press, 1975.

Robertson, D. W., Jr., "A Note on the Classical Origin of 'Circumstance' in the Medieval Confessional." *Studies in Philology* 43 (1946): 6–14.

———. *A Preface to Chaucer: Studies in Medieval Perspectives*. Princeton: Princeton University Press, 1962.

Rolle, Richard. *Richard Rolle: Prose and Verse, Edited from MS Longleat 29 and Related Manuscripts*, ed. S. J. Ogilvie-Thomson. EETS, o.s. 293. Oxford: Oxford University Press, 1988.

Root, Jerry. "'Space to speke': The Wife of Bath and the Discourse of Confession." *Chaucer Review* 28, no. 3 (1994): 252–74.

Roppolo, Joseph P. "The Converted Knight in Chaucer's 'Wife of Bath's Tale.'" *College English* 12, no. 5 (1951): 263–69.

Rosaldo, Michelle Zimbalist. "Woman, Culture, and Society: A Theoretical Overview." In *Woman, Culture, and Society*, ed. Michelle Zimbalist Rosaldo and Louise Lamphere, 17–42. Stanford: Stanford University Press, 1974.

Rosnow, Ralph L. "Gossip and Marketplace Psychology." *Journal of Communication* 27 (1977): 158–63.

Rosnow, Ralph L., and Gary Alan Fine. *Rumor and Gossip: The Social Psychology of Hearsay*. New York: Elsevier, 1976.

Rouse, Edward Clive. *Medieval Wall Paintings.* Princes Risborough, Eng.: Shire Publications, 1991.

Ruffolo, Laura. "Literary Authority and the Lists of Chaucer's *House of Fame:* Destruction and Definition Through Proliferation." *Chaucer Review* 27, no. 4 (1993): 325–41.

Rysman, Alexander. "How the 'Gossip' Became a Woman." *Journal of Communication* 27 (1977): 176–80.

Salter, Elizabeth. "The 'Troilus Frontispiece.'" In *Troilus and Crisyede: A Facsimile of Corpus Christi Cambridge MS 61,* ed. M. B. Parkes and Elizabeth Salter, 15–23. Cambridge: D. S. Brewer, 1978.

Salter, Elizabeth, and Derek Pearsall. "Pictorial Illustration of Late Medieval Poetic Texts: The Role of the Frontispiece or Prefatory Picture." In *Medieval Iconography and Narrative: A Symposium,* ed. Flemming G. Andersen, Esther Nyholm, Marianne Powell, and Flemming Talbo Stubkjer, 100–123. Odense: Odense University Press, 1980.

Sandison, Helen Estabrook, ed. *The "Chanson D'Aventure" in Middle English.* Bryn Mawr: Bryn Mawr College Press, 1913.

Scanlon, Larry. *Narrative, Authority, and Power: The Medieval Exemplum and the Chaucerian Tradition.* Cambridge: Cambridge University Press, 1994.

Schein, Sylvia. "Used and Abused: Gossip in Medieval Society." In *Good Gossip,* ed. Robert F. Goodman and Aaron Ben-Ze'ev, 139–53. Lawrence: University Press of Kansas, 1994.

Scheps, Walter. "'Up Roos our Hoost, and Was our Aller Cok': Harry Bailly's Taletelling Competition." *Chaucer Review* 10, no. 2 (1975): 113–28.

Schibanoff, Susan. "The New Reader and Female Textuality in Two Early Commentaries on Chaucer." *Studies in the Age of Chaucer* 10 (1988): 71–108.

Schlauch, Margaret. "The Marital Dilemma in the Wife of Bath's Tale." *PMLA* 61, no. 2 (1946): 416–30.

"Sent Ion þe Ewangelist in a boke þat he made þat men clepyn þe Apocalips." London, British Library, MS Additional 37677, fols. 61v–83v.

"Seynt Johon þe evangelist in his boke of pryuytes." London, British Library, MS Harley 6571, fols. 1r–78v.

Shahar, Shulamith. *Childhood in the Middle Ages.* London: Routledge, 1990.

Shaw, Judith. "The Influence of Canonical and Episcopal Reform on Popular Books of Instruction." In *The Popular Literature of Medieval England,* ed. Thomas J. Heffernan, 44–60. *Tennessee Studies in Literature* 28. Knoxville: University of Tennessee Press, 1985.

Simpson, James. "Chaucer as a European Writer." In *The Yale Companion to Chaucer,* ed. Seth Lerer, 55–86. New Haven: Yale University Press, 2006.

Skelton, John. *John Skelton: The Complete English Poems,* ed. John Scattergood. New Haven: Yale University Press, 1983.

Smith, D. Vance. "Chaucer as an English Writer." In *The Yale Companion to Chaucer,* ed. Seth Lerer, 87–121. New Haven: Yale University Press, 2006.

Smith, Warren S. "The Wife of Bath Debates Jerome." *Chaucer Review* 32, no. 2 (1997): 129–45.

Spacks, Patricia Meyer. *Gossip.* New York: Knopf, 1985.

Spargo, John Webster. *Juridical Folklore in England Illustrated by the Cucking-Stool.* Durham: Duke University Press, 1944.

Spearing, A. C., ed. *The Knight's Tale.* Cambridge: Cambridge University Press, 1966.

Speculum Christiani, ed. Gustaf Holmstedt. EETS, o.s. 182. London: Oxford University Press, 1933.

Speculum Sacerdotale, ed. Edward H. Weatherley. EETS, o.s. 200. London: Oxford University Press, 1936.

"Speculum Vitae: An Edition of British Museum Manuscript Royal 17 C.viii," ed. John W. Smeltz. Unpub. diss., Duquesne University, 1977.

Spencer, H. Leith. *English Preaching in the Late Middle Ages.* Oxford: Clarendon Press, 1993.

Stanton, Domna C. "Recuperating Women and the Man Behind the Screen." In *Sexuality and Gender in Early Modern Europe, Institutions, Texts, Images,* ed. James Grantham Turner, 247–65. Cambridge: Cambridge University Press, 1993.

Steele, Robert, ed. *Three Prose Versions of the Secreta Secretorum.* EETS, e.s. 74. London: Kegan Paul, Trench, Trübner, 1898.

Stock, Brian. *The Implications of Literacy: Written Language and Models of Interpretation in the Eleventh and Twelfth Centuries.* Princeton: Princeton University Press, 1983.

Strohm, Paul. *Hochon's Arrow: The Social Imagination of Fourteenth Century Texts.* Princeton: Princeton University Press, 1992.

———. "*Passioun, Lyf, Miracle, Legende:* Some Generic Terms in Middle English Hagiographical Narrative, Part II." *Chaucer Review* 10, no. 2 (1975): 154–71.

———. *Social Chaucer.* Cambridge: Harvard University Press, 1989.

Suls, Jerry M. "Gossip as Social Comparison." *Journal of Communication* 27 (1977): 164–68.

The Tale of Beryn, ed. F. J. Furnivall and W. G. Stone. EETS, e.s. 105. London: Kegan Paul, Trench, Trübner, 1909.

A Talk of Ten Wives on Their Husbands' Ware. In *Jyl of Breyntford's Testament,* ed. Frederick J. Furnivall, 29–33. London, 1871.

Tatlock, John S. P. "The Source of *The Legend,* and Other Chauceriana." *Studies in Philology* 18 (1921): 419–28.

Taylor, Karla. "Social Aesthetics and the Emergence of Civic Discourse from the *Shipman's Tale* to *Melibee.*" *Chaucer Review* 39, no. 3 (2005): 298–322.

Taylor, Steven M. "Wifely Wiles: Comic Unmasking in *Les Quinze Joyes de Mariage.*" In *New Images of Medieval Women: Essays Toward a Cultural Anthropology,* ed. Edelgard E. DuBruck, 287–302. Lewiston, N.Y.: Edwin Mellen Press, 1989.

Tentler, Thomas N. *Sin and Confession on the Eve of the Reformation.* Princeton: Princeton University Press, 1977.

Terrell, Katherine H. "Reallocation of Hermeneutic Authority in Chaucer's *House of Fame.*" *Chaucer Review* 31, no. 3 (1997): 279–89.

Thomas, Keith. *Religion and the Decline of Magic.* New York: Scribner's, 1971.

Thompson, John A. F. *The Later Lollards, 1414–1520.* London: Oxford University Press, 1965.

Thormann, Janet. "The Circulation of Desire in the 'Shipman's Tale.'" *Literature and Psychology* 39, no. 3 (1993): 1–15.

Der Treperel-Druck der Quinze Joyes de Mariage, ed. Arthur Fleig. Griefswald: Julius Abel, 1903.

Trigg, Stephanie. "Chaucer's Influence and Reception." In *The Yale Companion to Chaucer,* ed. Seth Lerer, 297–323. New Haven: Yale University Press, 2006.

Tubach, Frederic C. *Index Exemplorum: a Handbook of Medieval Religious Tales.* Helsinki: Suomalainen Tiedeakatemia, 1969.

Turner, Patricia A. *I Heard It Through the Grapevine: Rumor in African-American Culture.* Berkeley and Los Angeles: University of California Press, 1993.

Turville-Petre, Thorlac. *The Alliterative Revival.* Cambridge: D. S. Brewer, 1977.

Underdown, D. E. "The Taming of the Scold: The Enforcement of Partriarchal Authority in Early Modern England." In *Order and Disorder in Early Modern England,* ed. Anthony Fletcher and John Stevenson, 116–36. Cambridge: Cambridge University Press, 1985.

Utley, Francis. *The Crooked Rib: An Analytical Index to the Argument About Women in English and Scots Literature to the End of the Year 1568.* Columbus: Ohio State University, 1944.

Verba Seniorum. In *Patrologia Latina,* ed. J. P. Migne, vol. 73, col. 765, #43. Paris, 1849.

Wack, Mary. "Women, Work, and Plays in an English Medieval Town." In *Maids and Mistresses, Cousins and Queens: Women's Alliances in Early Modern England,* ed. Susan Frye and Karen Robertson, 33–51. Oxford: Oxford University Press, 1999.

Walker, Sue Sheridan. "Proof of Age of Feudal Heirs in Medieval England." *Mediaeval Studies* 35 (1973): 306–23.

Wallace, David. *Chaucerian Polity: Absolutist Lineages and Associational Forms in England and Italy.* Stanford: Stanford University Press, 1997.

———. "Chaucer's Body Politic: Social and Narrative Self-Regulation." *Exemplaria* 2, no. 1 (1990): 221–40.

Waters, Claire M. *Angels and Earthly Creatures: Preaching, Performance, and Gender in the Later Middle Ages.* Philadelphia: University of Pennsylvania Press, 2004.

Watson, Nicholas. "Censorship and Cultural Change in Late-Medieval England: Vernacular Theology, the Oxford Translation Debate, and Arundel's Constitutions of 1409." *Speculum* 70, no. 4 (1995): 822–64.

———. *Richard Rolle and the Invention of Authority.* Cambridge: Cambridge University Press, 1991.

Welsh, Andrew. "Story and Wisdom in Chaucer: The Physician's Tale and The Manciple's Tale." In *Manuscript, Narrative, Lexicon: Essays on Literary and Cultural Transmission in Honor of Whitney F. Bolton,* ed. Robert Boenig and Kathleen Davis, 76–95. Lewisburg, Pa.: Bucknell University Press, 2000.

Wenzel, Siegfried. *The Sin of Sloth: Acedia in Medieval Thought and Literature.* Chapel Hill: University of North Carolina Press, 1960.

———. "The Source of Chaucer's Seven Deadly Sins." *Traditio* 30 (1974): 351–78.

Westervelt, L. A. "The Mediaeval Notion of Janglery and Chaucer's *Manciple's Tale.*" *Southern Review* 14 (1981): 107–15.

White, Hugh. *Nature, Sex, and Goodness.* Oxford: Oxford University Press, 2000.

White, Luise. "Between Gluckman and Foucault: Historicizing Rumor and Gossip." *Social Dynamics* 20, no. 1 (1994): 75–92.

Whiting, Bartlett Jere. *Proverbs, Sentences, and Proverbial Phrases from English Writings Mainly Before 1500.* Cambridge: Belknap Press, 1968.

Willard, Charity Cannon. "Women and Marriage Around 1400: Three Views." *Fifteenth-Century Studies* 17 (1990): 475–84.

Wilson, Adrian. "The Ceremony of Childbirth and Its Interpretation." In *Women as Mothers in Pre-industrial England,* ed. Valerie Fildes, 68–107. London: Routledge, 1990.

———. "Participant or Patient? Seventeenth-Century Childbirth from the Mother's Point of View." In *Patients and Practitioners: Lay Perceptions of Medicine in Pre-industrial Society,* ed. Roy Porter, 129–44. Cambridge: Cambridge University Press, 1985.

Wilson, Peter J. "Filcher of Good Names: An Enquiry into Anthropology and Gossip." *Man: The Journal of the Royal Anthropological Institute* 9 (1973): 93–108.

Wise, F. Franklyn. *The Problem of Gossip: Guidelines for Christian Speech.* Kansas City: Beacon Hill Press of Kansas City, 1988.

Wogan-Browne, Jocelyn, Nicholas Watson, Andrew Taylor, and Ruth Evans, eds. *The Idea of the Vernacular: An Anthology of Middle English Literary Theory, 1280–1520.* University Park: The Pennsylvania State University Press, 1999.

Wood, Chauncey. "Speech, the Principle of Contraries, and Chaucer's Tales of the Manciple and Parson." *Mediaevalia* 6 (1980): 209–29.

Woodbridge, Linda. *Women and the English Renaissance: Literature and the Nature of Womankind, 1540–1620.* Urbana: University of Illinois Press, 1984.

Wyclif, John. *The English Works of Wyclif,* ed. F. D. Matthew. EETS, o.s. 74. London: Kegan Paul, Trench, Trübner, 1902.

———. *The Holy Bible: containing the Old and New Testaments, with the Apocryphal books, in the earliest English versions made from the Latin Vulgate by John Wycliffe and his followers,* ed. Rev. Josiah Forshall and Sir Frederic Madden. Oxford: Oxford University Press, 1850.

Yeager, R. F. "Aspects of Gluttony in Chaucer and Gower." *Philology Quarterly* 81 (1984): 42–53.

Yerkovich, Sally. "Gossiping as a Way of Speaking." *Journal of Communication* 27 (1977): 192–96.

Zieman, Katherine. "Chaucer's *Voys.*" *Representations* 60 (1997): 70–91.

INDEX

Made in the USA
Lexington, KY
05 October 2017